EASY GUITAR TAB

CHRISTMAS CAROLS

ISBN 978-1-4803-9300-4

HAL•LEONARD®
CORPORATION

7777 W. BLUEMOUND RD. P.O. BOX 13819 MILWAUKEE, WI 53213

In Australia Contact:
Hal Leonard Australia Pty. Ltd.
4 Lentara Court
Cheltenham, Victoria, 3192 Australia
Email: ausadmin@halleonard.com.au

Visit Hal Leonard Online at **www.halleonard.com**

Angels from the Realms of Glory

Words by James Montgomery
Music by Henry T. Smart

Strum Pattern: 4
Pick Pattern: 5

Verse
Moderately fast

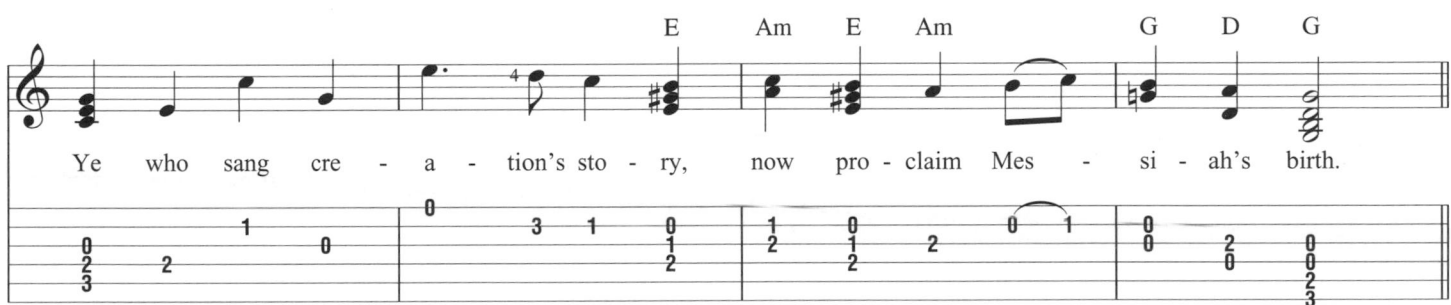

1. An - gels from the realms of glo - ry, wing your flight o'er all the earth.
2., 3., 4. *See additional lyrics*

Ye who sang cre - a - tion's sto - ry, now pro - claim Mes - si - ah's birth.

Chorus

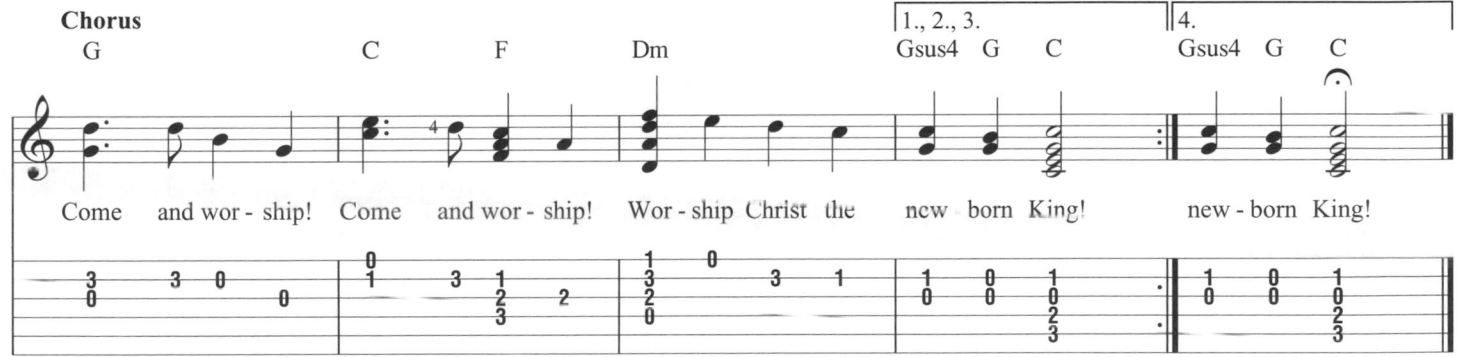

Come and wor - ship! Come and wor - ship! Wor - ship Christ the new - born King! new - born King!

Additional Lyrics

2. Shepherds in the fields abiding,
   Watching o'er your flocks by night,
   God with men is now residing,
   Yonder shines the infant light.

3. Sages, leave your contemplations,
   Brighter visions beam afar;
   Seek the great Desire of Nations;
   Ye have seen His natal star.

4. Saints, before the altar bending,
   Watching long in hope and fear,
   Suddenly the Lord, descending,
   In His temple shall appear.

Angels We Have Heard on High

Traditional French Carol
Translated by James Chadwick

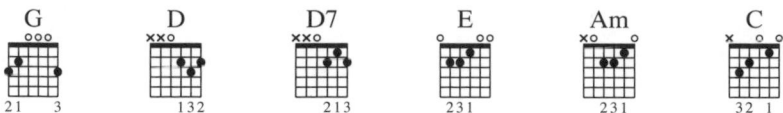

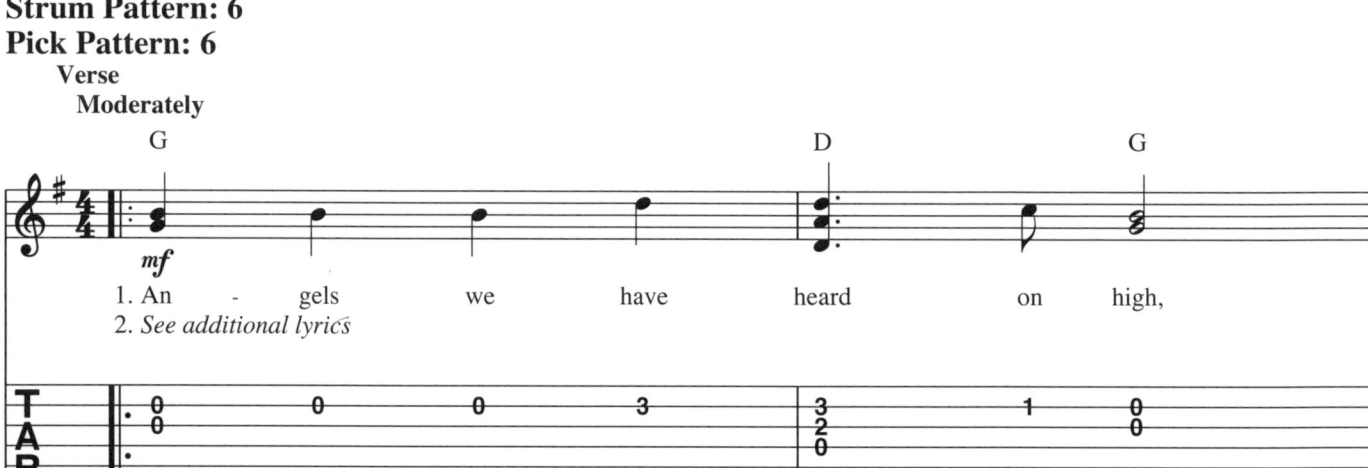

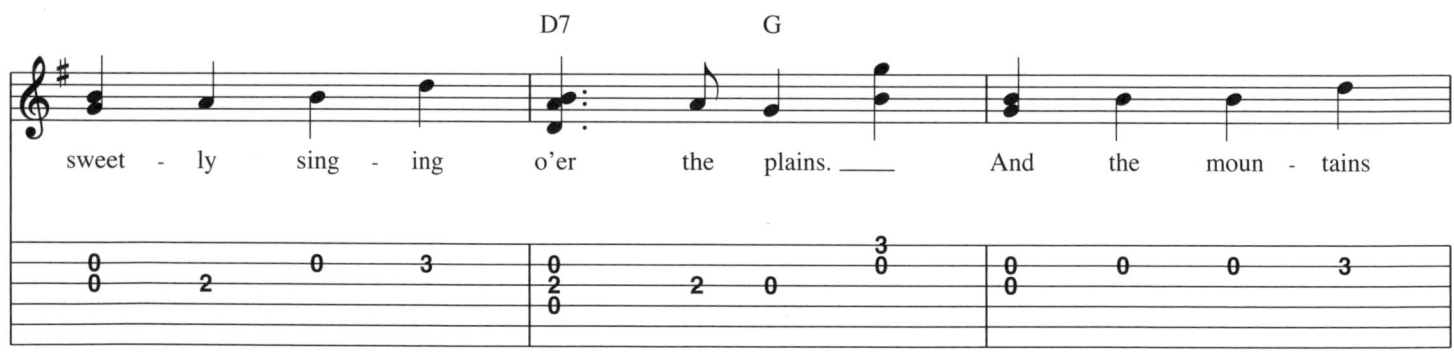

Chorus

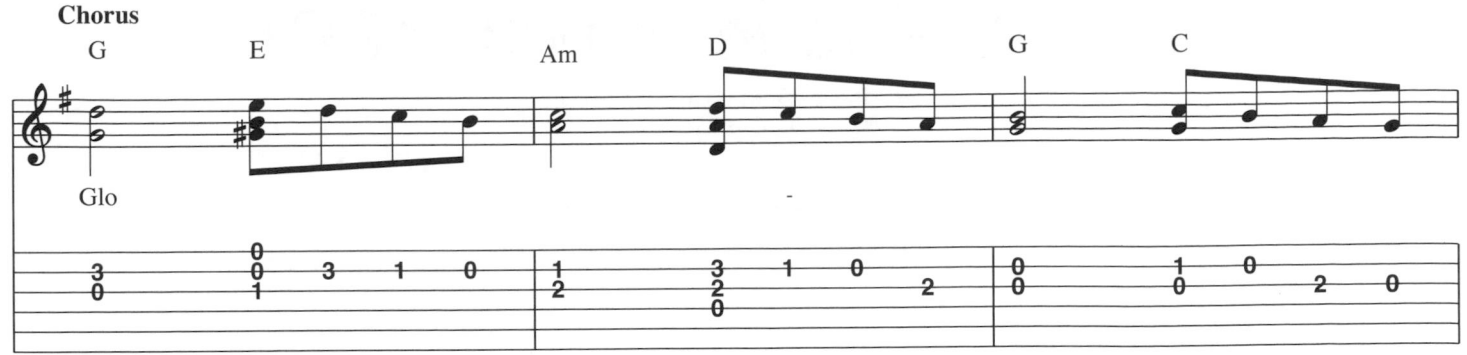

Glo -

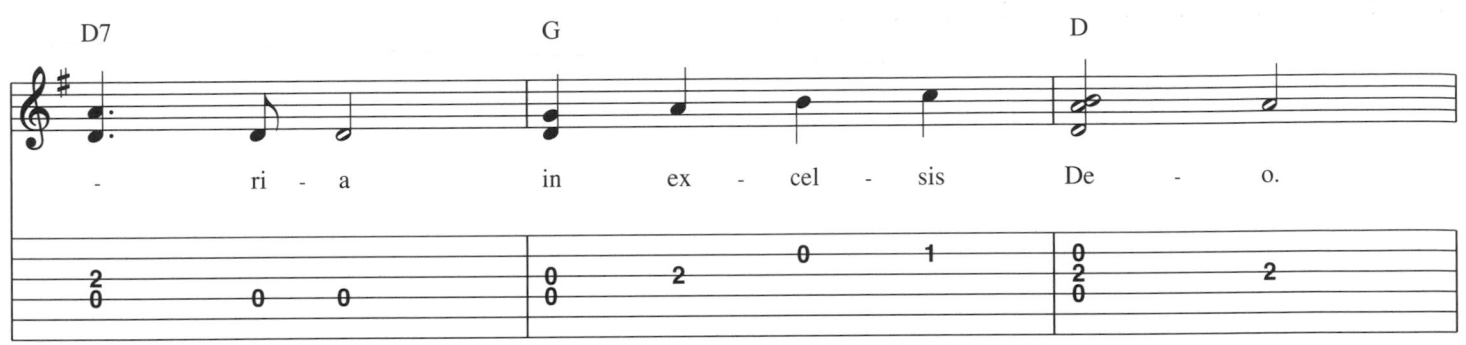

- ri - a in ex - cel - sis De - o.

Glo - ri - a

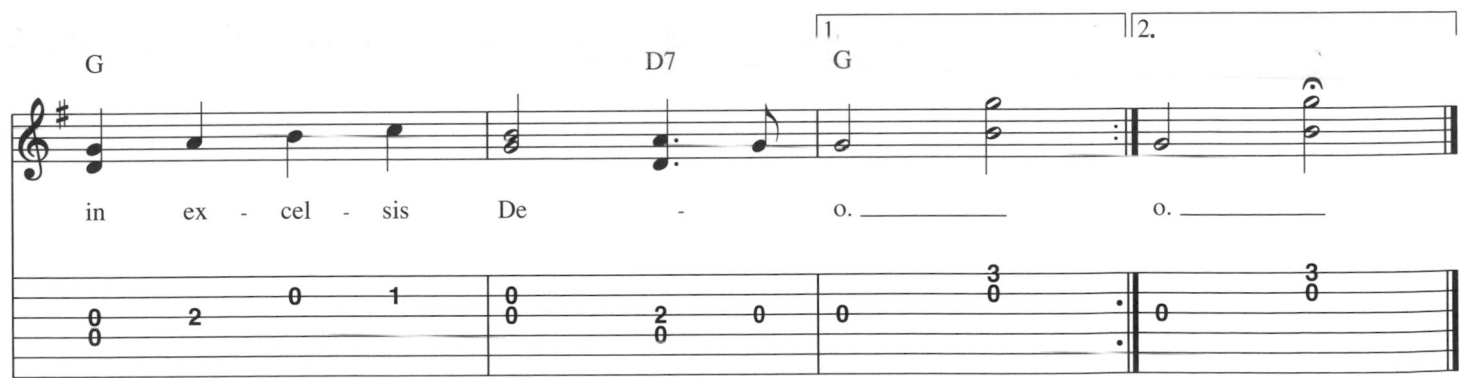

in ex - cel - sis De - o. _____ o. _____

Additional Lyrics

2. Shepherds why this jubilee?
   Why your joyous strains prolong?
   What the gladsome tidings be
   Which inspire your heavenly song?

As with Gladness Men of Old

Words by William Chatterton Dix
Music by Conrad Kocher

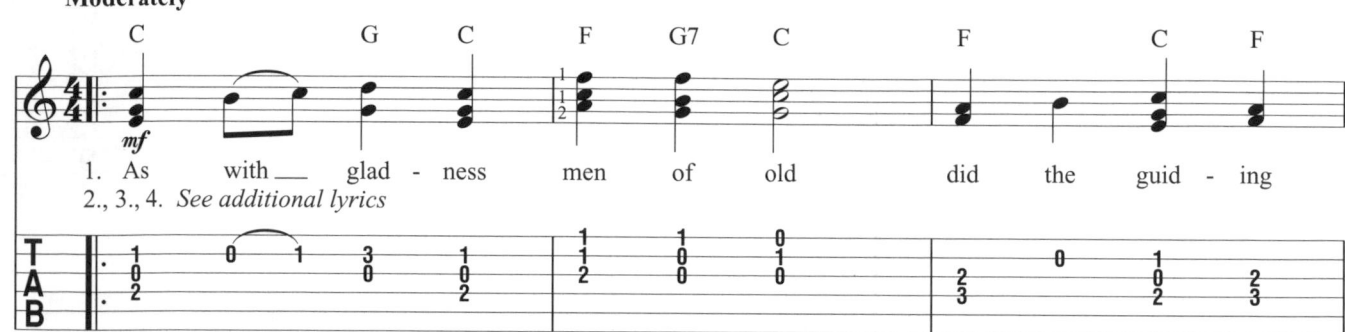

Strum Pattern: 4
Pick Pattern: 4

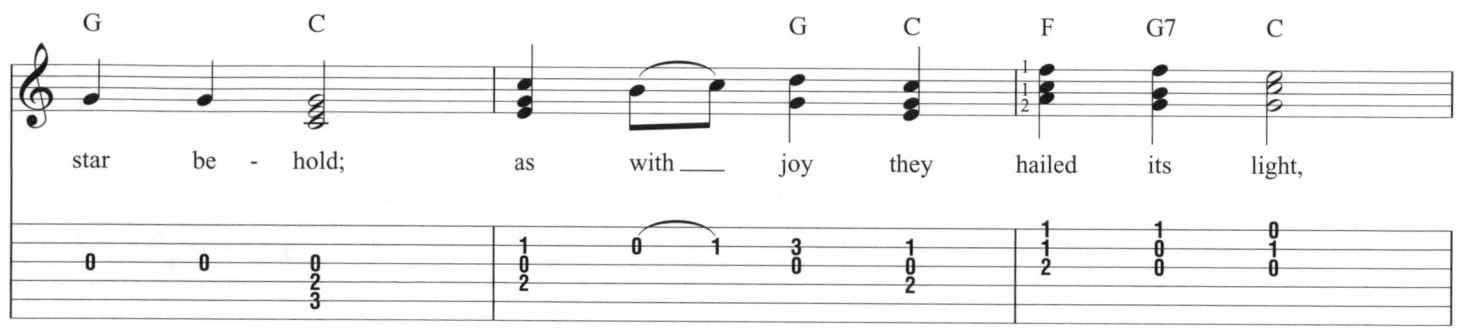

1. As with ___ glad - ness men of old did the guid - ing
2., 3., 4. *See additional lyrics*

star be - hold; as with ___ joy they hailed its light,

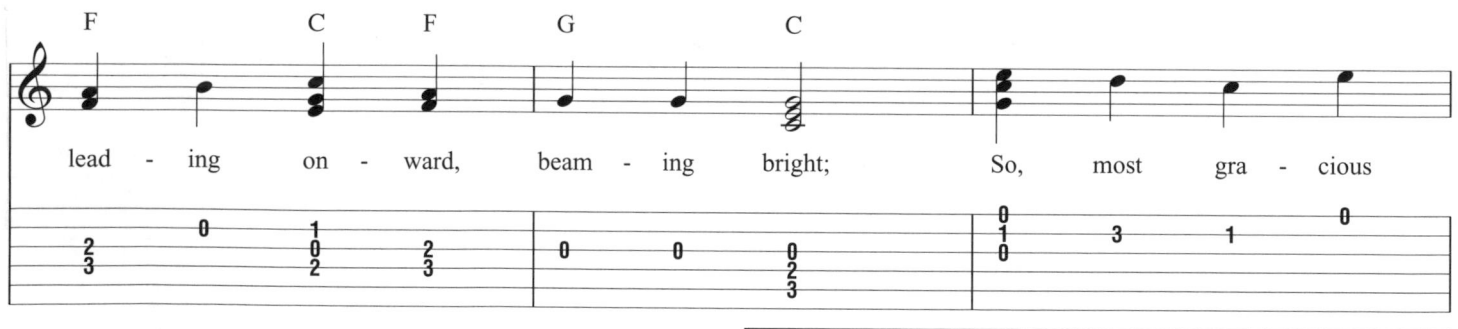

lead - ing on - ward, beam - ing bright; So, most gra - cious

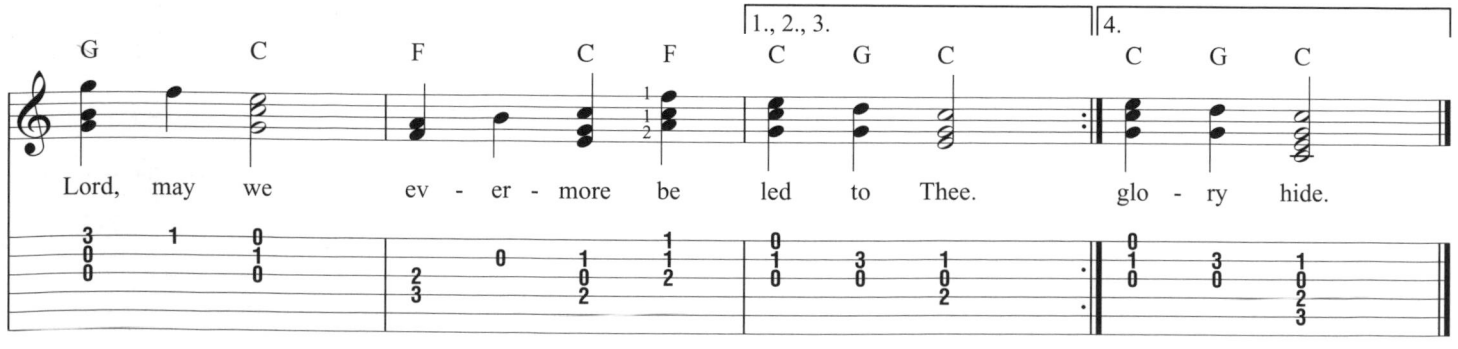

Lord, may we ev - er - more be led to Thee. glo - ry hide.

Additional Lyrics

2. As with joyful steps they sped,
To that lowly manger bed,
There to bend the knee before
Him who Heaven and Earth adore,
So may we with willing feet
Ever seek thy mercy seat.

3. As they offered gifts most rare
At that manger rude and bare,
So may we with holy joy,
Pure and free from sin's alloy,
All our costliest treasures bring,
Christ, to Thee, our heavenly King.

4. Holy Jesus, every day
Keep us in the narrow way;
And, when earthly things are past,
Bring our ransomed souls at last
Where they need no star to guide,
Where no clouds Thy glory hide.

Away in a Manger

Traditional
Words by John T. McFarland (v.3)
Music by William J. Kirkpatrick

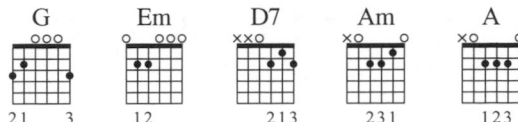

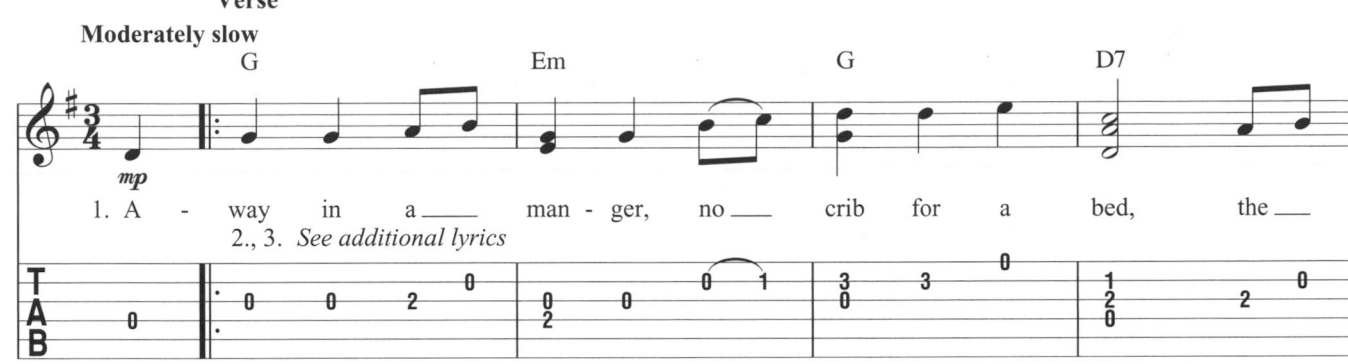

Strum Pattern: 8
Pick Pattern: 7

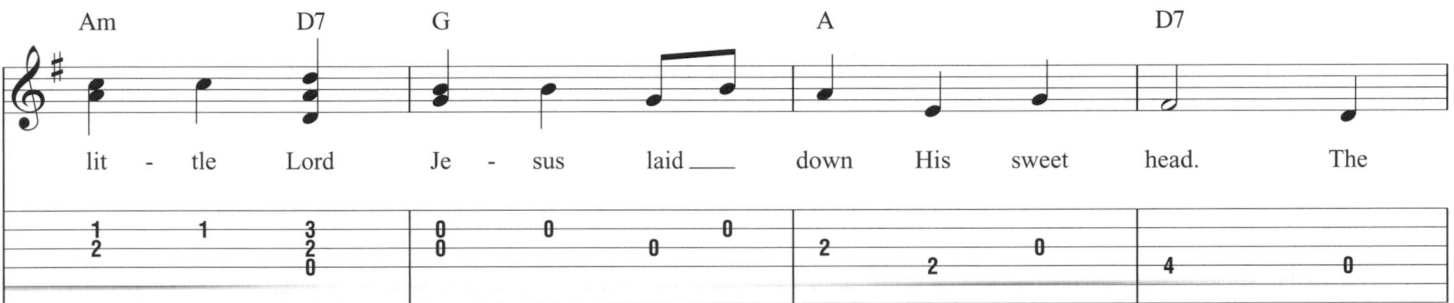

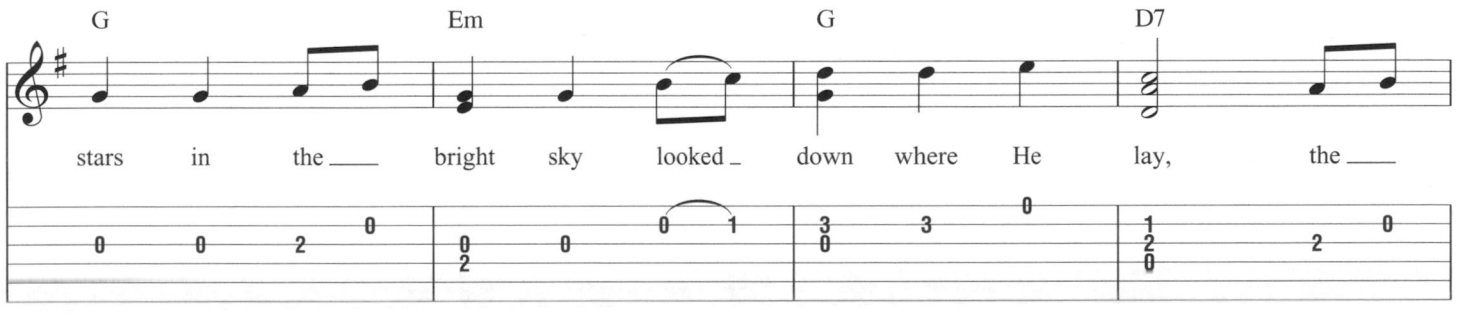

Additional Lyrics

2. The cattle are lowing, the Baby awakes,
   But little Lord Jesus, no crying He makes.
   I love Thee, Lord Jesus, look down from the sky,
   And stay by my side until morning is nigh.

3. Be near me, Lord Jesus; I ask Thee to stay
   Close by me forever and love me, I pray.
   Bless all the dear children in Thy tender care,
   And fit us for heaven to live with Thee there.

Away in a Manger

Words by John T. McFarland (v.3)
Music by James R. Murray

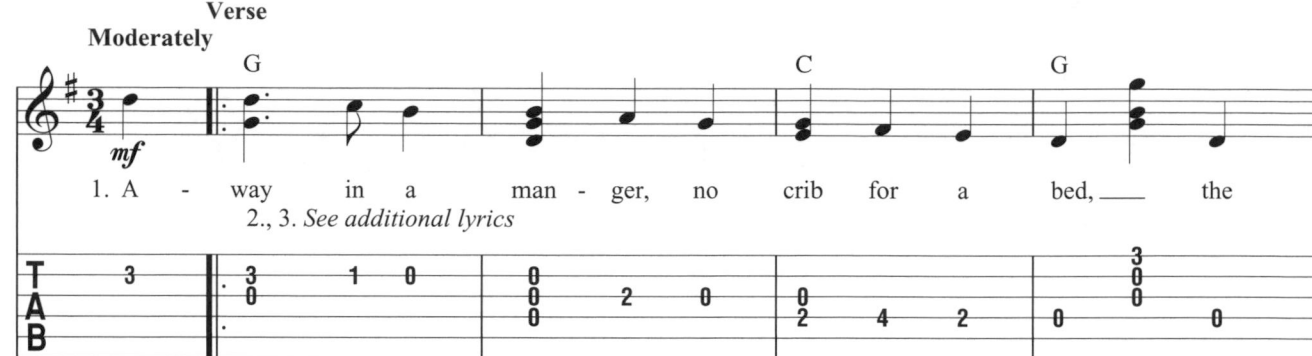

Strum Pattern: 7
Pick Pattern: 7

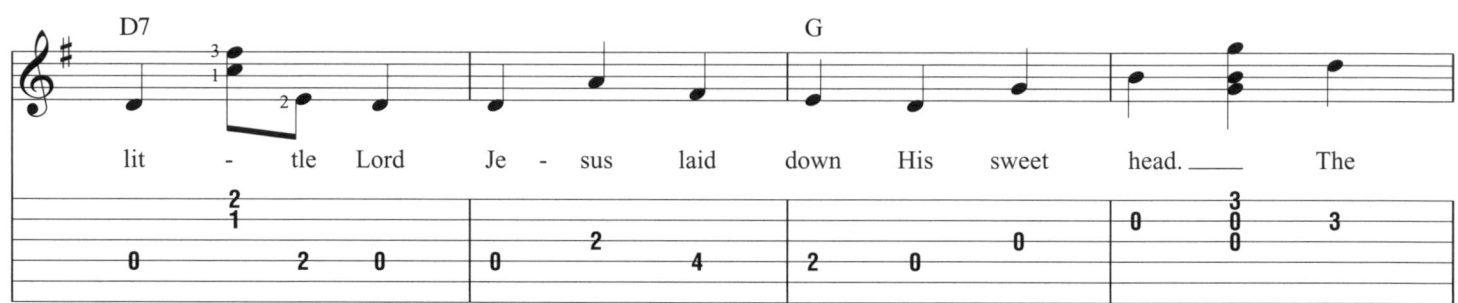

1. A - way in a man - ger, no crib for a bed, ___ the
2., 3. See additional lyrics

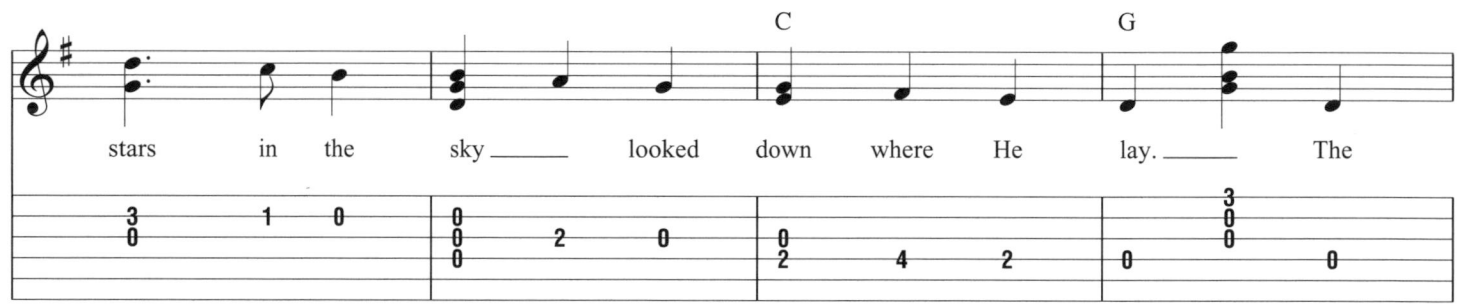

lit - tle Lord Je - sus laid down His sweet head. ___ The

stars in the sky ___ looked down where He lay. ___ The

lit - tle Lord Je - sus, a - sleep on the hay. 2. The   there.

Additional Lyrics

2. The cattle are lowing, the baby awakes,
   But little Lord Jesus, no crying He makes.
   I love thee, Lord Jesus, look down from the sky
   And stay by my cradle 'til morning is nigh.

3. Be near me, Lord Jesus, I ask Thee to stay
   Close by me forever, and love me, I pray.
   Bless all the dear children in Thy tender care,
   And fit us for heaven to live with Thee there.

Christ Was Born on Christmas Day

Traditional

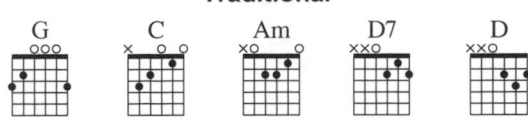

* **Strum Pattern: 10**
* **Pick Pattern: 10**

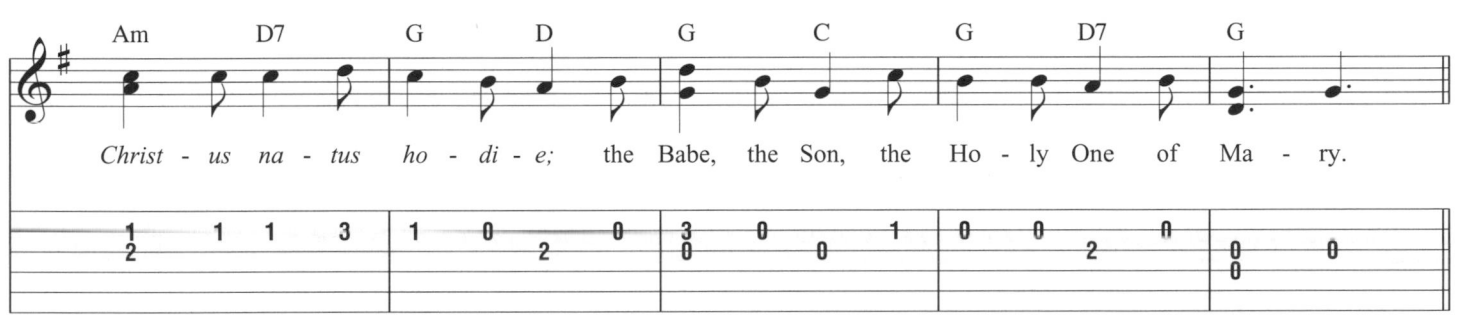

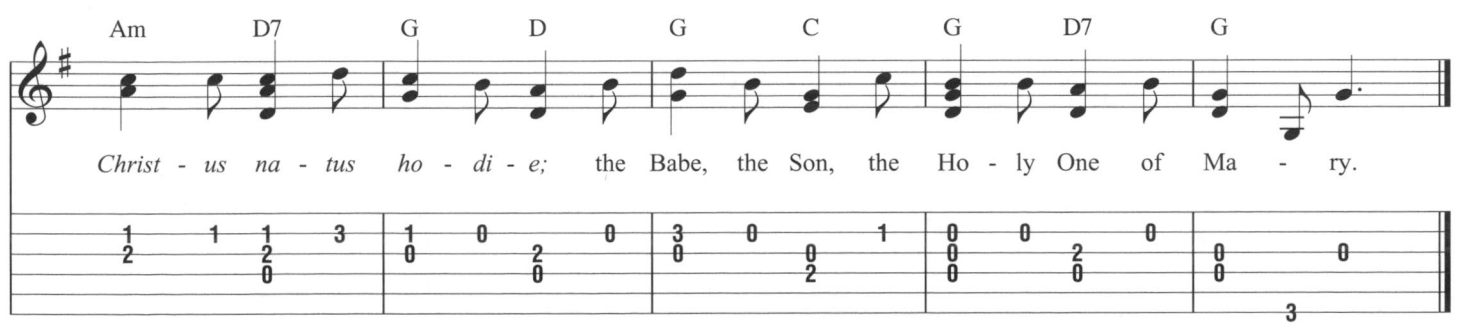

Bring a Torch, Jeannette, Isabella

17th Century French Provencal Carol

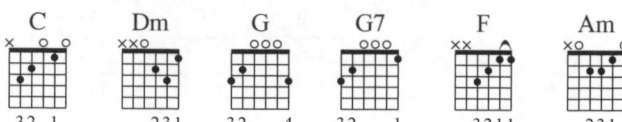

Strum Pattern: 7
Pick Pattern: 8

Verse
Moderately fast

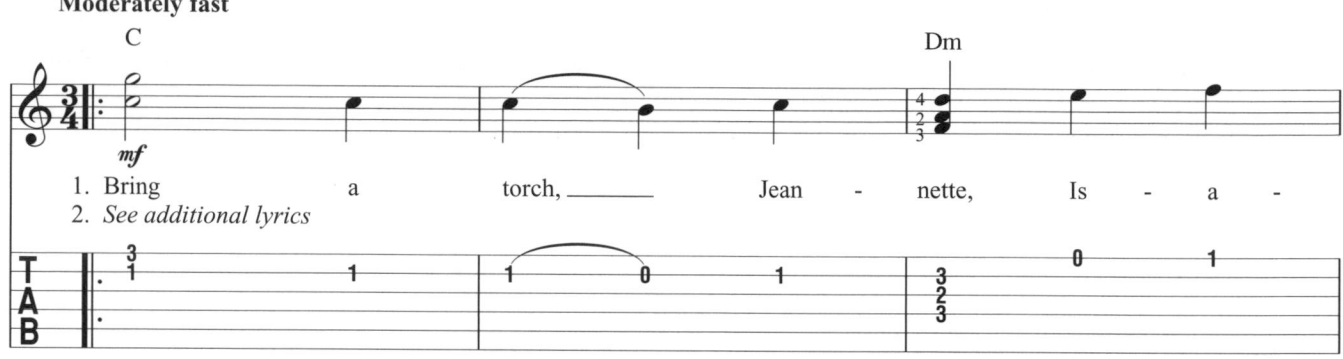

1. Bring a torch, _____ Jean - nette, Is - a -
2. *See additional lyrics*

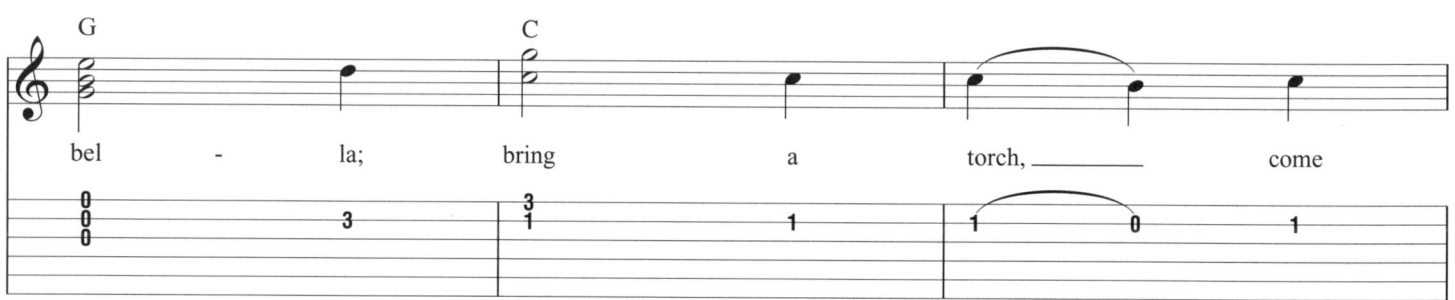

bel - la; bring a torch, _____ come

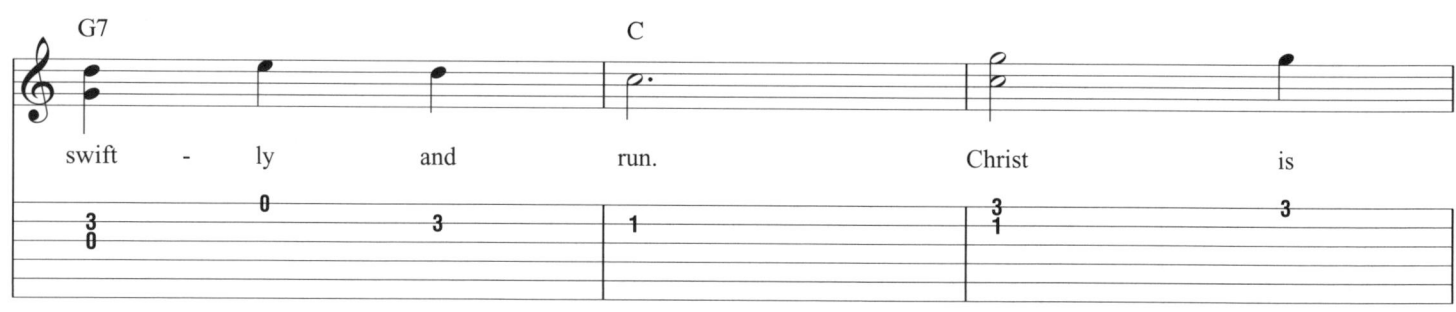

swift - ly and run. Christ is

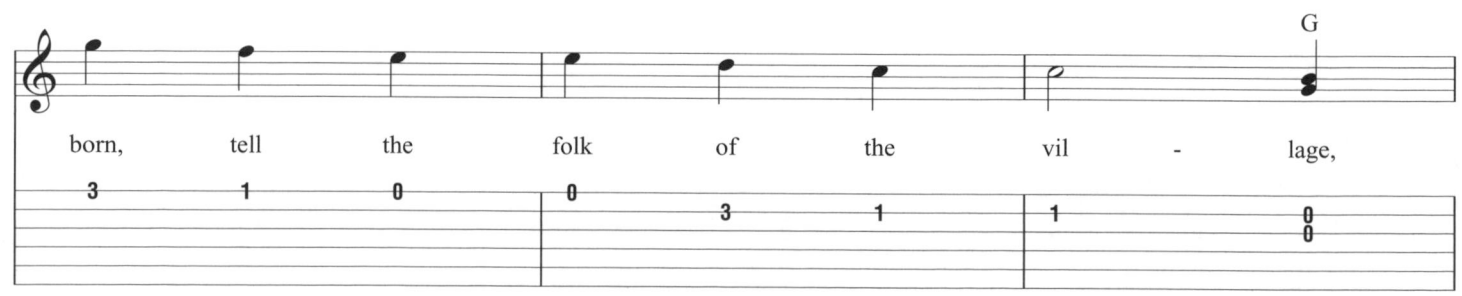

born, tell the folk of the vil - lage,

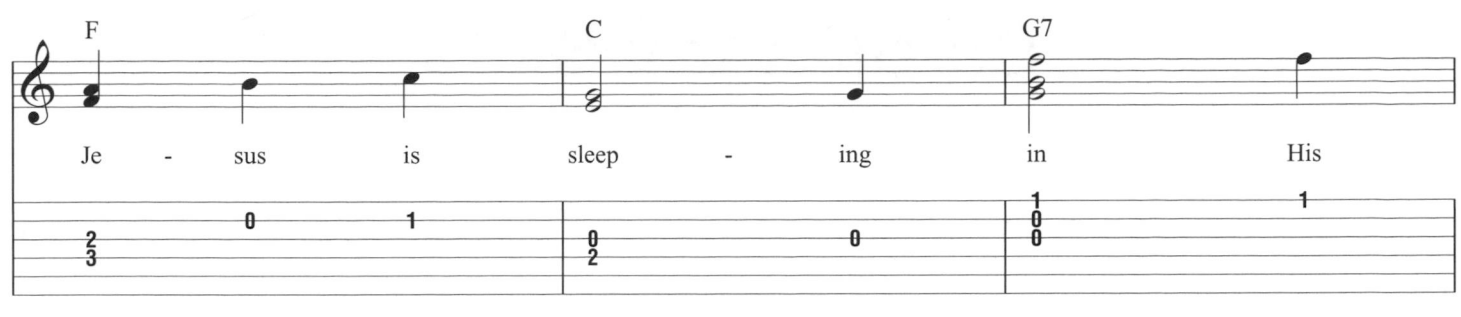

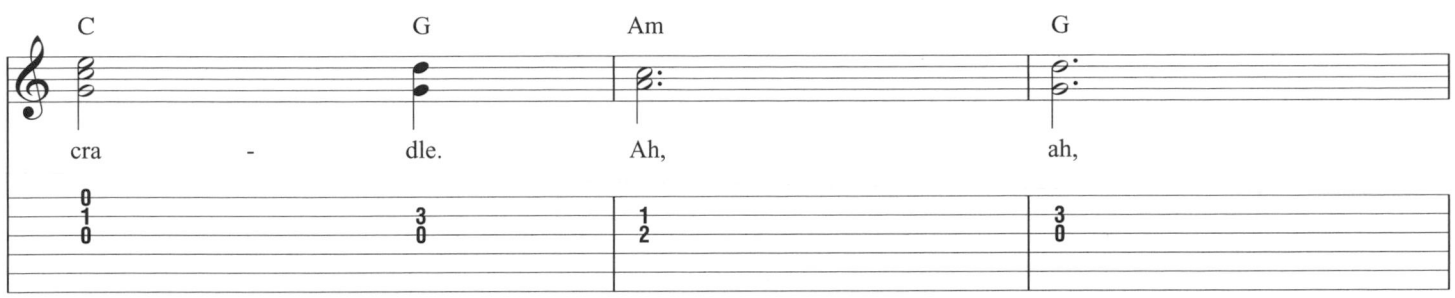

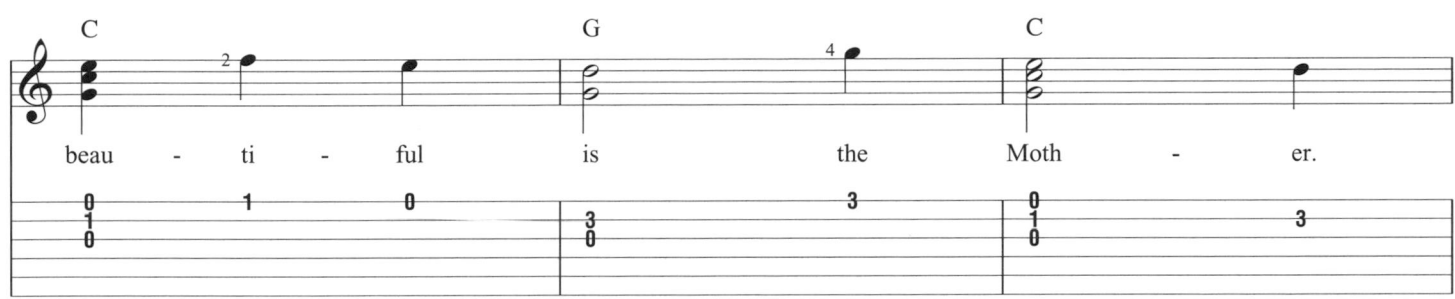

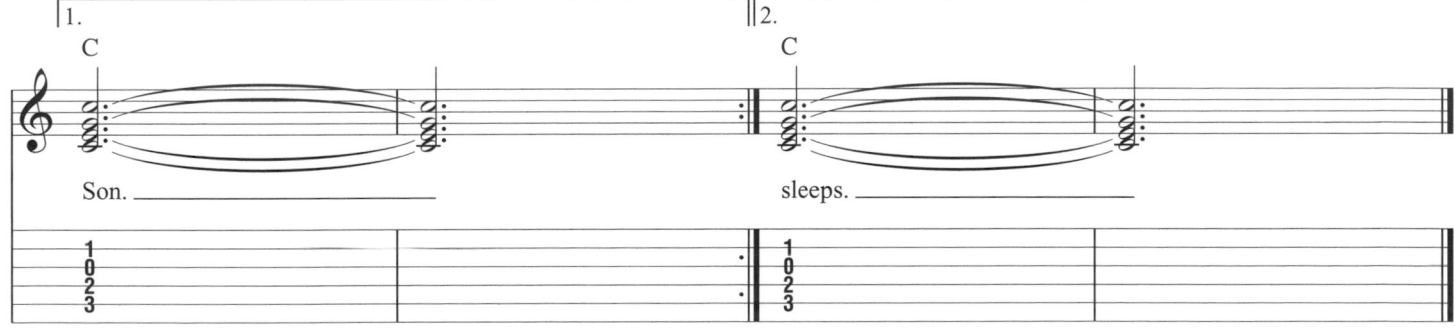

Additional Lyrics

2. Hasten now, good folk of the village,
   Hasten now, the Christ Child to see.
   You will find Him asleep in a manger,
   Quietly come and whisper softly.
   Hush, hush, peacefully now He slumbers,
   Hush, hush, peacefully now He sleeps.

Carol of the Bells

Ukrainian Christmas Carol

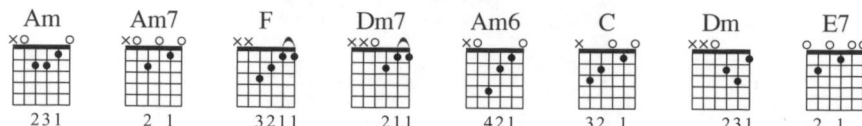

Strum Pattern: 7
Pick Pattern: 7

Verse
Fast

Hark to the bells, hark to the bells, tell - ing us all Je - sus is King!

Strong - ly they chime, sound with a rhyme, Christ - mas is here, wel - come the King!

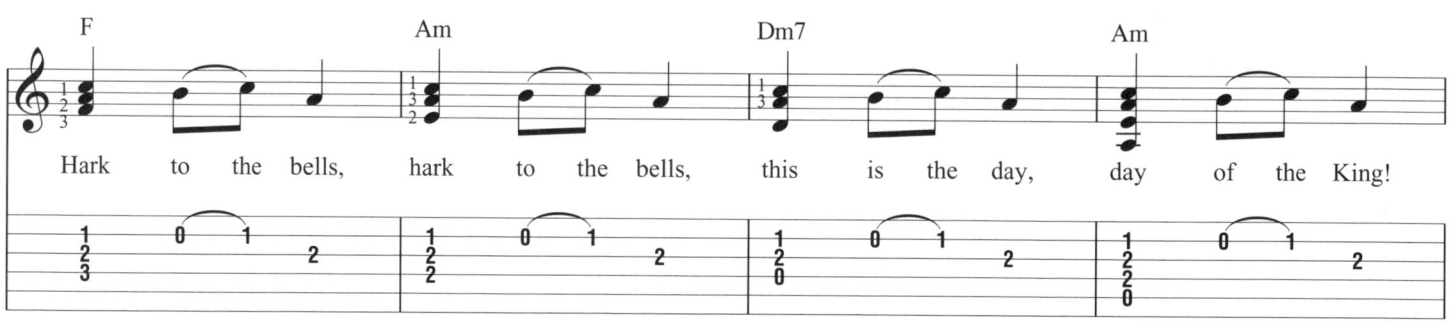

Hark to the bells, hark to the bells, this is the day, day of the King!

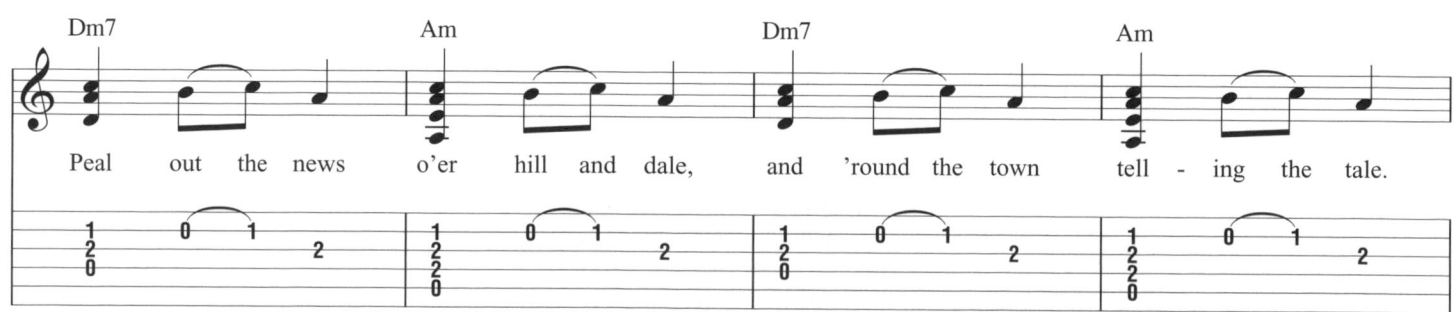

Peal out the news o'er hill and dale, and 'round the town tell - ing the tale.

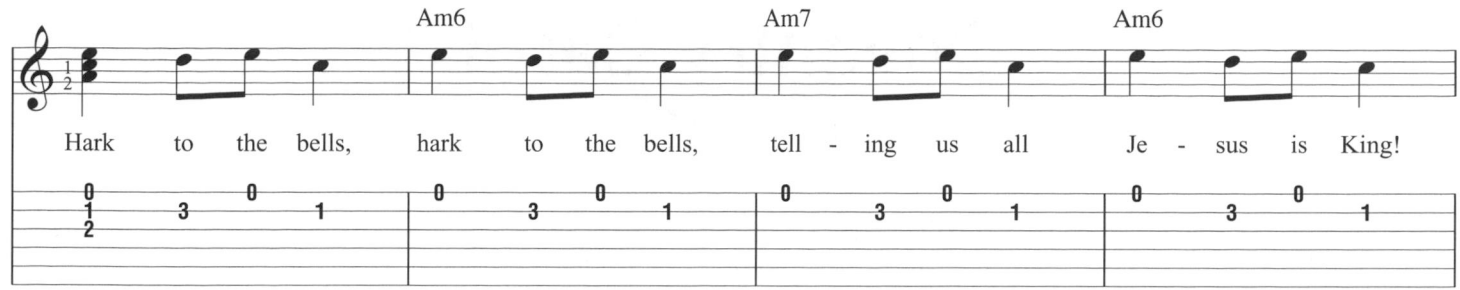

Hark to the bells, hark to the bells, tell - ing us all Je - sus is King!

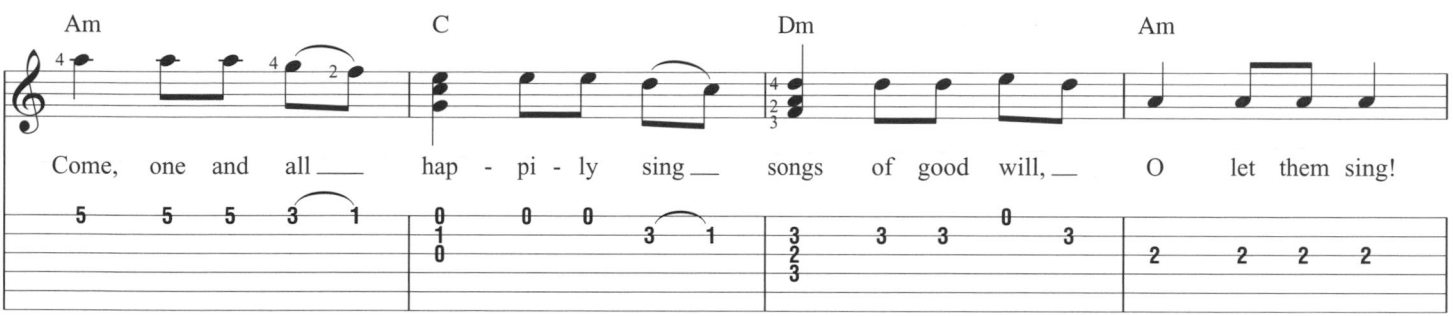

Come, one and all ___ hap - pi - ly sing ___ songs of good will, ___ O let them sing!

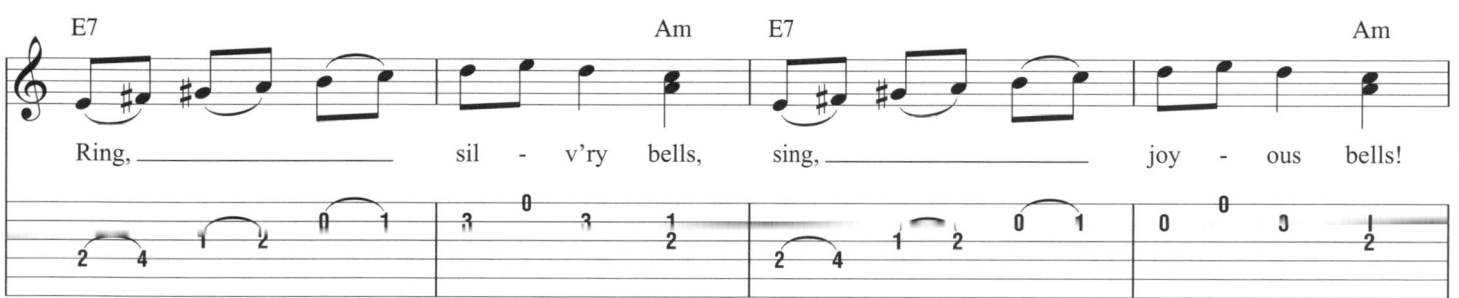

Ring, _____ sil - v'ry bells, sing, _____ joy - ous bells!

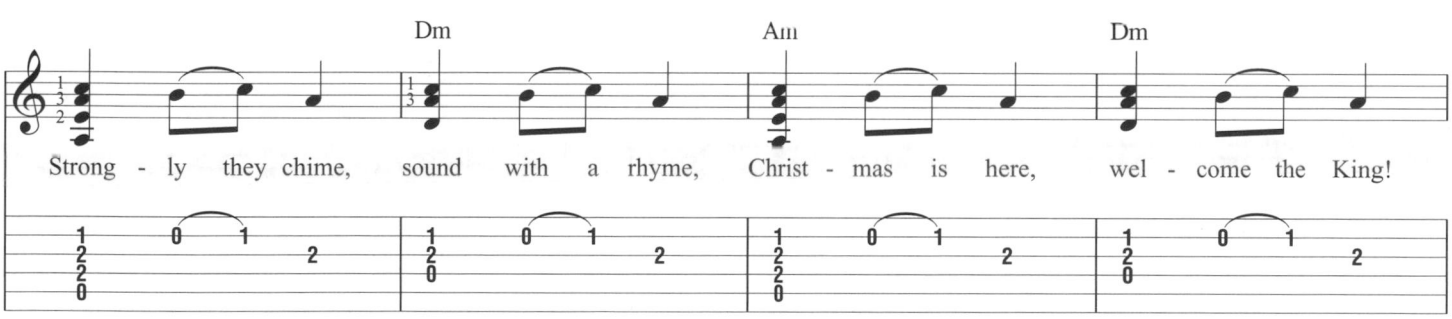

Strong - ly they chime, sound with a rhyme, Christ - mas is here, wel - come the King!

Hark to the bells, hark to the bells, tell - ing us all Je - sus is King! Ring, ring ___ bells. ___

Coventry Carol

Words by Robert Croo
Traditional English Melody

 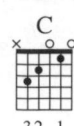 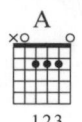  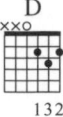

Strum Pattern: 7, 9
Pick Pattern: 7, 9

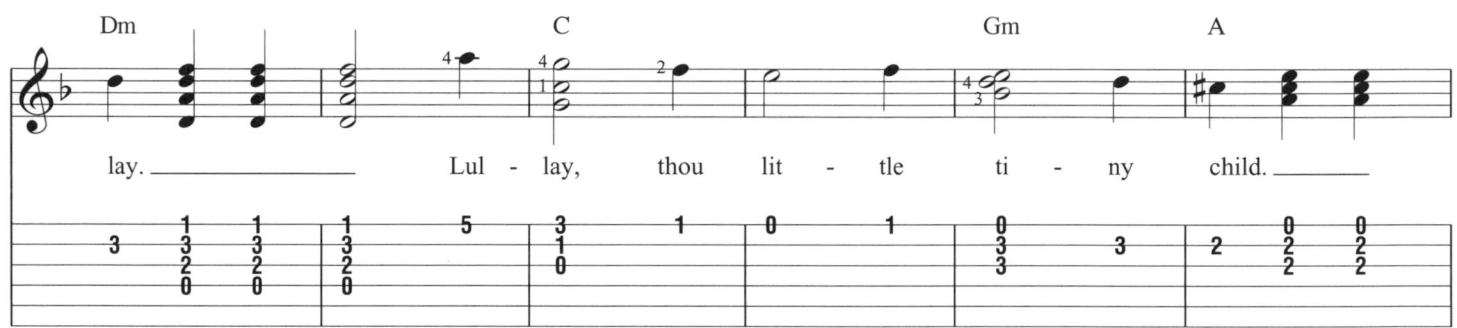

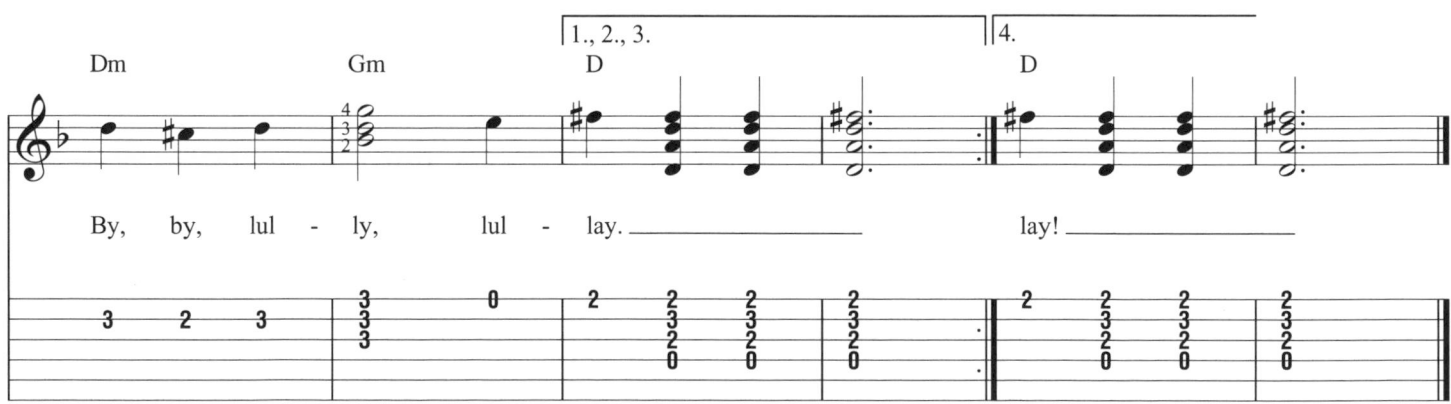

Additional Lyrics

2. Oh, sisters too,
   How may we do,
   For to preserve this day?
   This poor youngling,
   For whom we sing
   By, by, lully, lullay.

3. Herod the king,
   In his raging,
   Charged he hath this day.
   His men of might,
   In his own sight,
   All young children to slay.

4. That woe is me,
   Poor child for thee!
   And ever morn and day,
   For thy parting
   Neither say nor sing
   By, by, lully, lullay!

Deck the Hall

Traditional Welsh Carol

Strum Pattern: 4, 6
Pick Pattern: 5, 6

1. Deck the hall with boughs of hol-ly; fa, la, la, la, la, la, la, la, la.
2., 3. *See additional lyrics*

'Tis the sea-son to be jol-ly; fa, la, la, la, la, la, la, la, la.

Don we now our gay ap-par-el; fa, la, la, la, la, la, la, la, la. ____

Troll the an-cient yule-tide car-ol; fa, la, la, la, la, la, la, la, la. ____ la, la, la. ____

Additional Lyrics

2. See the blazing yule before us;
Fa, la, la, la, la, la, la, la, la.
Strike the harp and join the chorus;
Fa, la, la, la, la, la, la, la, la.
Follow me in merry measure;
Fa, la, la, la, la, la, la, la, la, la.
While I tell of Yuletide treasure;
Fa, la, la, la, la, la, la, la, la.

3. Fast away the old year passes;
Fa, la, la, la, la, la, la, la, la.
Hail the new ye lads and lasses;
Fa, la, la, la, la, la, la, la, la.
Sing we joyous, all together;
Fa, la, la, la, la, la, la, la, la.
Heedless of the wind and weather;
Fa, la, la, la, la, la, la, la, la.

Ding Dong! Merrily on High!

French Carol

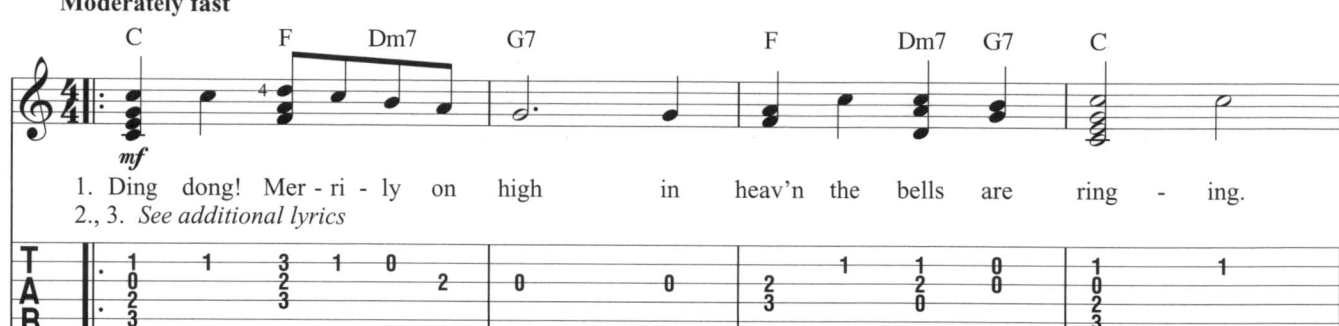

Strum Pattern: 4
Pick Pattern: 4

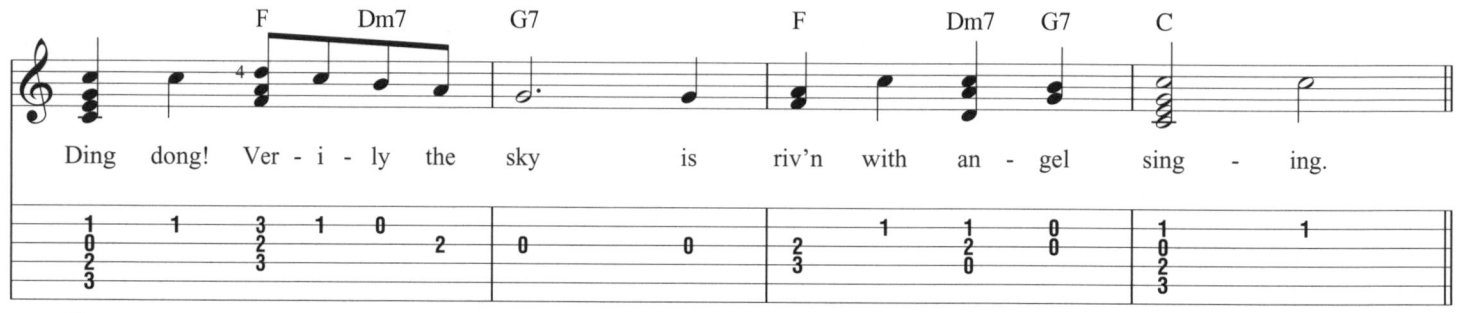

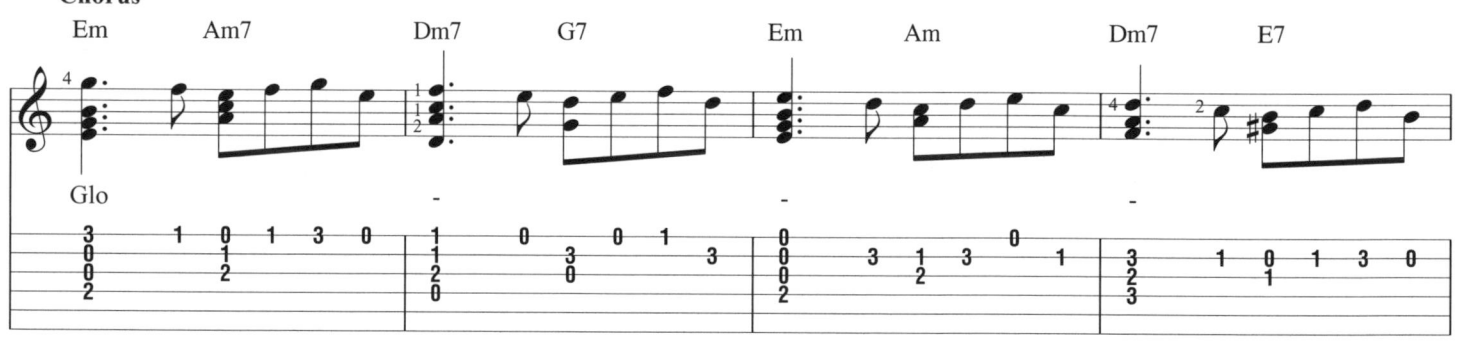

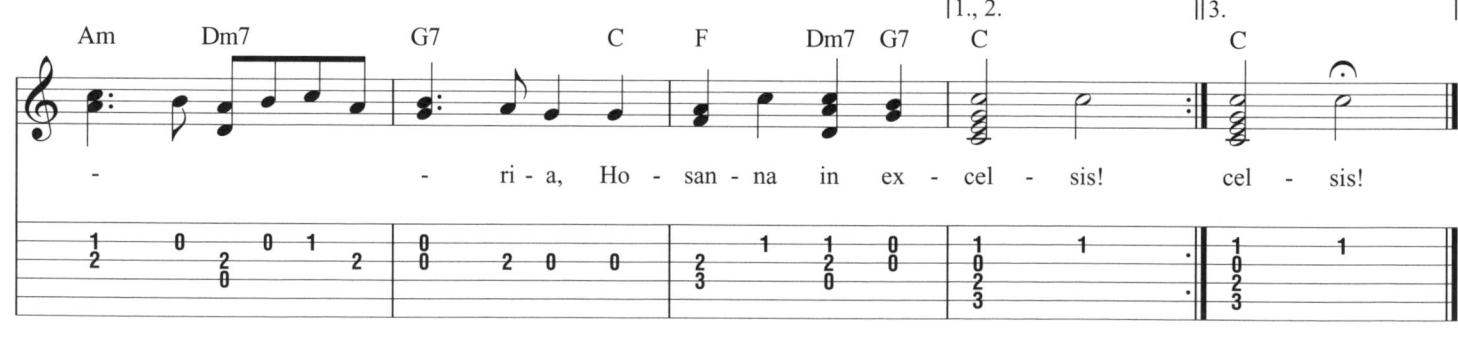

Additional Lyrics

2. E'en so here below, below, let steeple bells be swinging,
   And i-o, i-o, i-o, by priest and people singing.

3. Pray you, dutifully prime your matin chime, ye ringers;
   May you beautifully rime your evetime song, ye singers.

The Friendly Beasts

Traditional English Carol

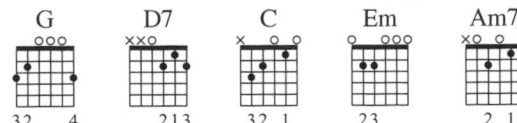

Strum Pattern: 7
Pick Pattern: 8

Verse
Moderately

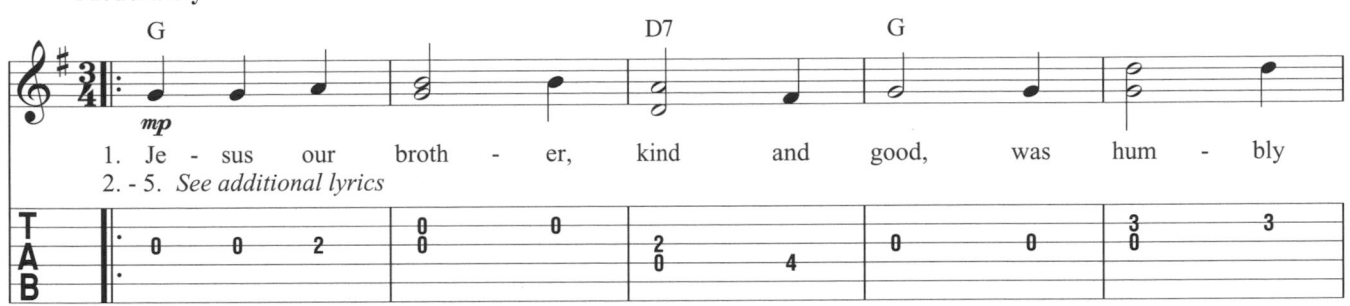

1. Je - sus our broth - er, kind and good, was hum - bly
2. - 5. *See additional lyrics*

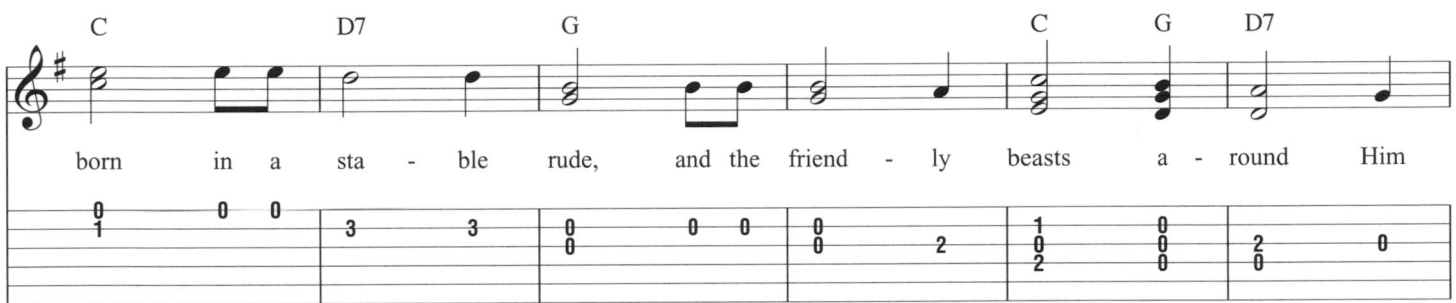

born in a sta - ble rude, and the friend - ly beasts a - round Him

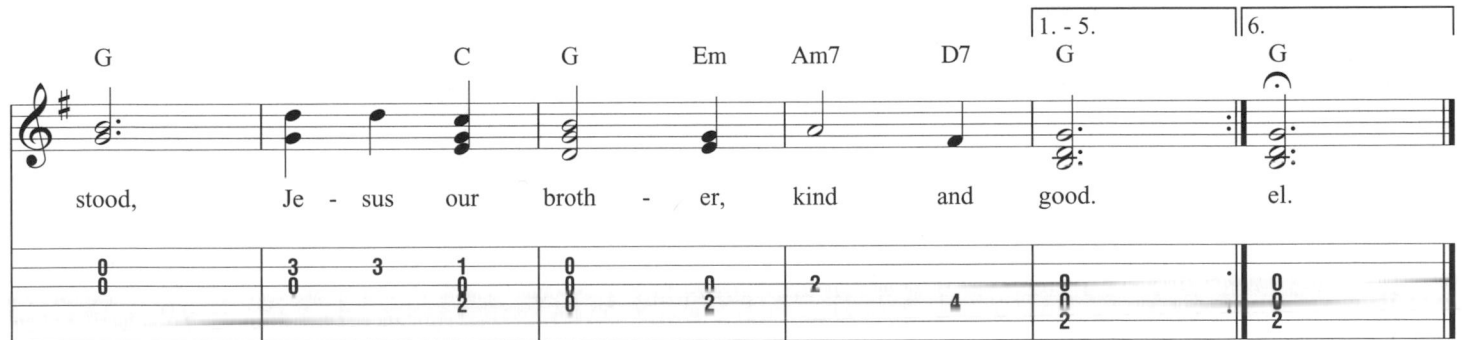

stood, Je - sus our broth - er, kind and good. el.

Additional Lyrics

2. "I," said the donkey, shaggy and brown,
   "I carried his mother up hill and down.
   I carried his mother to Bethlehem town."
   "I," said the donkey, shaggy and brown.

3. "I," said the cow, all white and red,
   "I gave Him my manger for His bed.
   I gave Him my hay to pillow His head."
   "I," said the cow, all white and red.

4. "I," said the sheep with the curly horn,
   "I gave Him my wool for His blanket warm.
   He wore my coat on Christmas morn."
   "I," said the sheep with the curly horn.

5. "I," said the dove from the rafters high,
   "I cooed Him to sleep that He would not cry.
   We cooed Him to sleep, my mate and I."
   "I," said the dove from the rafters high.

6. Thus every beast by some good spell,
   In the stable dark was glad to tell
   Of the gift he gave Emmanuel,
   The gift he gave Emmanuel.

The First Noël

17th Century English
Music from W. Sandys' *Christmas Carols*

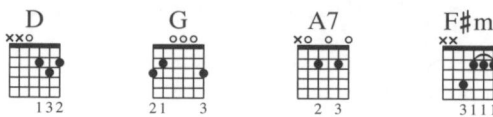

Strum Pattern: 7, 8
Pick Pattern: 8, 9

Verse
Moderately slow

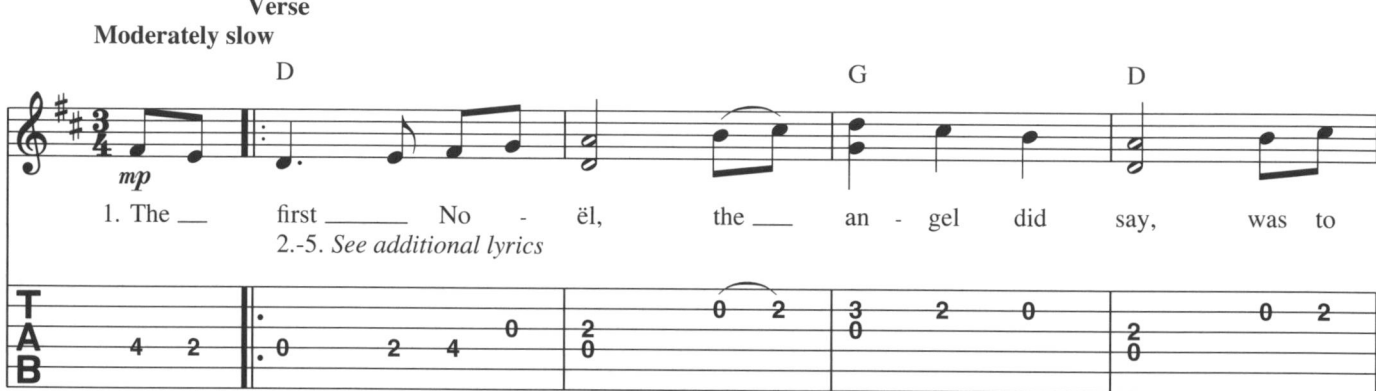

1. The ___ first _____ No - ël, the ___ an - gel did say, was to
2.-5. *See additional lyrics*

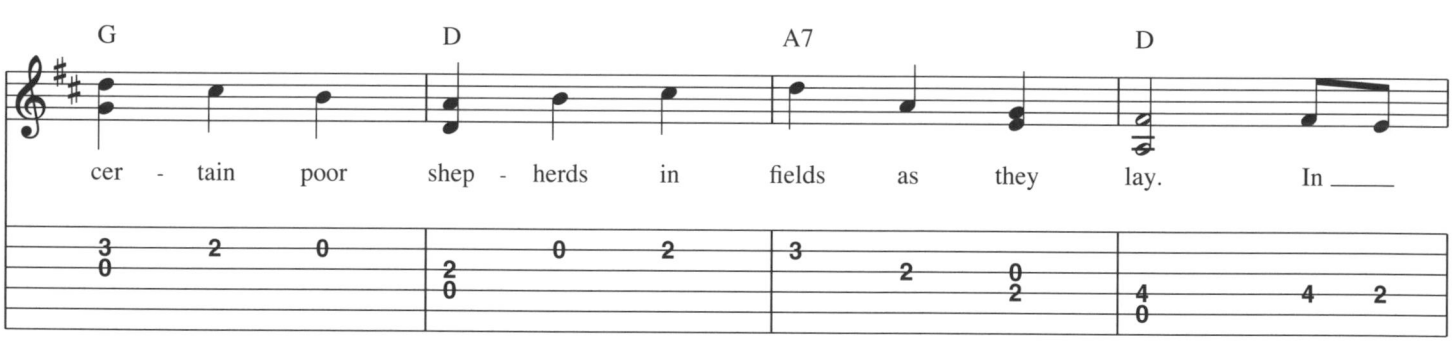

cer - tain poor shep - herds in fields as they lay. In _____

fields _____ where ___ they ___ lay ___ keep - ing their sheep, ___ on a

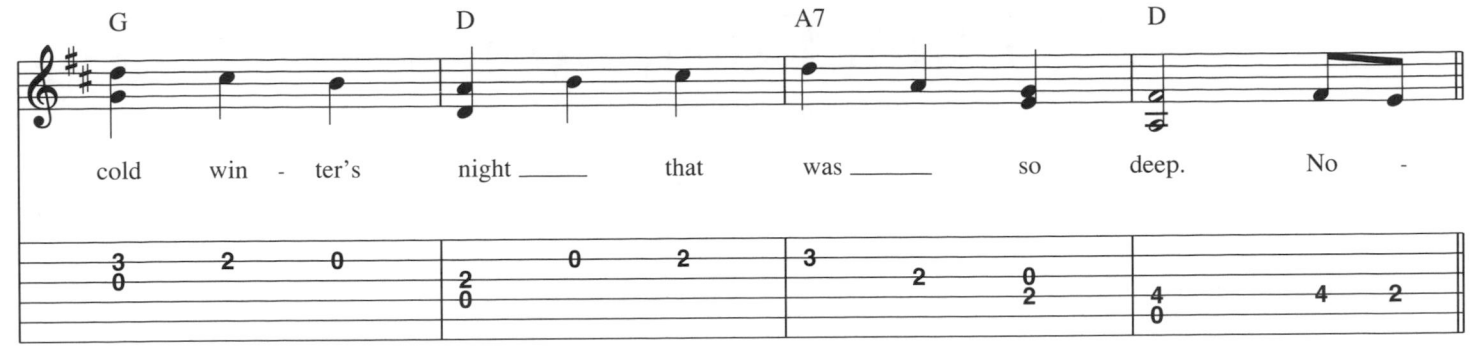

cold win - ter's night _____ that was _____ so deep. No -

Chorus

ël, _____ No - ël, No - ël, No - ël, _____

born is the King _____ of Is - ra - el. 2. They _ el.

Additional Lyrics

2. They looked up and saw a star
   Shining in the East, beyond them far.
   And to the earth it gave great light,
   And so it continued both day and night.

3. And by the light of that same star,
   Three wise man came from country far;
   To seek for a King was their intent,
   And to follow the star wherever it went.

4. This star drew nigh to the northwest,
   O'er Bethlehem it took its rest;
   And there it did both stop and stay,
   Right over the place where Jesus lay.

5. Then entered in those wise men three,
   Full reverently upon their knee;
   And offered there in His presence,
   Their gold and myrrh and frankincense.

Fum, Fum, Fum

Traditional Catalonian Carol

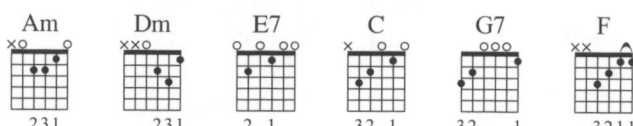

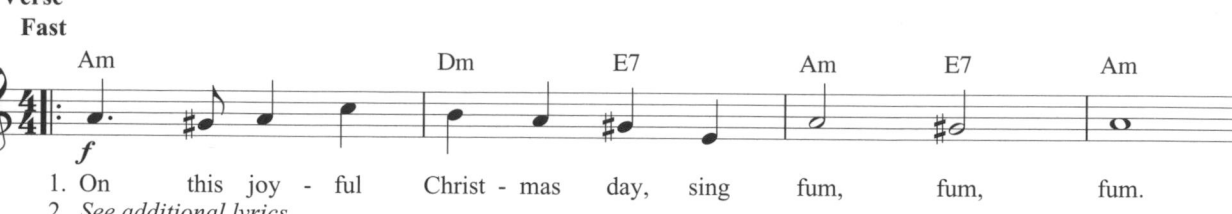

Strum Pattern: 3
Pick Pattern: 3

Verse
Fast

1. On this joy - ful Christ - mas day, sing fum, fum, fum.
2. *See additional lyrics*

On this joy - ful Christ - mas day, sing fum, fum, fum. For a bless - ed Babe was

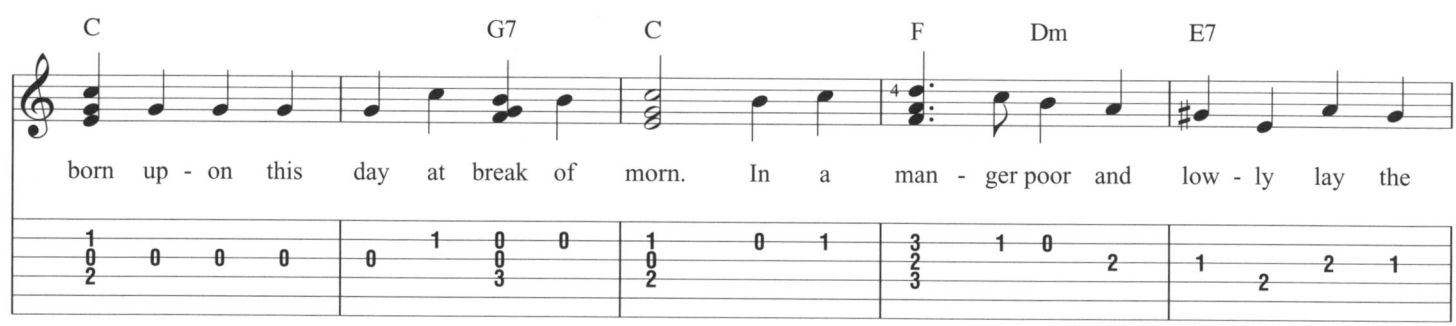

born up - on this day at break of morn. In a man - ger poor and low - ly lay the

Son of God most ho - ly. Fum, fum, fum. fum.

*Use Pattern 10

Additional Lyrics

2. Thanks to God for holidays, sing fum, fum, fum.
   Thanks to God for holidays, sing fum, fum, fum.
   Now we all our voices raise.
   And sing a song of grateful praise.
   Celebrate in song and story, all the wonders of His glory.
   Fum, fum, fum.

Go, Tell It on the Mountain

African-American Spiritual
Verses by John W. Work, Jr.

Strum Pattern: 3, 4
Pick Pattern: 1, 4

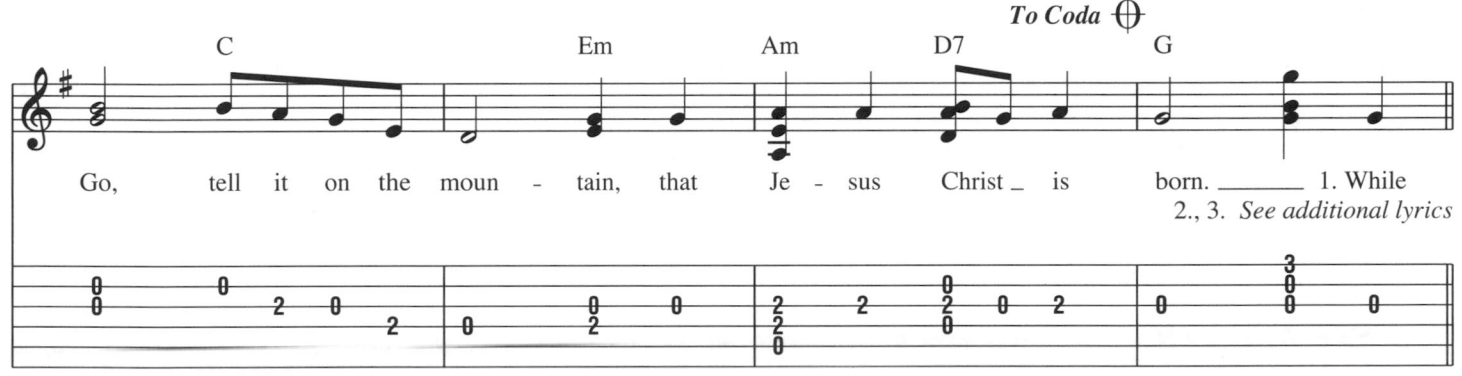

Additional Lyrics

2. The shepherds feared and trembled
   When, lo! above the earth
   Rang out the angel chorus
   That hailed our Savior's birth.

3. Down in a lowly manger
   Our humble Christ was born.
   And God sent us salvation
   That blessed Christmas morn.

God Rest Ye Merry, Gentlemen

19th Century English Carol

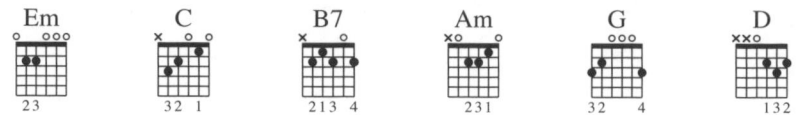

Strum Pattern: 3, 5
Pick Pattern: 3, 4

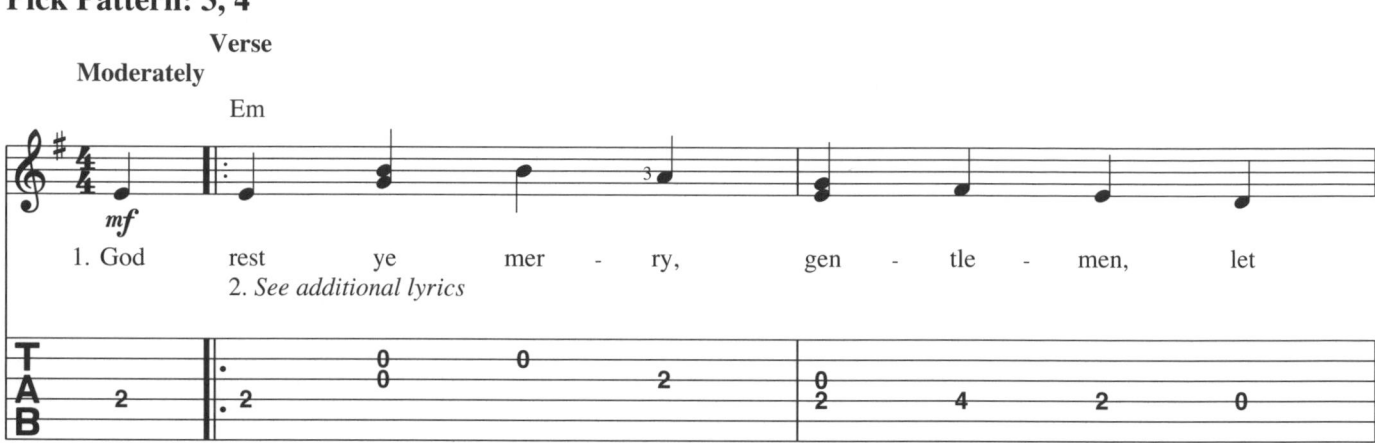

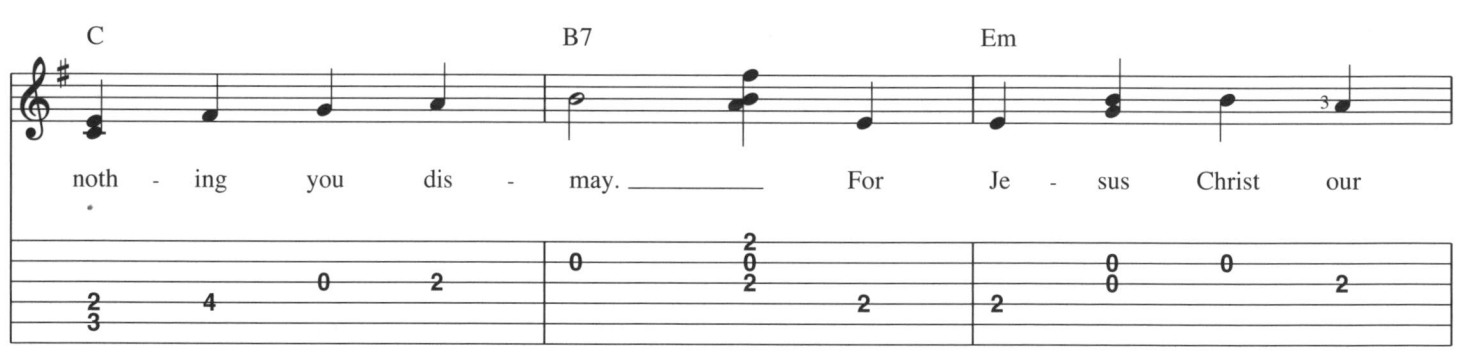

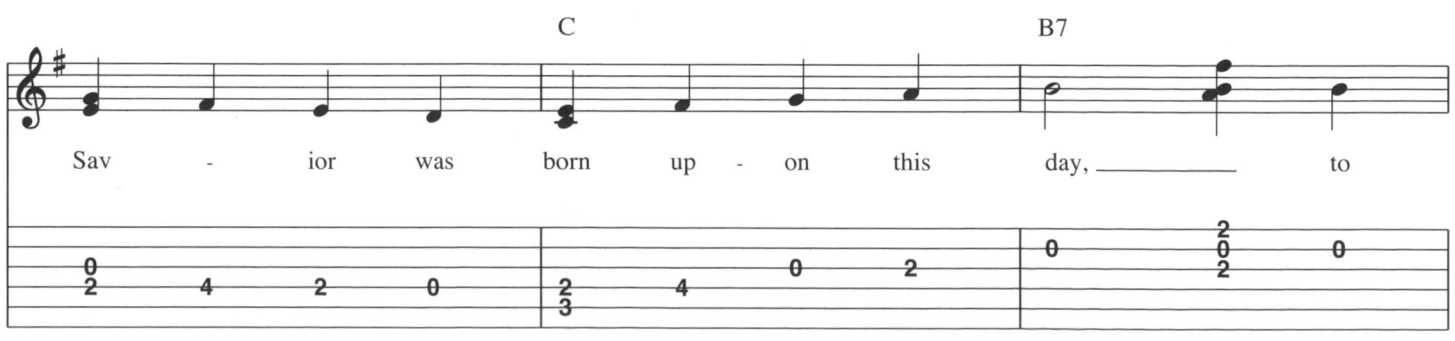

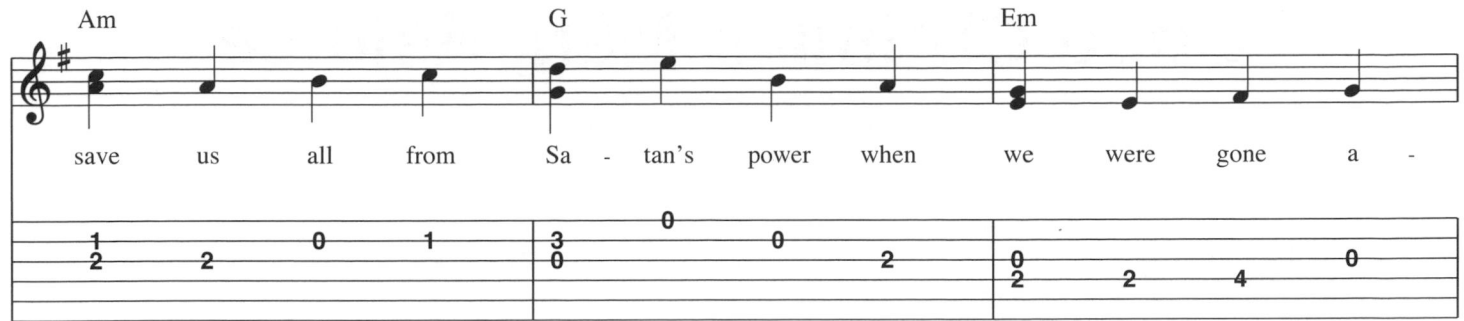

save us all from Sa - tan's power when we were gone a -

Chorus

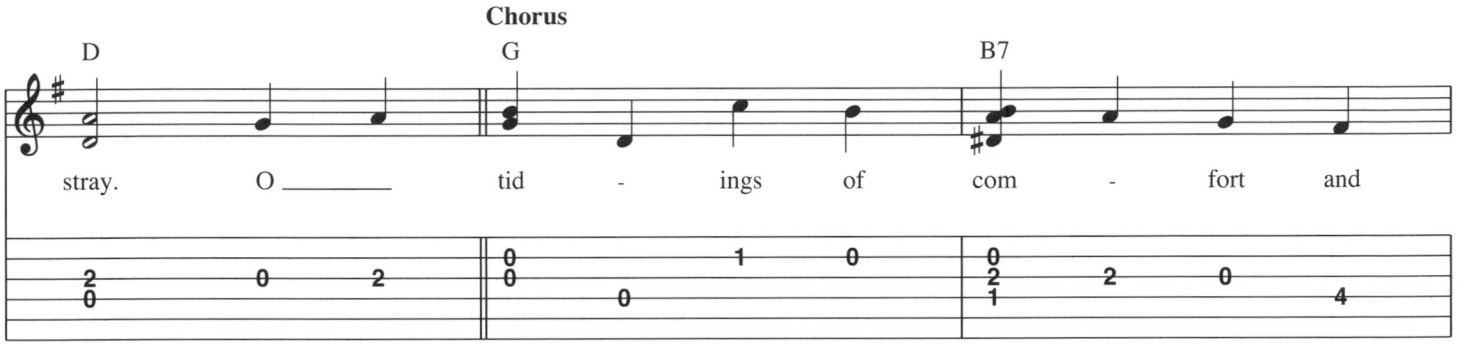

stray. O _____ tid - ings of com - fort and

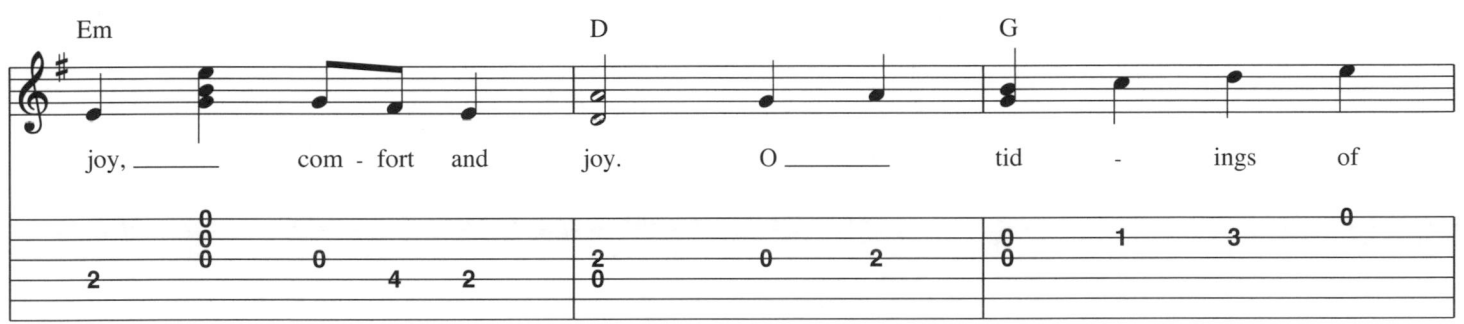

joy, _____ com - fort and joy. O _____ tid - ings of

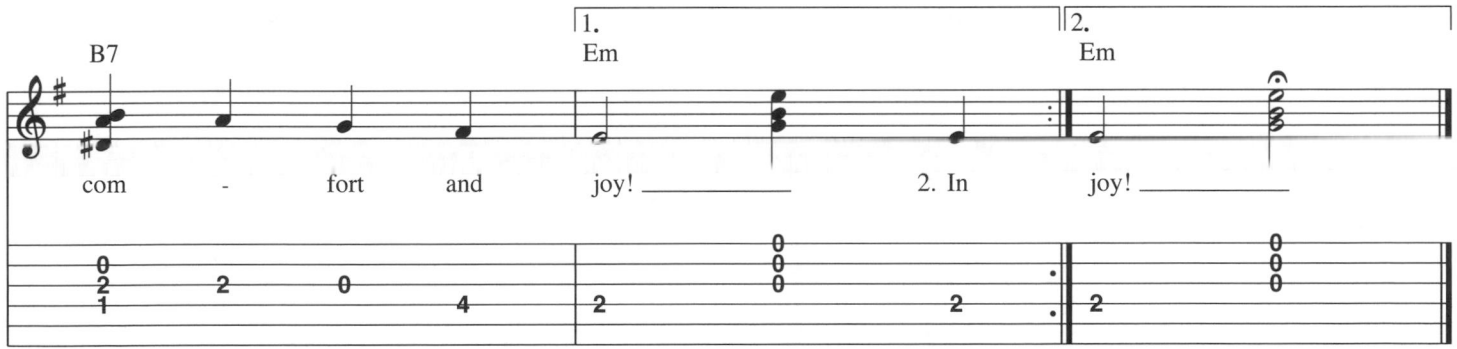

com - fort and joy! _____ 2. In joy! _____

Additional Lyrics

2. In Bethlehem, in Jewry
   This blessed babe was born
   And laid within a manger
   Upon this blessed morn
   To which His mother Mary
   Did nothing take in scorn.

Good Christian Men, Rejoice

14th Century Latin Text
Translated by John Mason Neale
14th Century German Melody

Strum Pattern: 7
Pick Pattern: 7

Verse
Moderately slow, in 2

1. Good Chris - tian men, re - joic _____ with heart and soul and voice. _____
2., 3. *See additional lyrics*

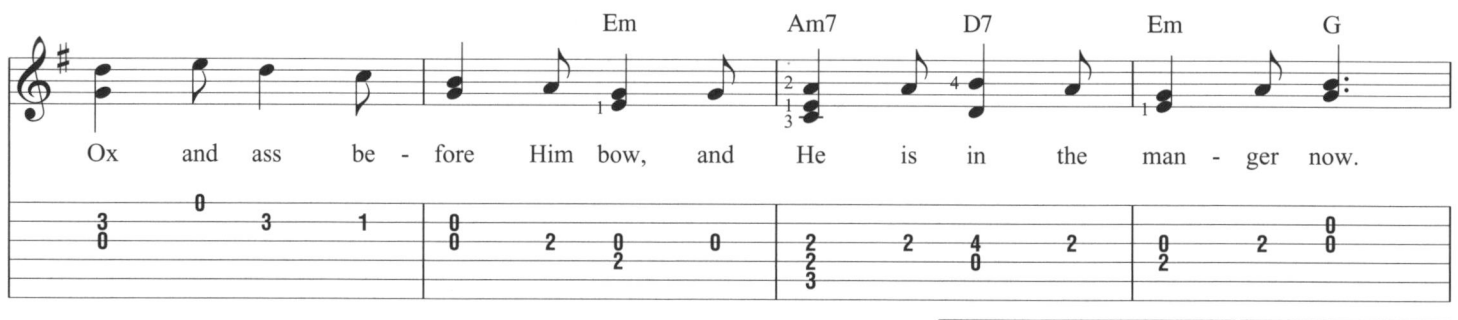

Give ye heed to what we say: News! News! Je - sus Christ is born to - day!

Ox and ass be - fore Him bow, and He is in the man - ger now.

Christ is born to - day! _____ Christ is born to - day. _____ 2. Good save!

Additional Lyrics

2. Good Christian men, rejoice
   With heart and soul and voice.
   Now ye hear of endless bliss: Joy! Joy!
   Jesus Christ was born for this.
   He hath op'd the heavenly door,
   And man is blessed evermore.
   Christ was born for this!
   Christ was born for this!

3. Good Christian men, rejoice
   With heart and soul and voice.
   Now ye need not fear the grave: Peace! Peace!
   Jesus Christ was born to save!
   Calls you one and calls you all,
   To gain His everlasting hall.
   Christ was born to save!
   Christ was born to save!

Hear Them Bells

Words and Music by D.S. McCosh

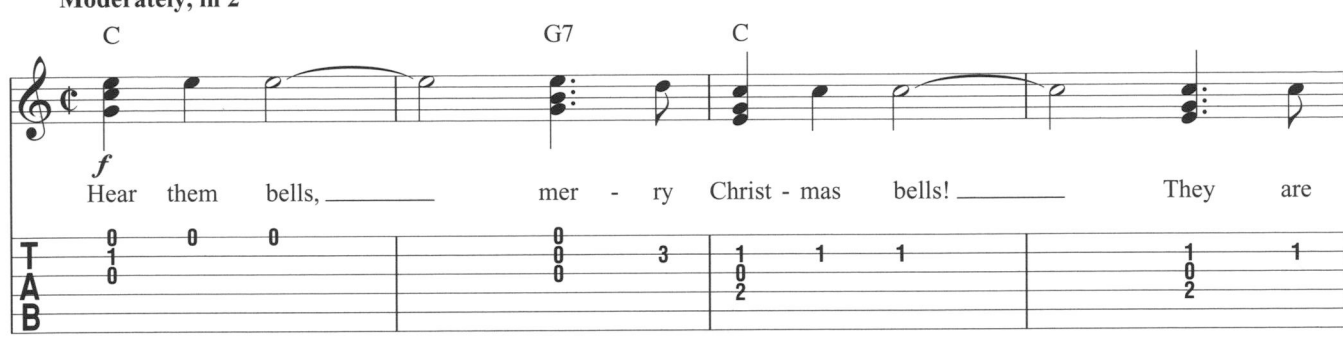

Strum Pattern: 3
Pick Pattern: 3

Verse
Moderately, in 2

Hear them bells, _____ mer - ry Christ - mas bells! _____ They are

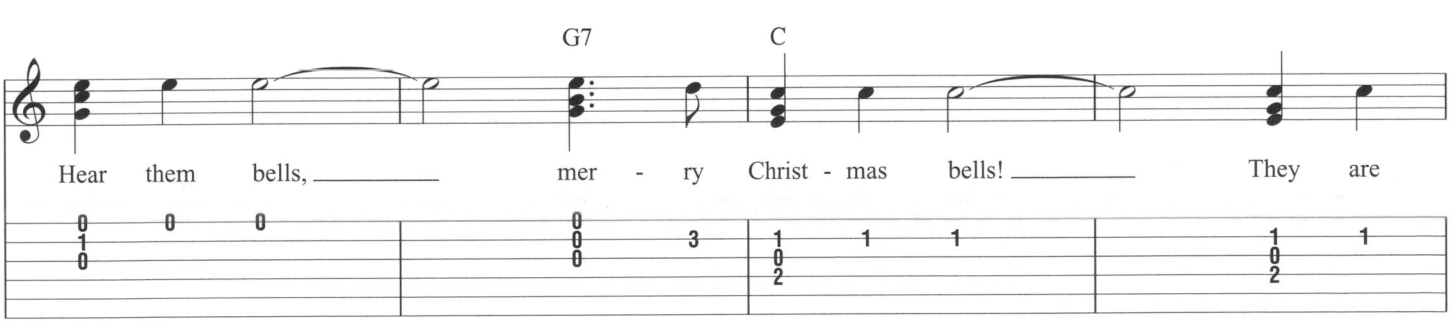

ring - ing out the e - vil of the sword. _____

Hear them bells, _____ mer - ry Christ - mas bells! _____ They are

ring - ing in the glo - ry of the Lord! _____

Good King Wenceslas

Words by John M. Neale
Music by Piae Cantiones

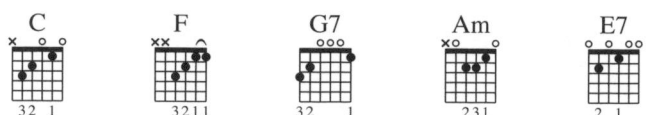

Strum Pattern: 3, 4
Pick Pattern: 3, 5

Verse
Moderately fast

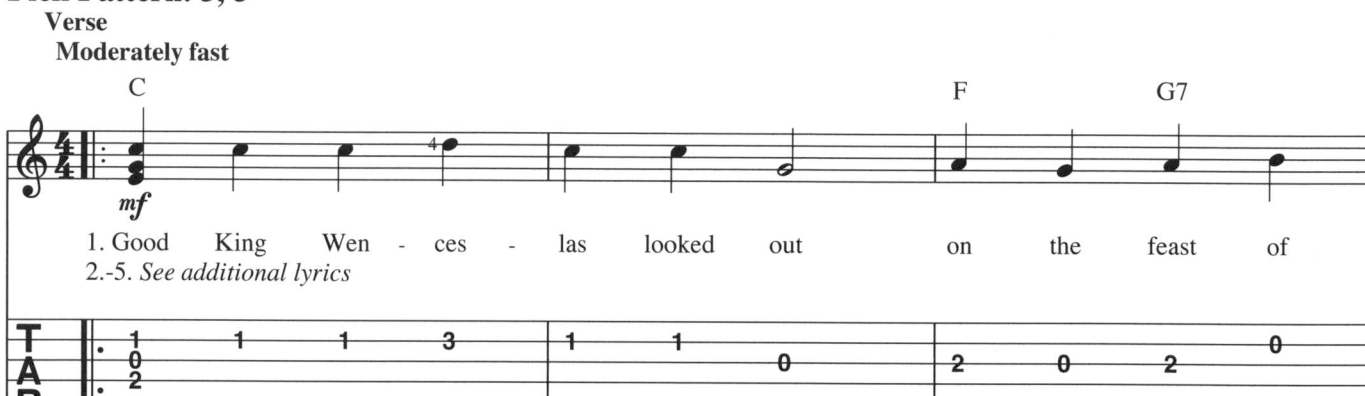

1. Good King Wen - ces - las looked out on the feast of
2.-5. *See additional lyrics*

Ste - phen; when the snow lay 'round a - bout, deep and crisp and e - ven. Bright - ly shone the

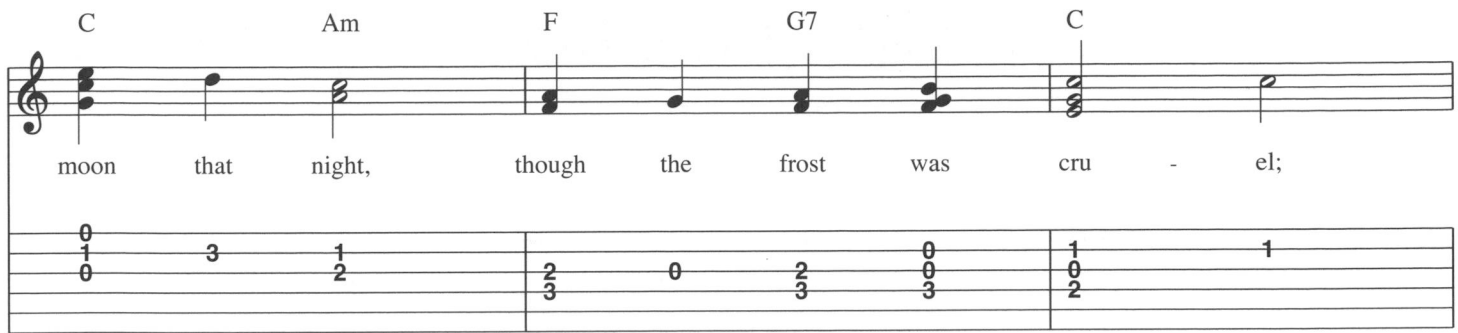

moon that night, though the frost was cru - el;

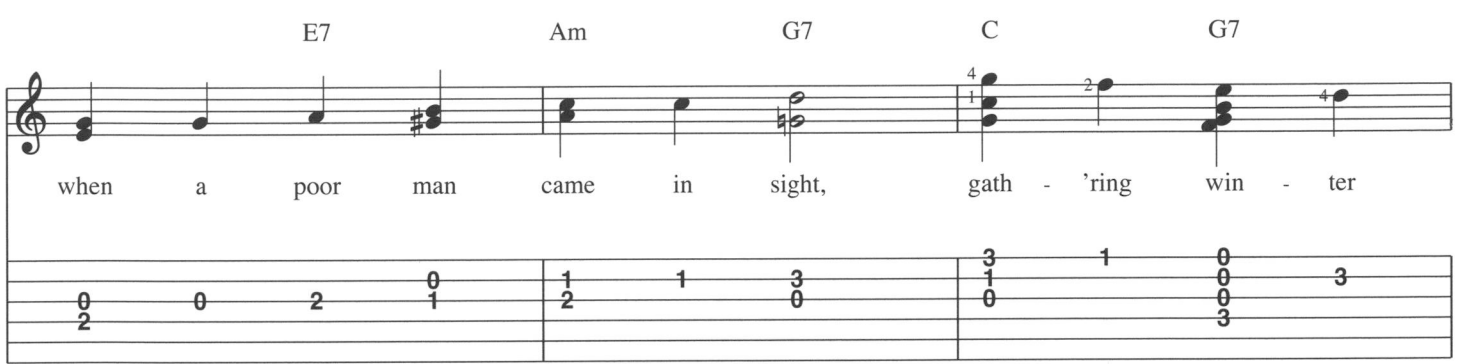

when a poor man came in sight, gath - 'ring win - ter

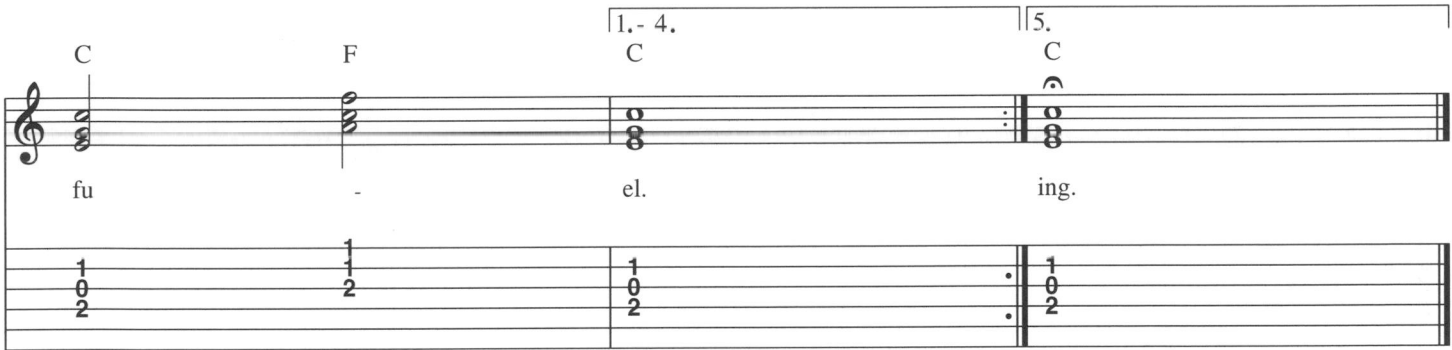

fu - el. ing.

Additional Lyrics

2. "Hither page, and stand by me,
   If thou know'st it, telling;
   Yonder peasant, who is he?
   Where and what his dwelling?"
   "Sire, he lives a good league hence,
   Underneath the mountain;
   Right against the forest fence,
   By Saint Agnes' fountain."

3. "Bring me flesh, and bring me wine,
   Bring me pine-logs hither;
   Thou and I will see him dine,
   When we bear them thither."
   Page and monarch forth they went,
   Forth they went together;
   Through the rude winds wild lament,
   And the bitter weather.

4. "Sire, the night is darker now,
   And the wind blows stronger;
   Fails my heart, I know not how,
   I can go not longer."
   "Mark my footsteps, my good page,
   Tread thou in them boldly:
   Thou shalt find the winter's rage
   Freeze thy blood less coldly."

5. In his master's steps he trod,
   Where the snow lay dinted;
   Heat was in the very sod
   Which the saint has printed.
   Therefore, Christian men, be sure,
   Wealth or rank possessing;
   Ye who now will bless the poor,
   Shall yourselves find blessing.

Hallelujah Chorus

By George Frideric Handel

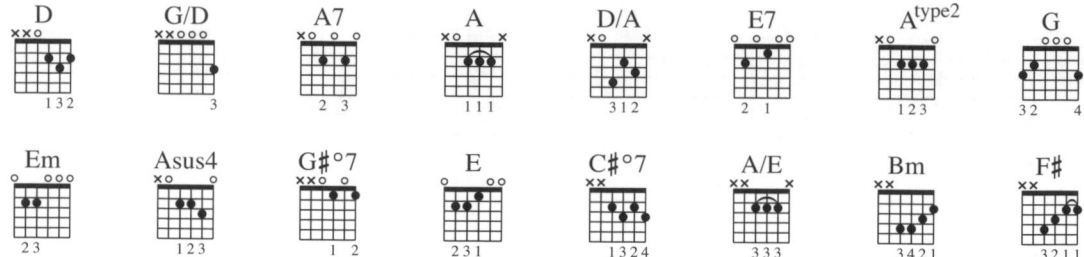

Strum Pattern: 4
Pick Pattern: 4

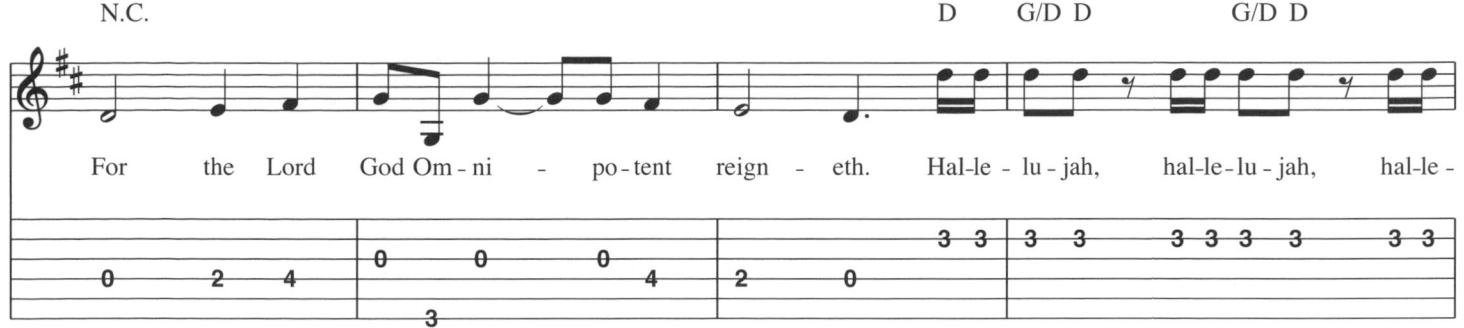

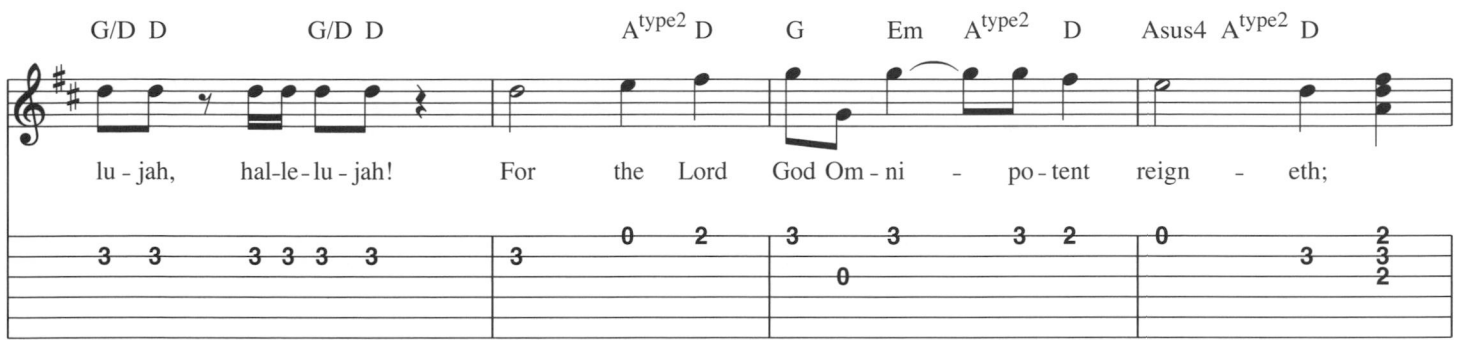

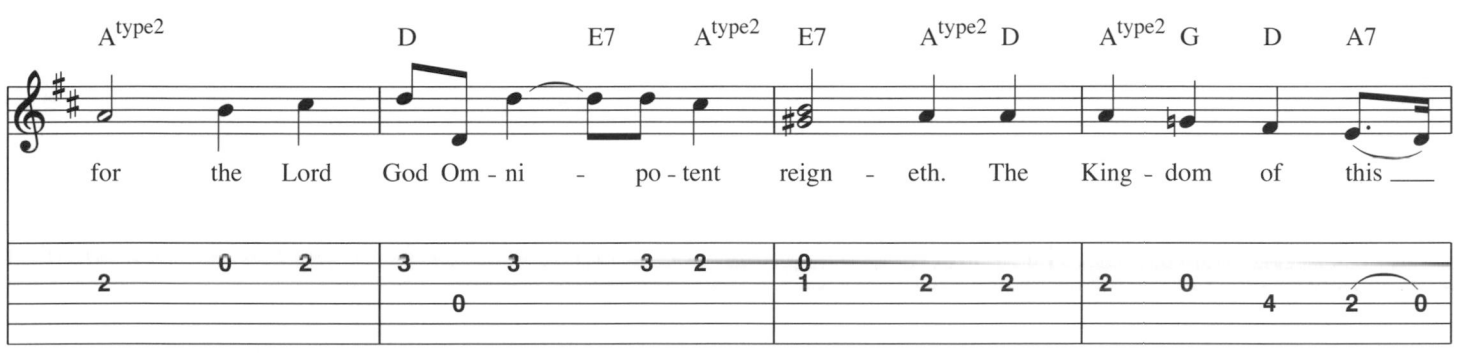

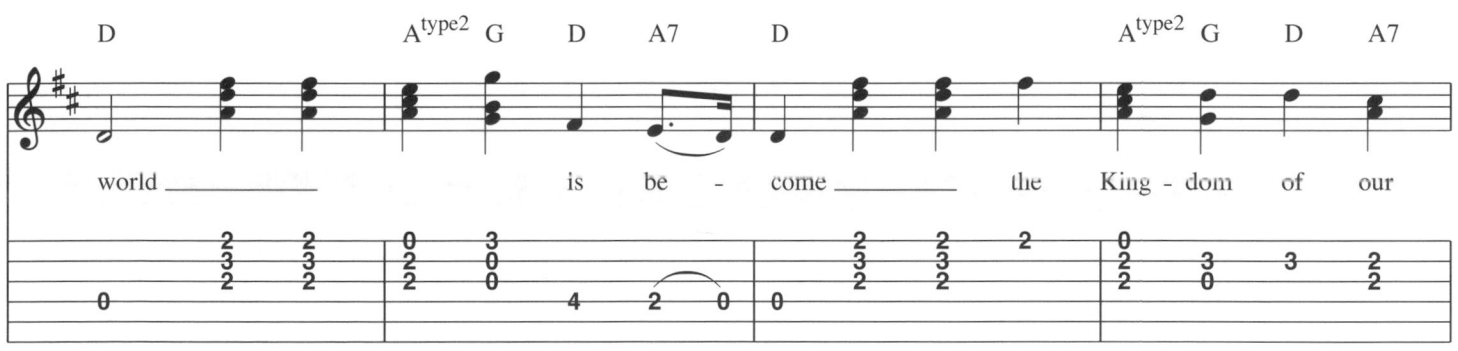

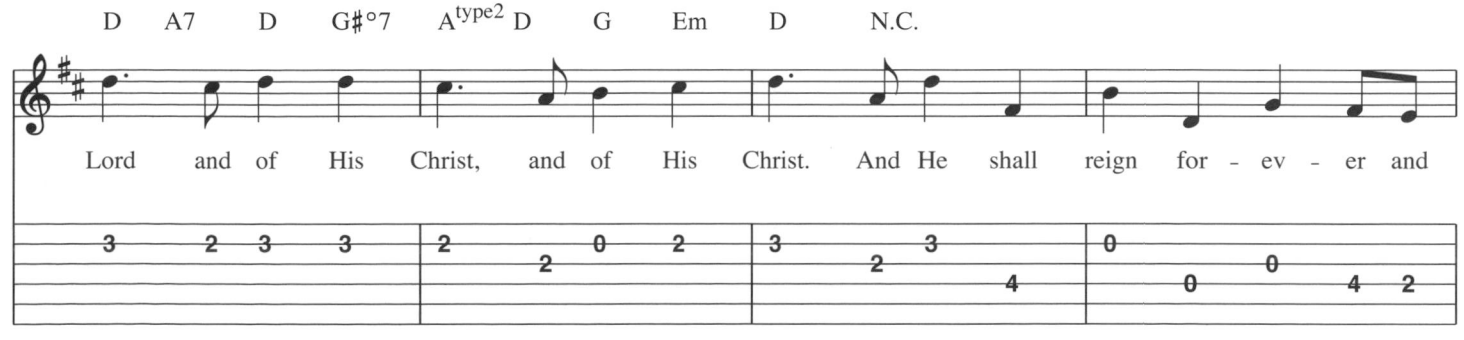

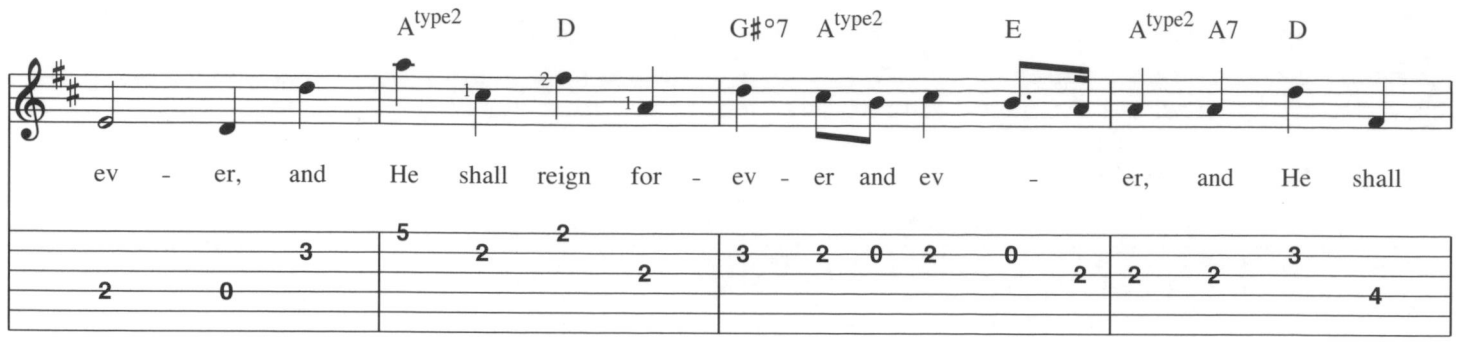

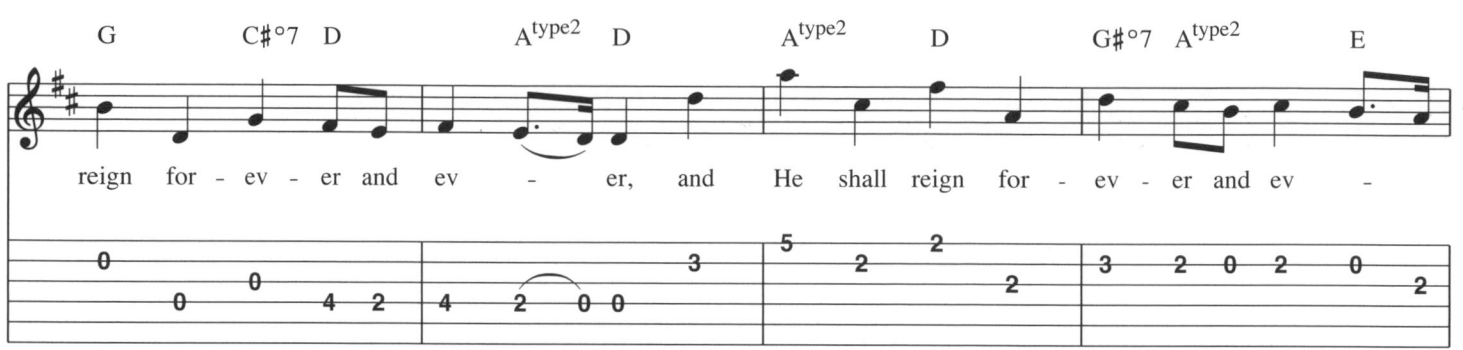

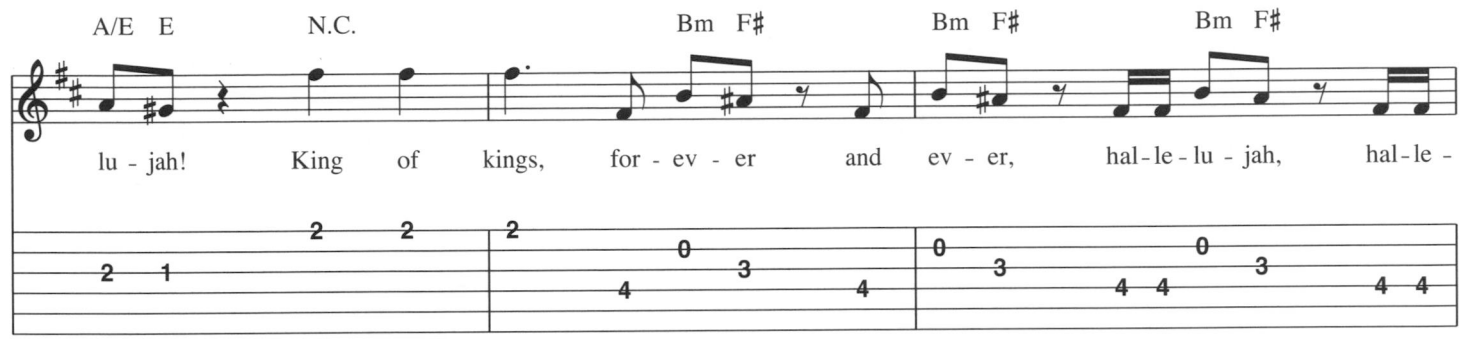

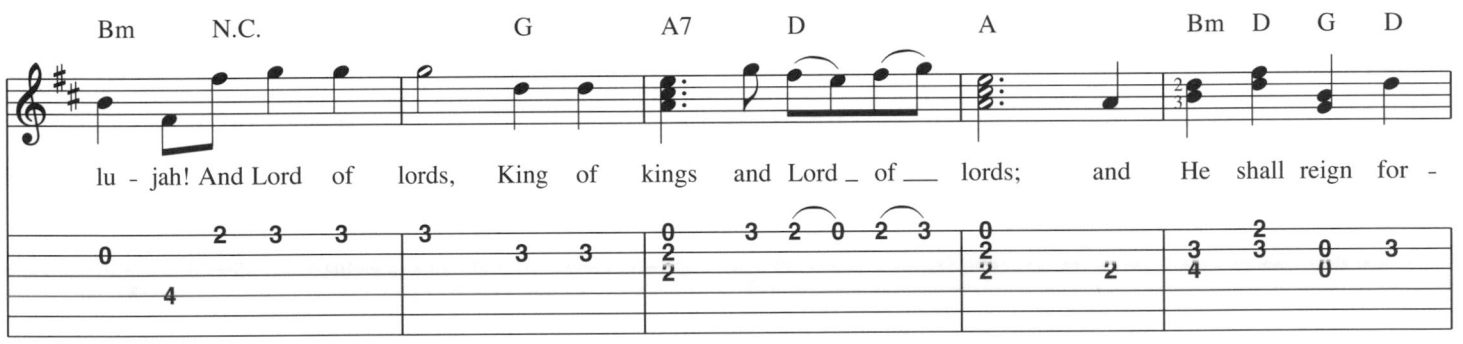

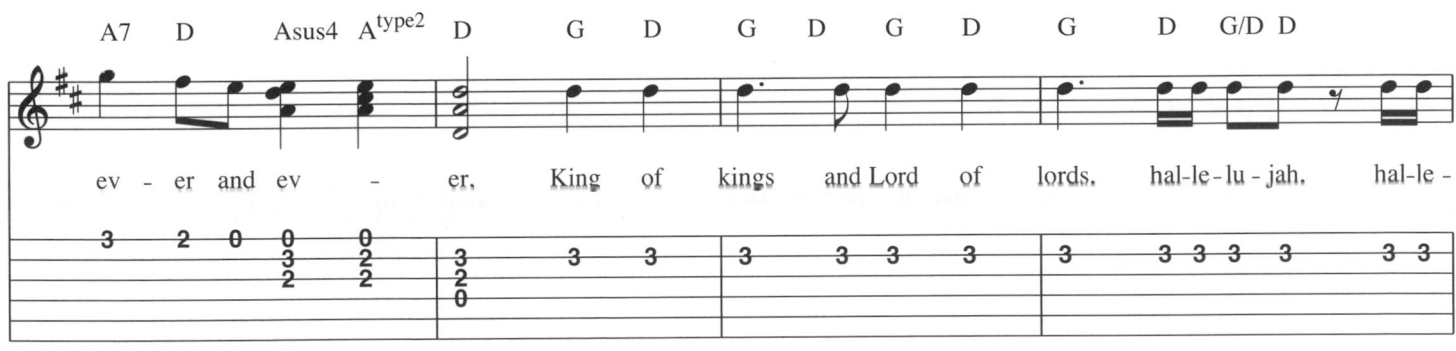

Hark! The Herald Angels Sing

Words by Charles Wesley
Altered by George Whitefield
Music by Felix Mendelssohn-Bartholdy
Arranged by William H. Cummings

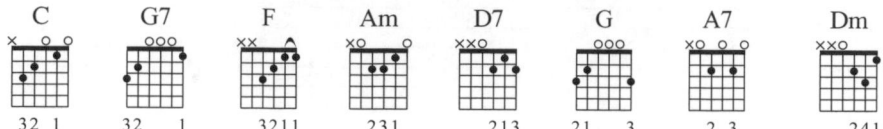

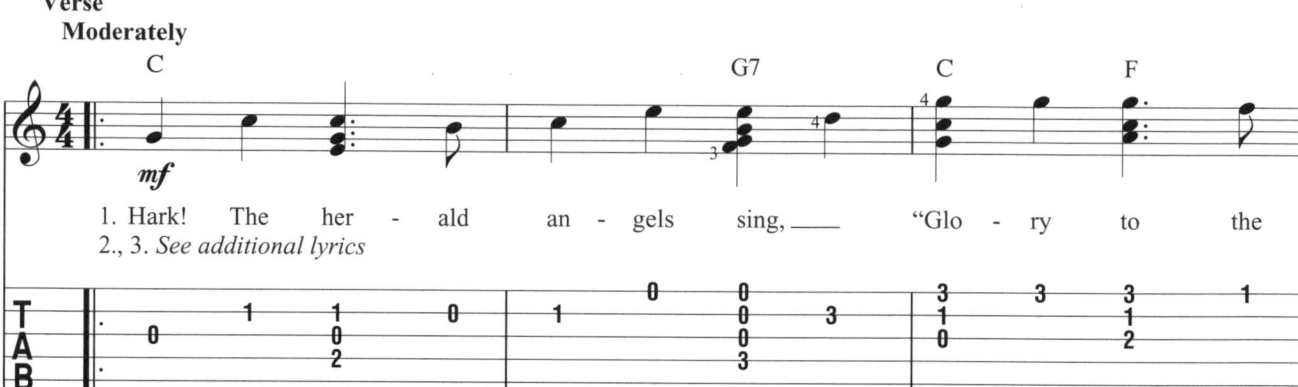

Strum Pattern: 3, 2
Pick Pattern: 3, 4

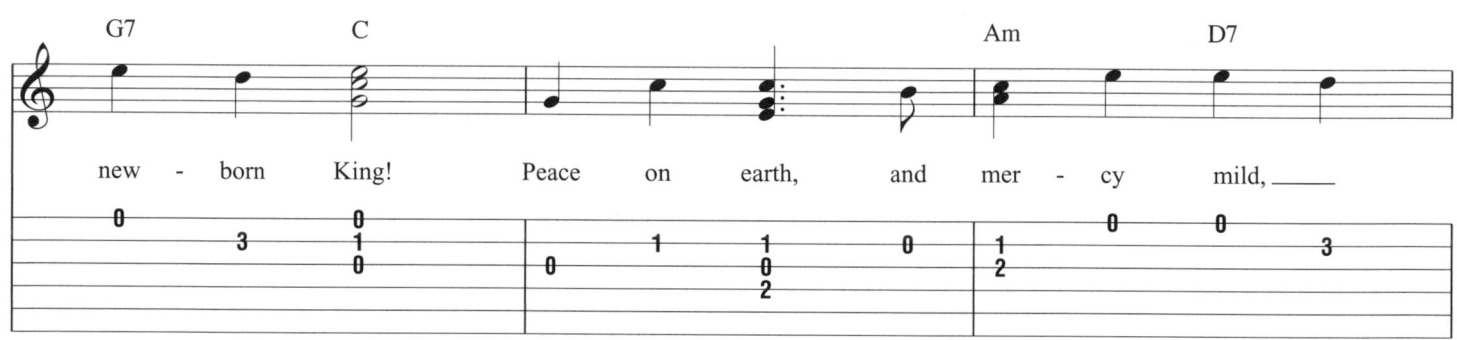

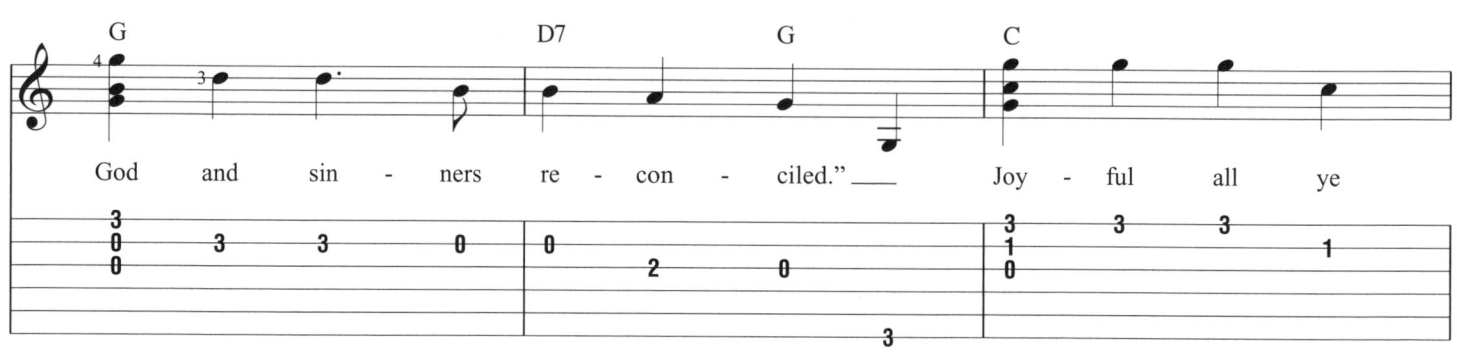

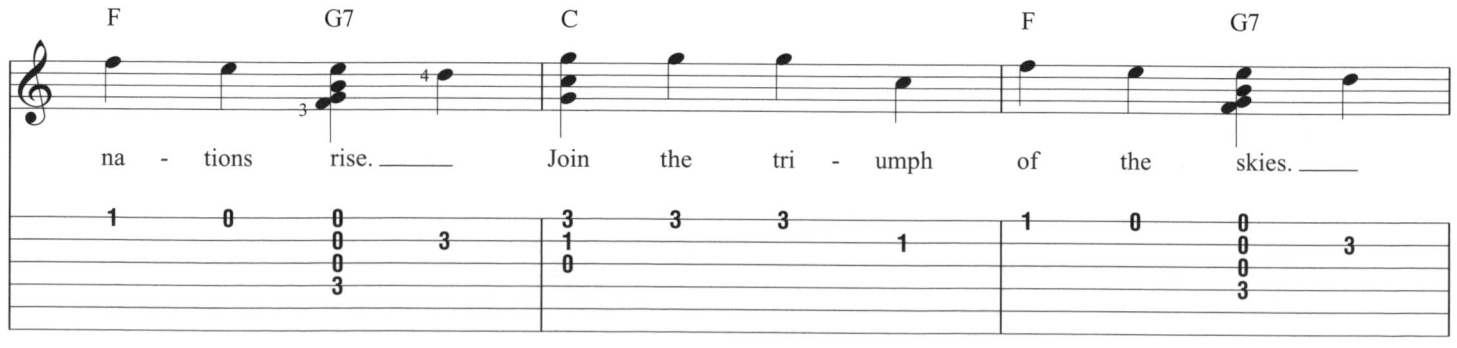

With th'an - gel - ic host pro - claim, ___ "Christ is ___ born in

Beth - le - hem." Hark! The her - ald an - gels sing,

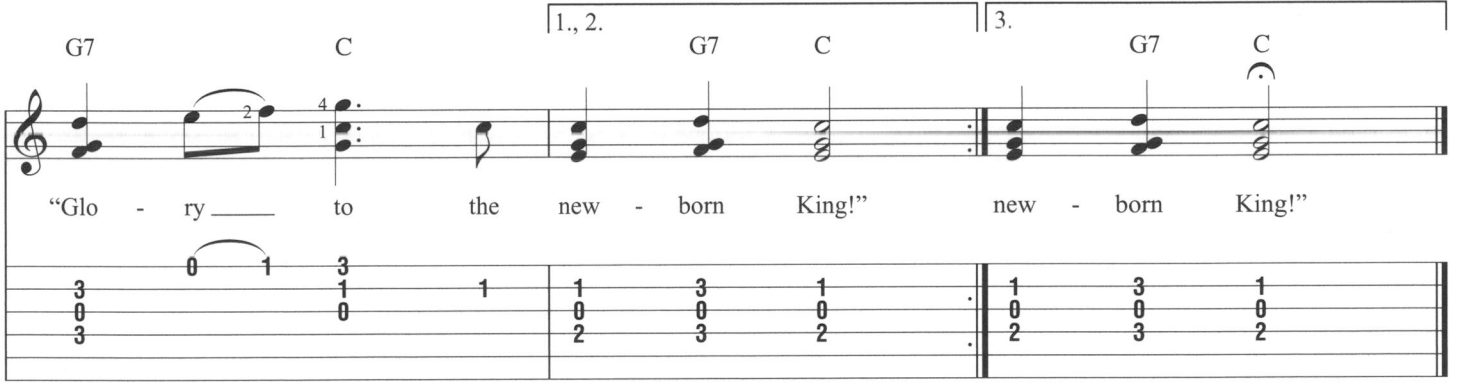

"Glo - ry ___ to the new - born King!" new - born King!"

Additional Lyrics

2. Christ, by highest heav'n adored,
   Christ, the everlasting Lord;
   Late in time behold Him come,
   Offspring of the Virgin's womb.
   Veil'd in flesh the Godhead see,
   Hail th'Incarnate Deity.
   Pleased as Man with man to dwell,
   Jesus, our Emmanuel!
   Hark! The herald angels sing,
   "Glory to the newborn King!"

3. Mild, He lays His glory by,
   Born that man no more may die.
   Born to raise the sons of earth,
   Born to give them second birth.
   Ris'n with healing in His wings,
   Light and life to all He brings.
   Hail the Son of Righteousness!
   Hail the heav'n-born Prince of Peace!
   Hark! The herald angels sing,
   "Glory to the newborn King!"

Hear, O Shepherds

Traditional Croation Carol

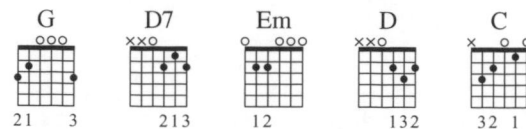

Strum Pattern: 4
Pick Pattern: 3

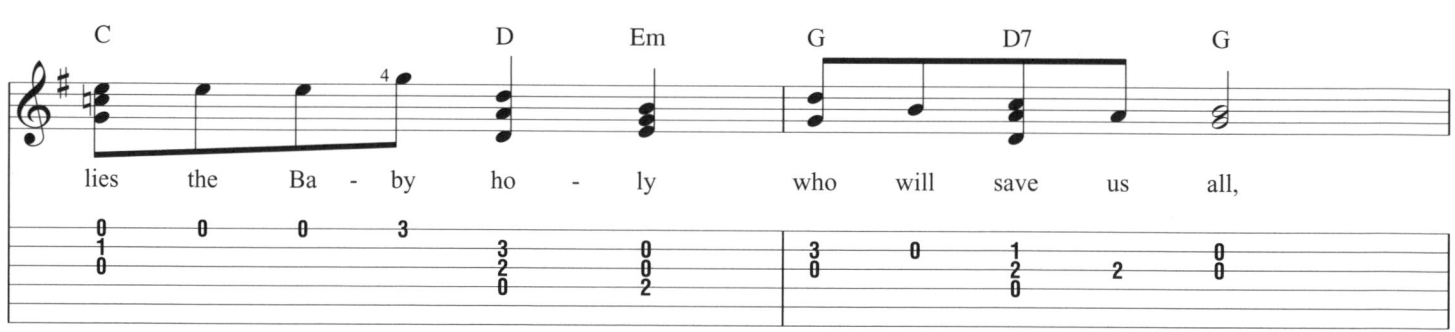

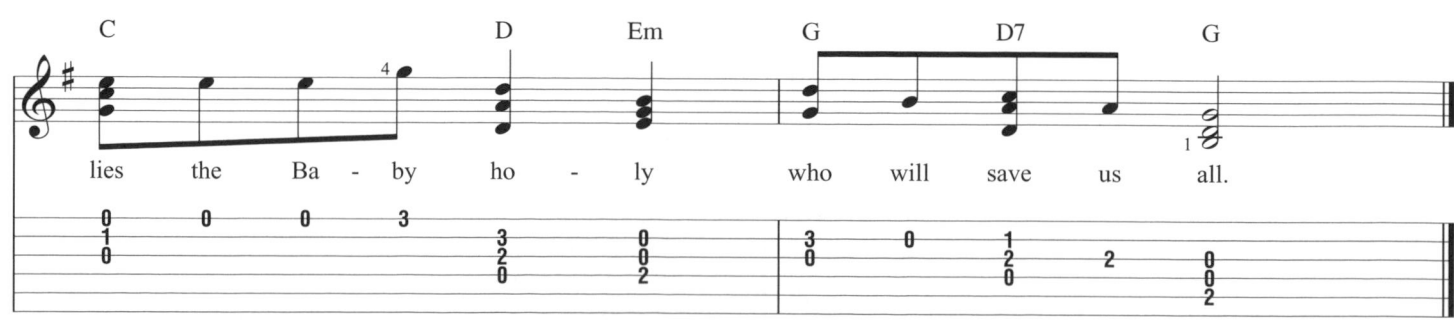

The Holly and the Ivy

18th Century English Carol

Strum Pattern: 8
Pick Pattern: 8

Additional Lyrics

2. The holly bears a blossom,
   As white as lily flow'r,
   And Mary bore sweet Jesus Christ,
   To be our sweet Savior.

3. The holly bears a berry,
   As red as any blood,
   And Mary bore sweet Jesus Christ,
   To do poor sinners good.

I Heard the Bells on Christmas Day

Words by Henry Wadsworth Longfellow
Music by John Baptiste Calkin

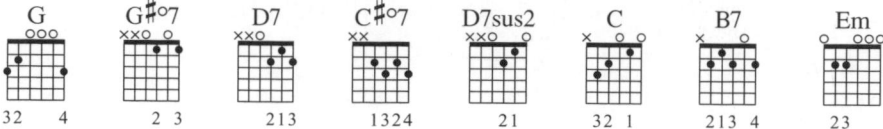

Strum Pattern: 4
Pick Pattern: 4

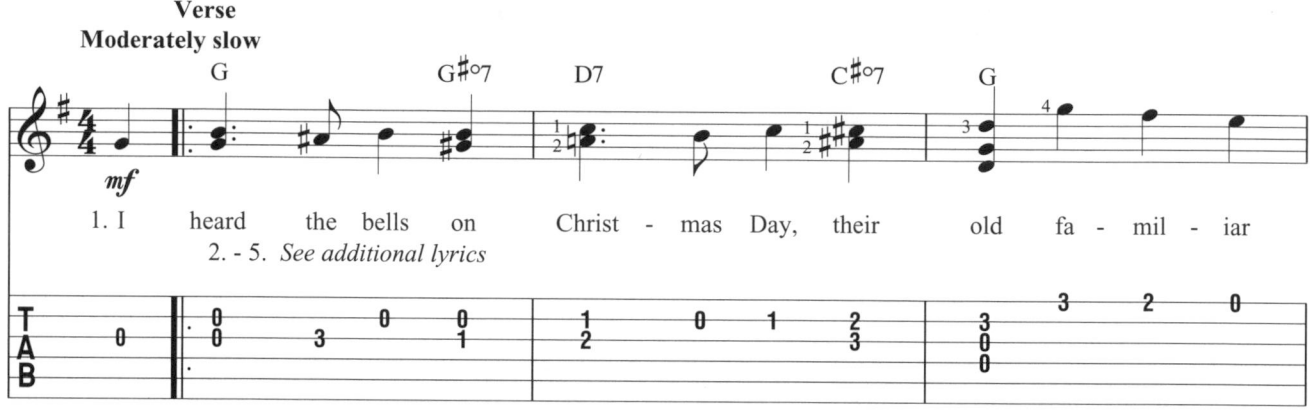

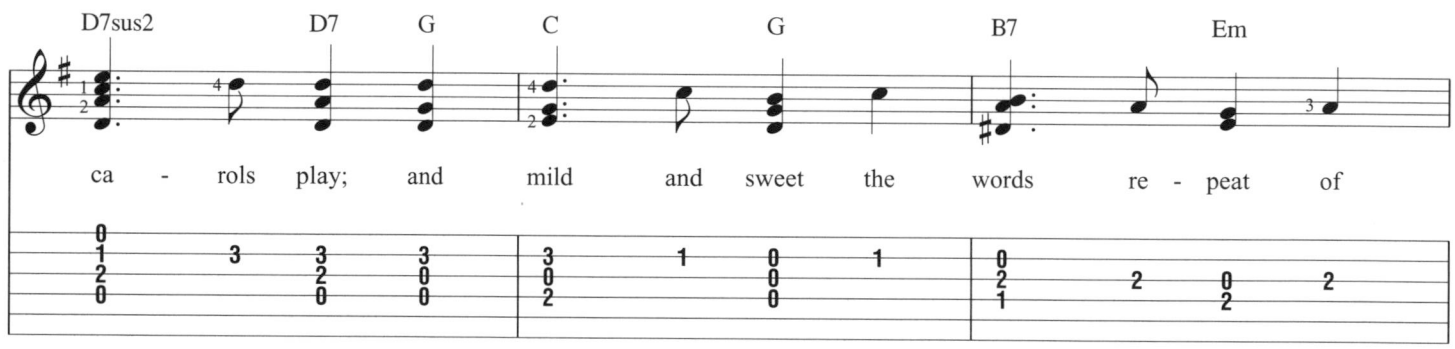

Additional Lyrics

2. I thought as now this day had come,
   The belfries of all Christendom
   Had rung so long the unbroken song
   Of peace on earth, good will to men.

3. And in despair I bow'd my head:
   "There is no peace on earth," I said,
   "For hate is strong, and mocks the song
   Of peace on earth, good will to min."

4. Then pealed the bells more loud and deep:
   "God is not dead, nor doth He sleep;
   The wrong shall fail, the right prevail,
   With peace on earth, good will to men."

5. Till ringing, singing on it's way,
   The world revolved from night to day,
   A voice, a chime, a chant sublime,
   Of peace on earth, good will to men!

I Saw Three Ships

Tradional English Carol

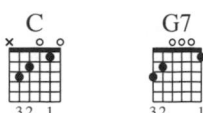

Strum Pattern: 7, 8
Pick Pattern: 8, 9

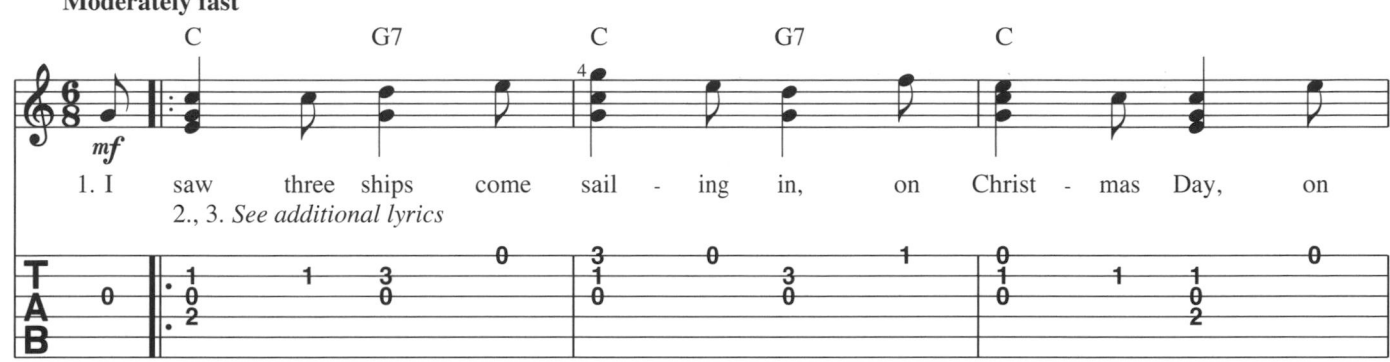

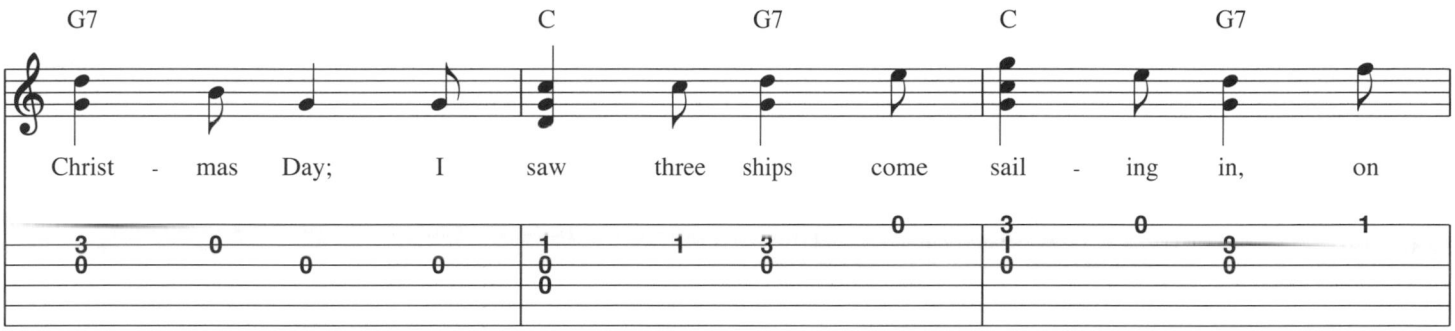

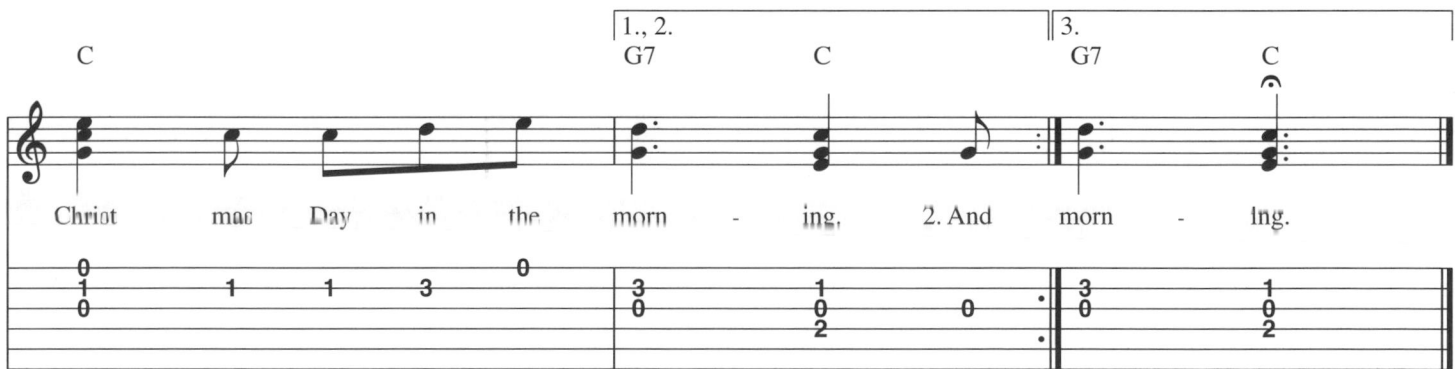

Additional Lyrics

2. And what was in those ships, all three,
   On Christmas Day, on Christmas Day;
   And what was in those ships, all three,
   On Christmas Day in the morning?

3. The Virgin Mary and Christ were there,
   On Christmas Day, on Christmas Day;
   The Virgin Mary and Christ were there,
   On Christmas Day in the morning.

Irish Carol

Traditional Irish Carol

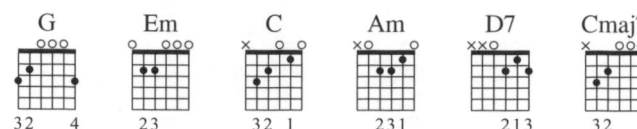

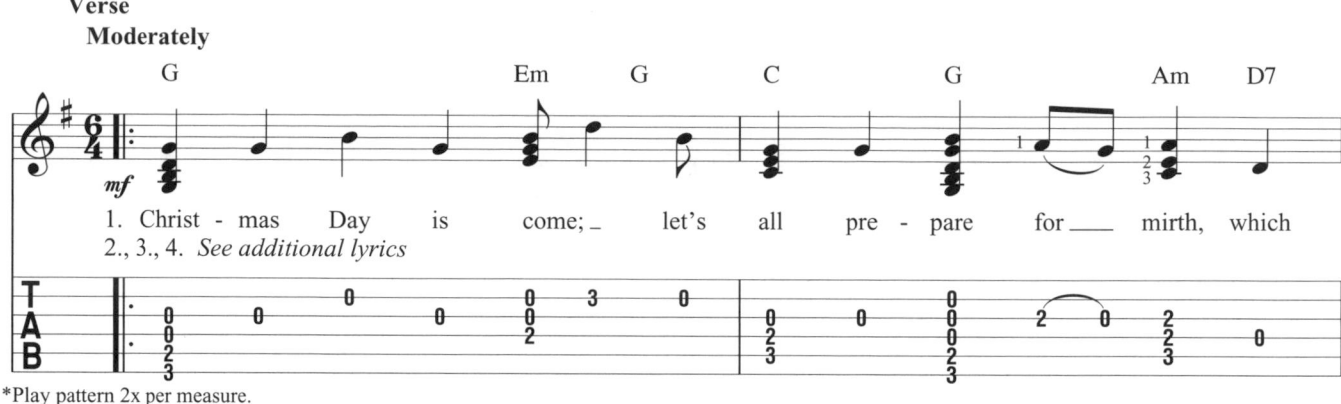

*Strum Pattern: 3
*Pick Pattern: 3

Verse
Moderately

1. Christ - mas Day is come; _ let's all pre - pare for __ mirth, which
2., 3., 4. *See additional lyrics*

*Play pattern 2x per measure.

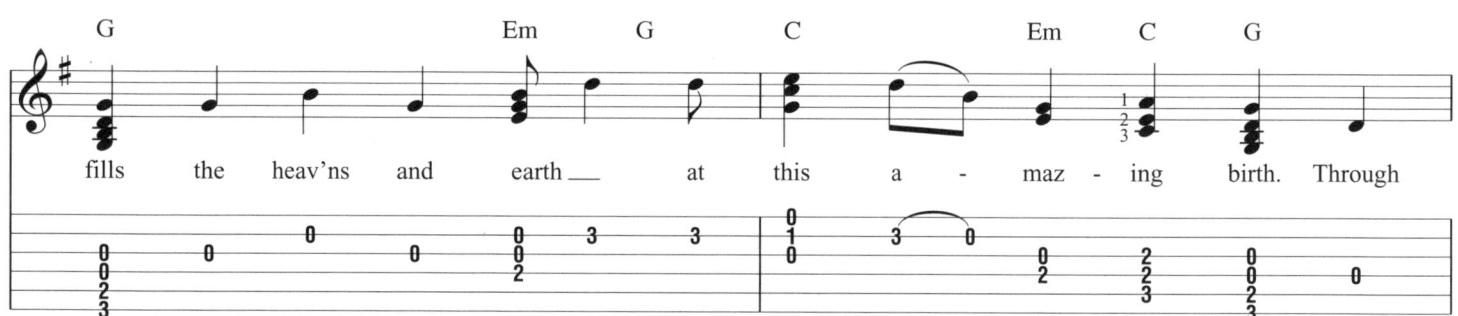

fills the heav'ns and earth __ at this a - maz - ing birth. Through

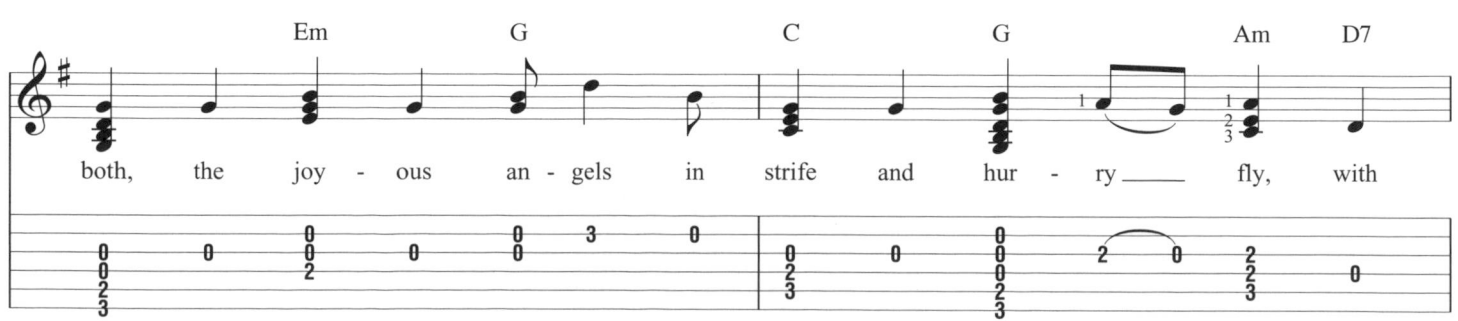

both, the joy - ous an - gels in strife and hur - ry __ fly, with

glo - ry and ho - san - nas, all Ho - ly ___ do they cry. In

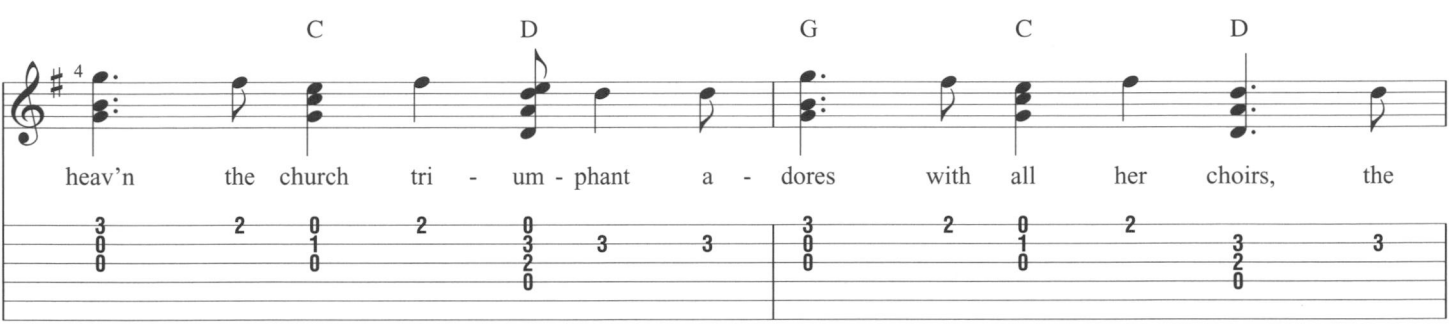

heav'n the church tri - um - phant a - dores with all her choirs, the

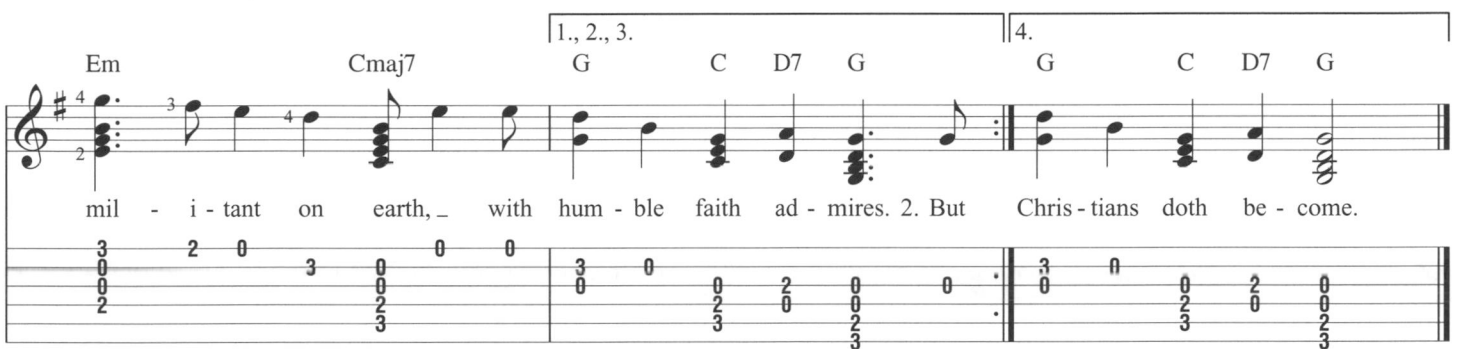

mil - i - tant on earth, _ with hum - ble faith ad - mires. 2. But Chris - tians doth be - come.

Additional Lyrics

2. But why should we rejoice? Should we not rather mourn
   To see the Hope of nations thus in a stable born?
   Where are His crown and sceptre, where is His throne sublime?
   Where is His train majestic that should the stars outshine?
   Is there no sumptuous palace, nor any inn at all,
   To lodge His heav'nly mother, but in a filthy stall?

3. O cease, ye blessed angels, such clam'rous joys to make!
   Though midnight silence favours, the shepherds are awake.
   And you, O glorious star that with new splendor brings,
   From the remotest parts three learned eastern Kings.
   Turn somewhere else your lustre, your rags elsewhere display,
   For Herod may slay the Babe, and Christ must straight away.

4. If we would then rejoice, let's cancel the old score.
   And purposing amendment, resolve to sin no more.
   For mirth can ne'er content us, without a conscience clear,
   And thus we'll find true pleasure in all the usual cheer.
   In dancing, sporting, rev'ling with masquerade and drum,
   So Christmas merry be, as Christians doth become.

It Came Upon the Midnight Clear

Words by Edmund Hamilton Sears
Music by Richard Storrs Willis

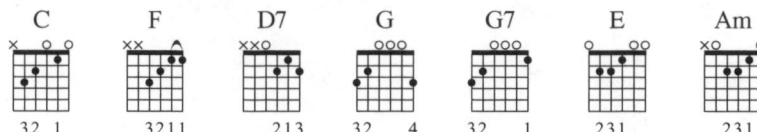

Strum Pattern: 7, 8
Pick Pattern: 7, 9

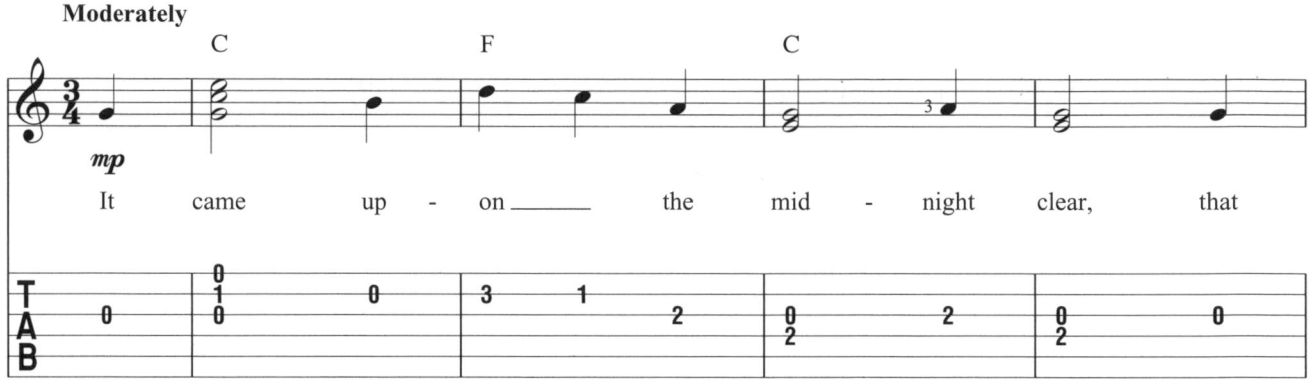

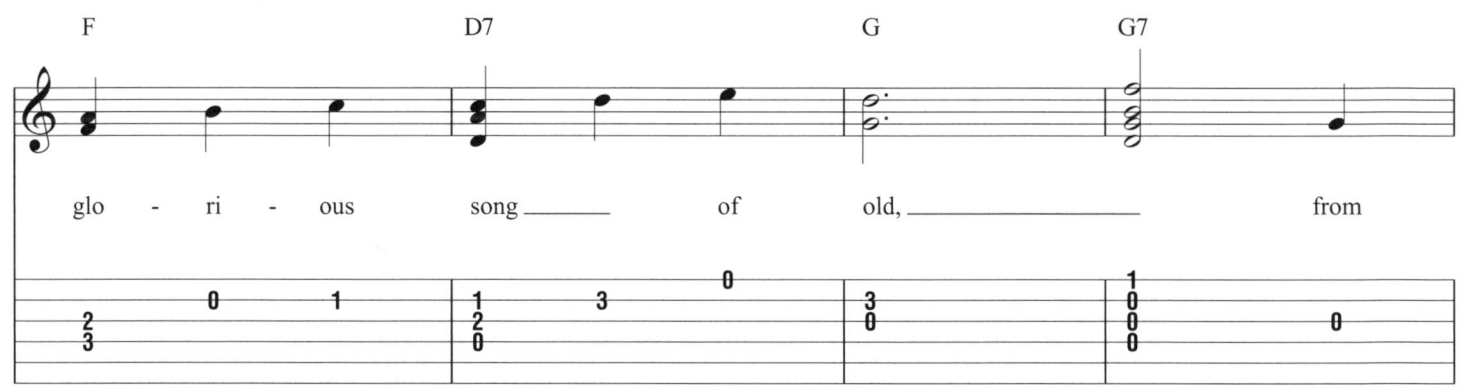

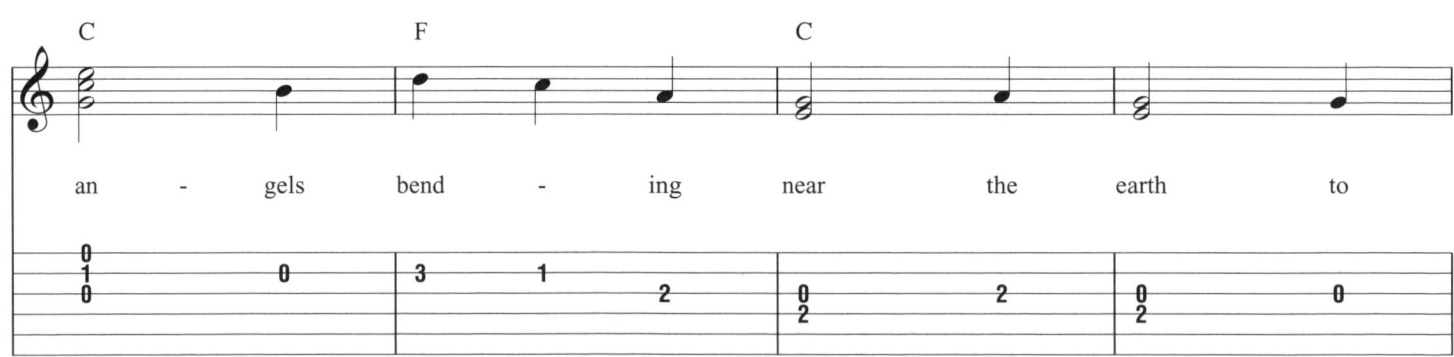

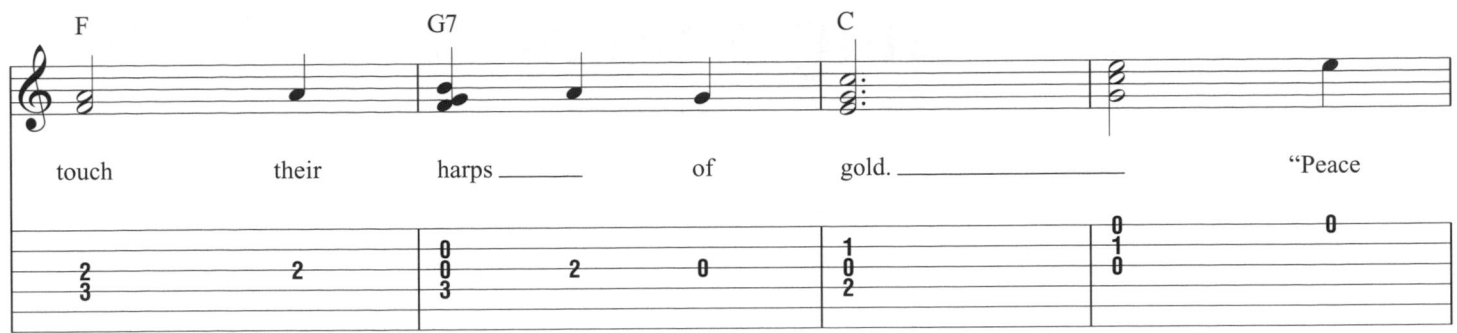

touch their harps _____ of gold. _____ "Peace

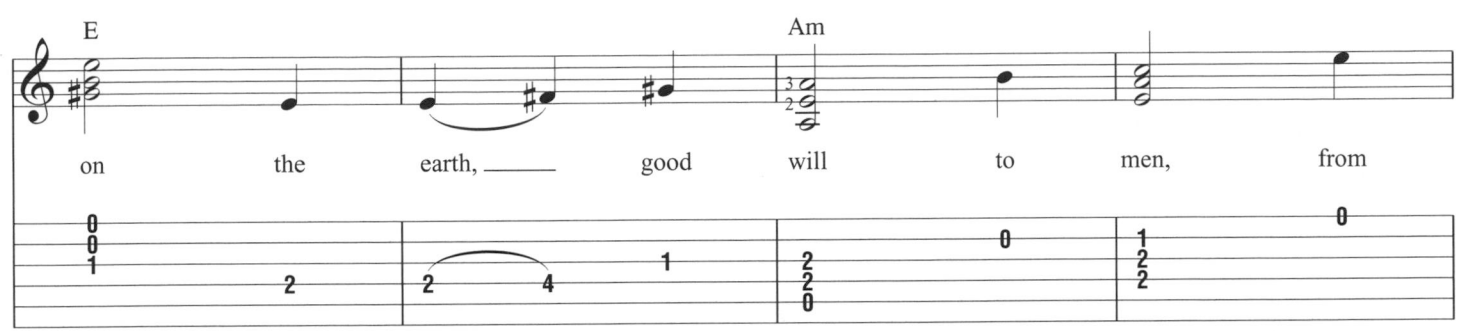

on the earth, _____ good will to men, from

heav - en's all gra - cious King." _____ The

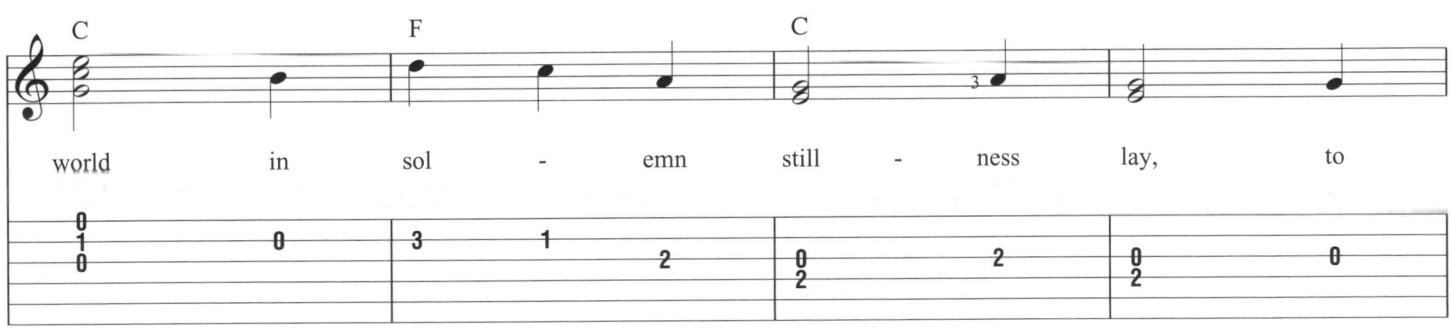

world in sol - emn still - ness lay, to

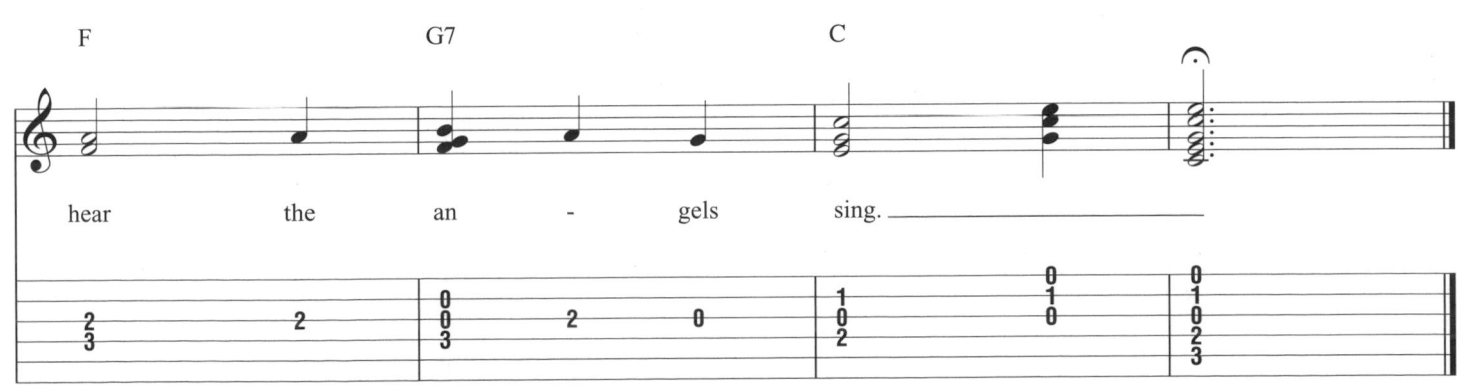

hear the an - gels sing. _____

Jingle Bells

Words and Music by J. Pierpont

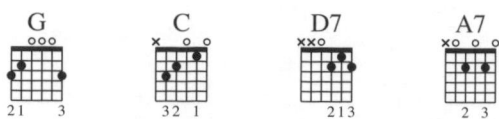

Strum Pattern: 2, 3
Pick Pattern: 3, 4

Verse
Fast

1. Dash - ing through the snow, _____ in a one horse o - pen sleigh, _____
2., 3. *See additional lyrics*

o'er the fields we go, laugh - ing all the way. _____

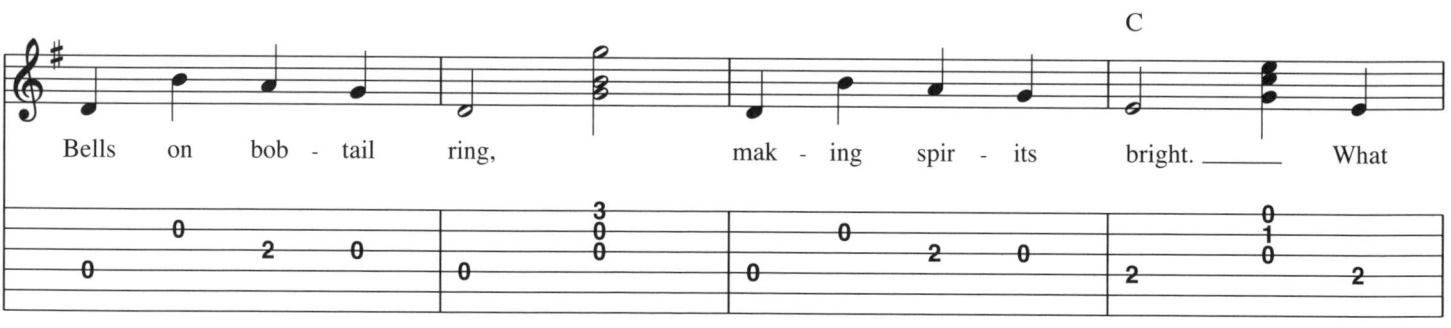

Bells on bob - tail ring, mak - ing spir - its bright. _____ What

fun it is to ride and sing a sleigh - ing song to - night! Oh!

Chorus

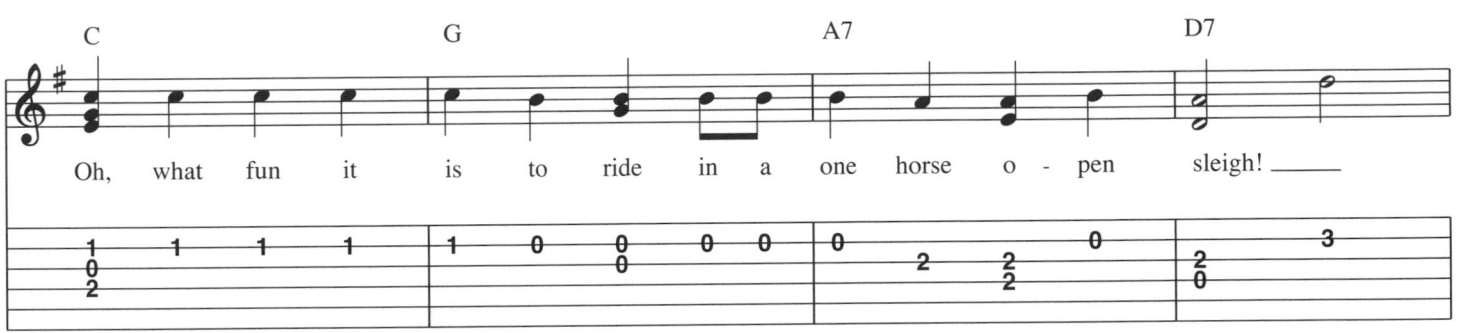

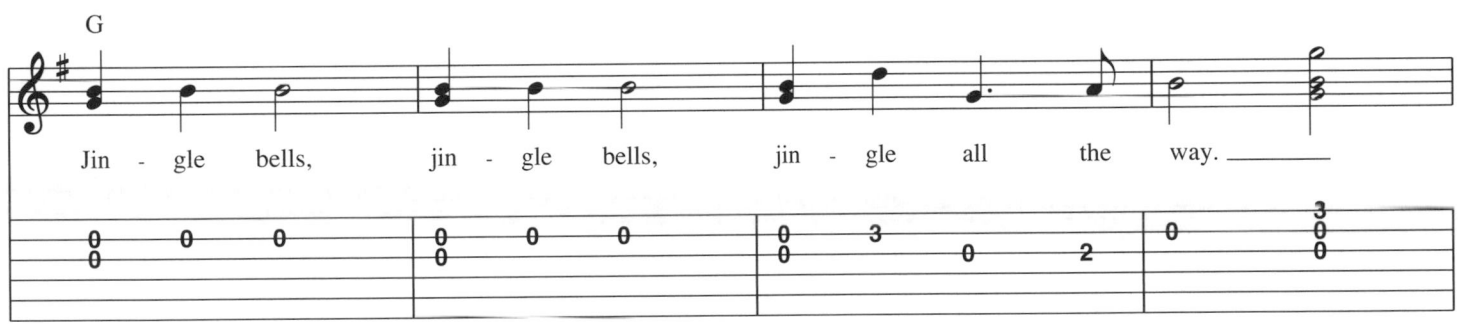

Additional Lyrics

2. A day or two ago, I thought I'd take a ride,
   And soon Miss Fannie Bright was sitting by my side.
   The horse was lean and lank,
   Misfortune seemed his lot.
   He got into a drifted bank and we, we got upshot! Oh!

3. Now the ground is white, go it while you're young.
   Take the girls tonight and sing this sleighing song.
   Just get a bobtail bay,
   Two-forty for his speed.
   Then hitch him to an open sleigh and
   Crack, you'll take the lead! Oh!

Jolly Old St. Nicholas

Traditional 19th Century American Carol

Strum Pattern: 4
Pick Pattern: 4

Verse
Fast

1. Jol - ly old Saint Nich - o - las, lean your ear this way.
2., 3. *See additional lyrics*

Don't you tell a sin - gle soul what I'm going to say.

Christ - mas Eve is com - ing soon, now, you dear old man,

whis - per what you'll bring to me; tell me if you can. best.

Additional Lyrics

2. When the clock is striking twelve, when I'm fast asleep,
Down the chimney broad and black, with your pack you'll creep.
All the stockings you will find hanging in a row.
Mine will be the shortest one, you'll be sure to know.

3. Johnny wants a pair of skates; Susy wants a sled.
Nellie wants a picture book, yellow, blue and red.
Now I think I'll leave to you what to give the rest.
Choose for me, dear Santa Claus.
You will know the best.

O Christmas Tree

Traditional German Carol

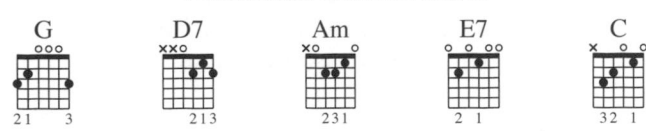

Strum Pattern: 7, 8
Pick Pattern: 8, 9

Verse
Moderately

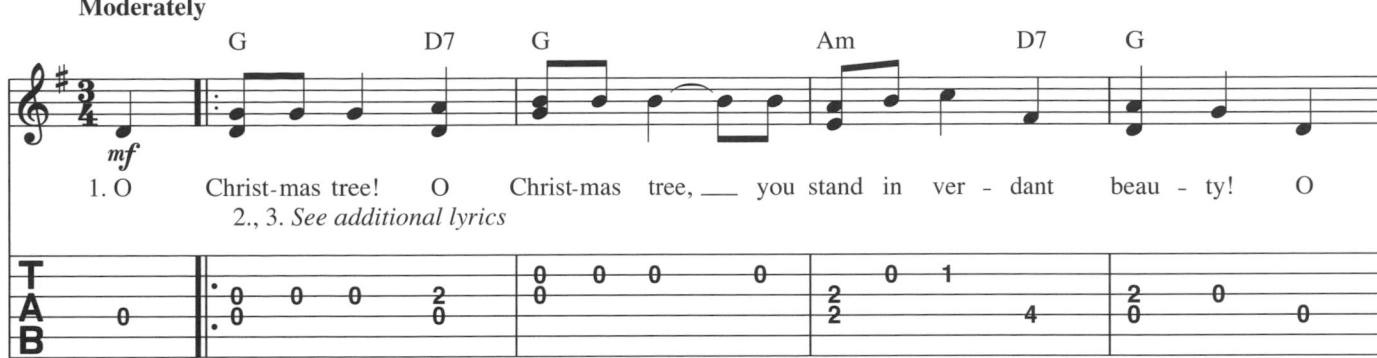

1. O Christ-mas tree! O Christ-mas tree, ___ you stand in ver - dant beau - ty! O

2., 3. See additional lyrics

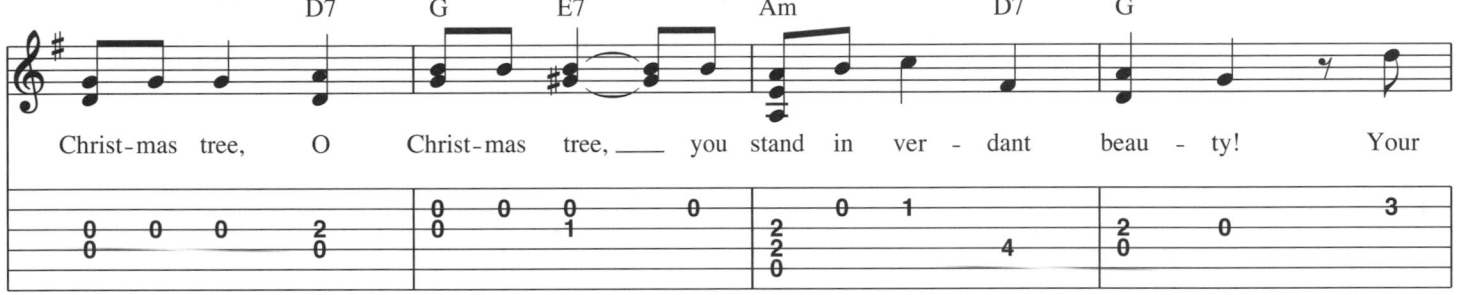

Christ-mas tree, O Christ-mas tree, ___ you stand in ver - dant beau - ty! Your

boughs are green ___ in sum-mer's glow, ___ and do not fade ___ in win - ter's snow. O

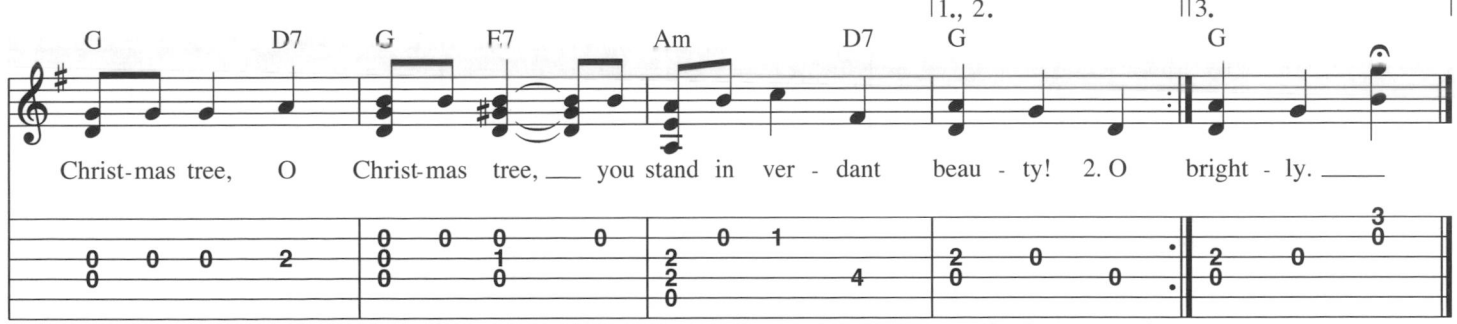

Christ-mas tree, O Christ-mas tree, ___ you stand in ver - dant beau - ty! 2. O bright - ly. ___

Additional Lyrics

2. O Christmas tree! O Christmas tree,
   Much pleasure doth thou bring me!
   O Christmas tree! O Christmas tree,
   Much pleasure does thou bring me!
   For every year the Christmas tree
   Brings to us all both joy and glee.
   O Christmas tree, O Christmas tree,
   Much pleasure doth thou bring me!

3. O Christmas tree! O Christmas tree,
   Thy candles shine out brightly!
   O Christmas Tree, O Christmas tree,
   Thy candles shine out brightly!
   Each bough doth hold its tiny light
   That makes each toy to sparkle bright.
   O Christmas tree, O Christmas tree,
   Thy candles shine out brightly.

Joy to the World

Words by Isaac Watts
Music by George Frideric Handel
Adapted by Lowell Mason

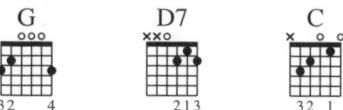

Strum Pattern: 3
Pick Pattern: 3

Verse
Moderately fast

1. Joy to the World! The Lord is
2. *See additional lyrics*

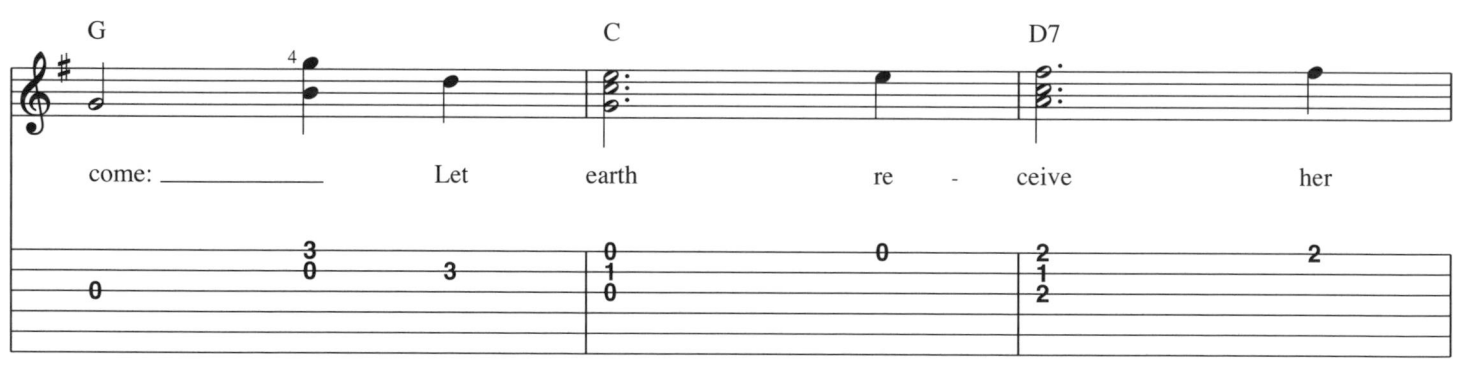

come: _____ Let earth re - ceive her

King. Let ev - 'ry _____ heart _____ pre -

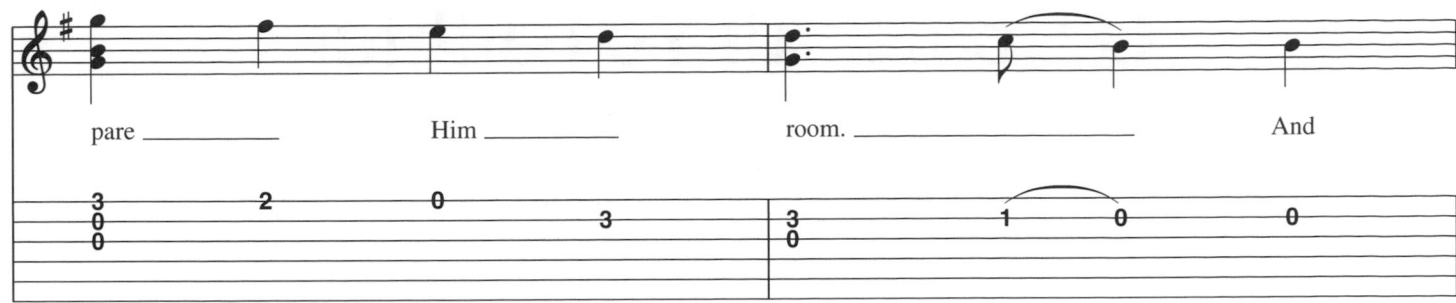

pare _____ Him _____ room. _____ And

heav - en and na - ture ___ sing, and ___ heav - en and na - ture ___

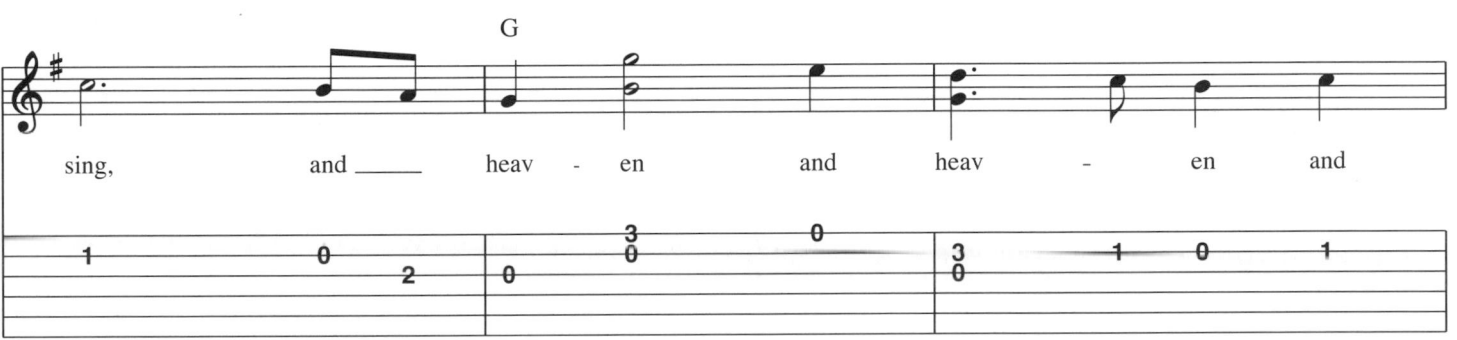

sing, and _____ heav - en and heav - en and

na - ture sing. _____ love. _____

Additional Lyrics

2. He rules the world with truth and grace
And makes the nations prove
The glories of His righteousness
And wonders of His love,
And wonders of His love,
And wonders, wonders of His love.

O Come, All Ye Faithful
(Adeste Fideles)

Music by John Francis Wade
Latin Words translated by Frederick Oakeley

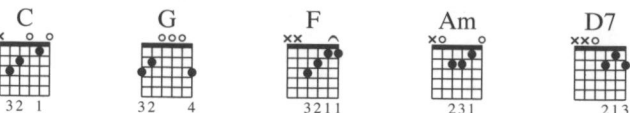

Strum Pattern: 4
Pick Pattern: 5

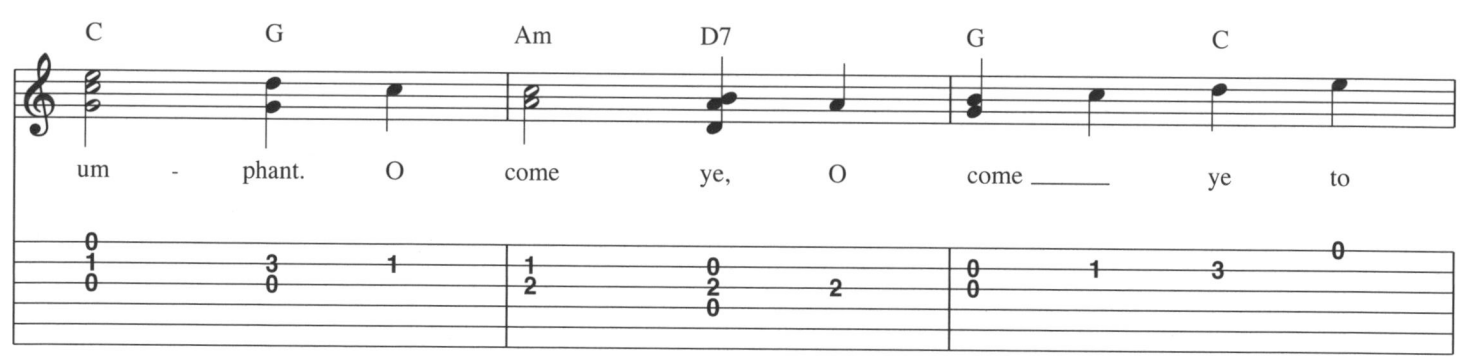

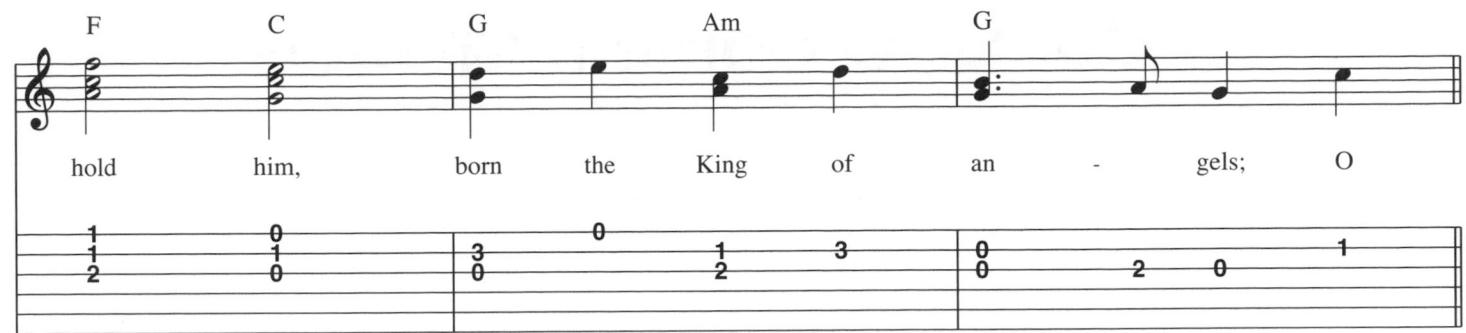

hold him, born the King of an - gels; O

Chorus

come, let us a - dore him. O come, let us a -

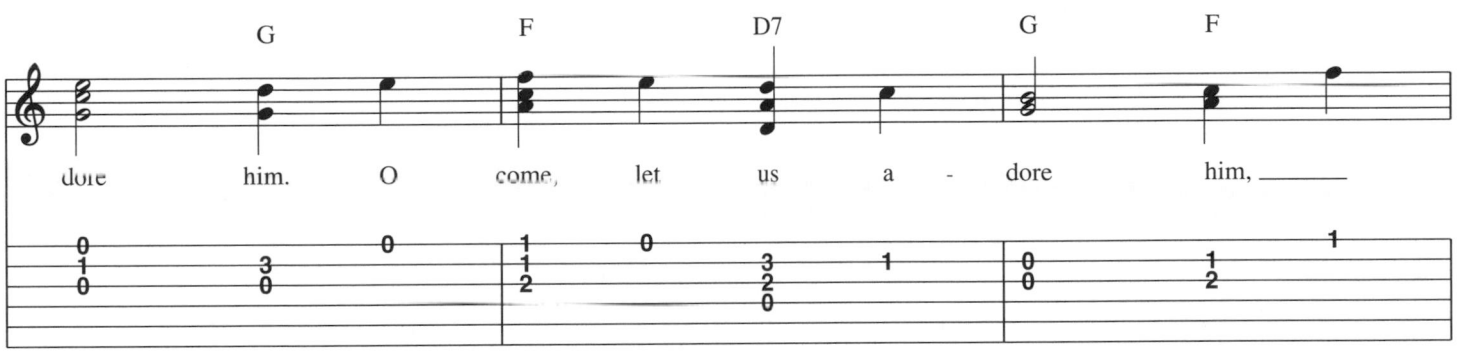

dore him. O come, let us a - dore him, _____

Christ, _____ the Lord! Lord!

Additional Lyrics

2. Sing choirs of angels, sing in exultation.
   O sing all ye citizens of heaven above.
   Glory to God in the highest.

O Come, O Come Immanuel

Plainsong, 13th Century
Words translated by John M. Neale and Henry S. Coffin

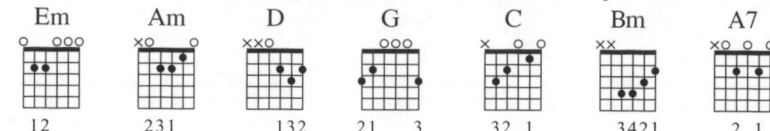

Strum Pattern: 4, 3
Pick Pattern: 3

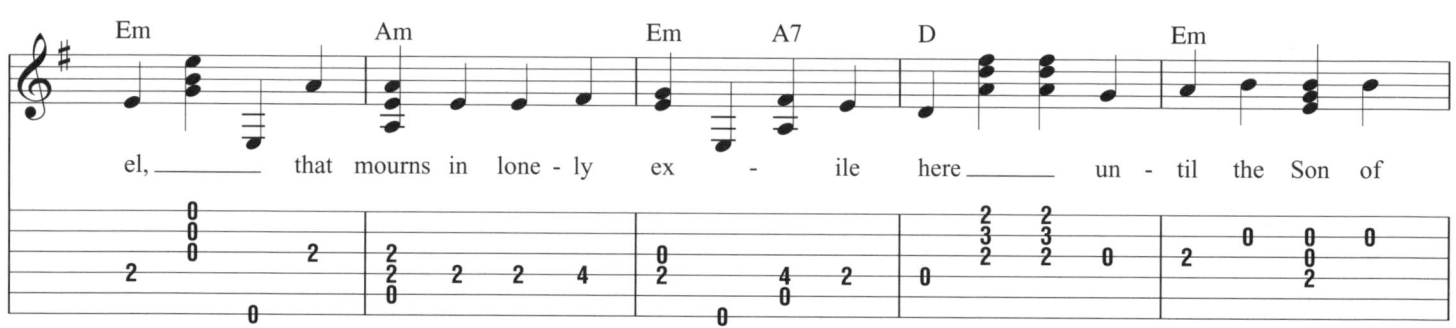

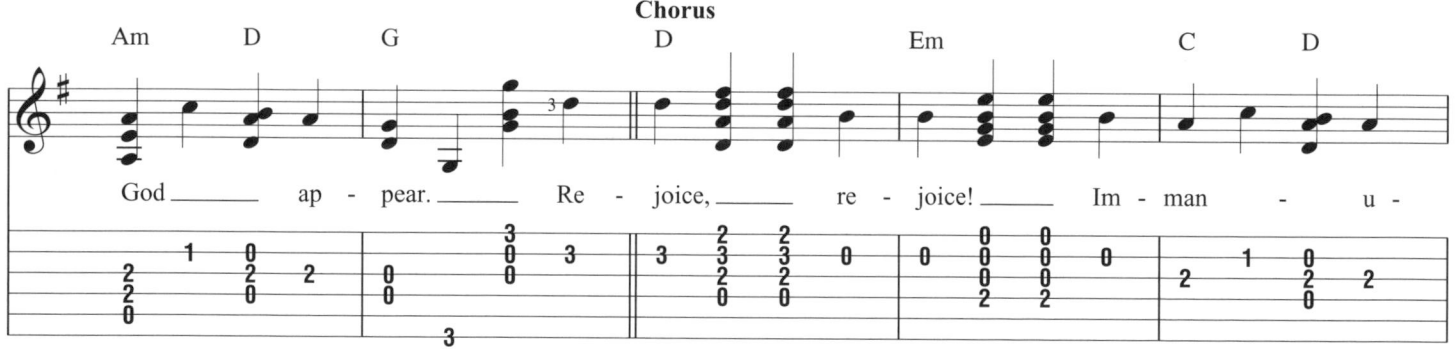

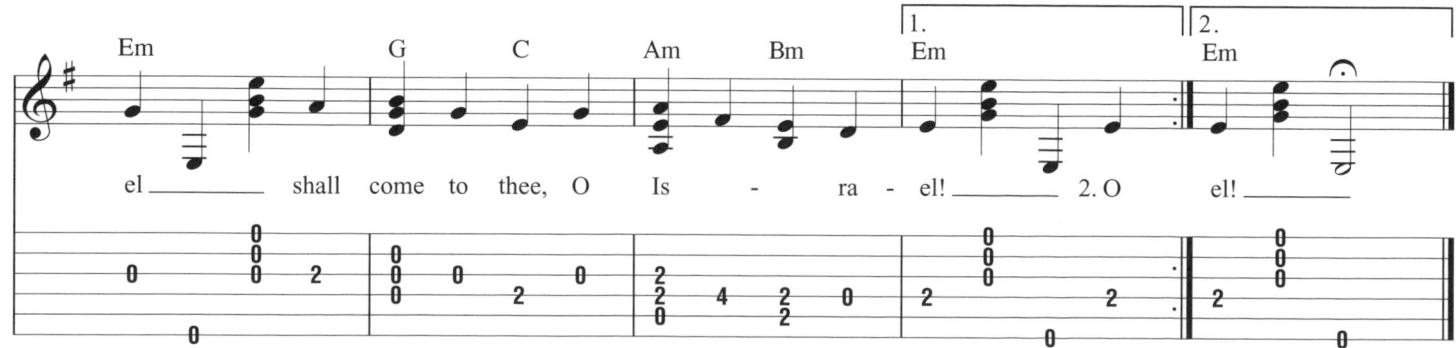

Additional Lyrics

2. O come, Thou Key of David, come
And open wide our heav'nly home.
Make safe the way that leads on high
And close the path to misery.

O Holy Night

French Words by Placide Cappeau
English Words by John S. Dwight
Music by Adolphe Adam

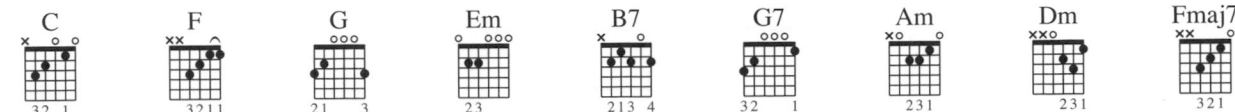

Strum Pattern: 8, 9
Pick Pattern: 8, 9

Verse
Slowly

1. O ho - ly night _____ the stars are bright - ly shin -
2. Tru - ly He taught us to love _____ one an - oth -

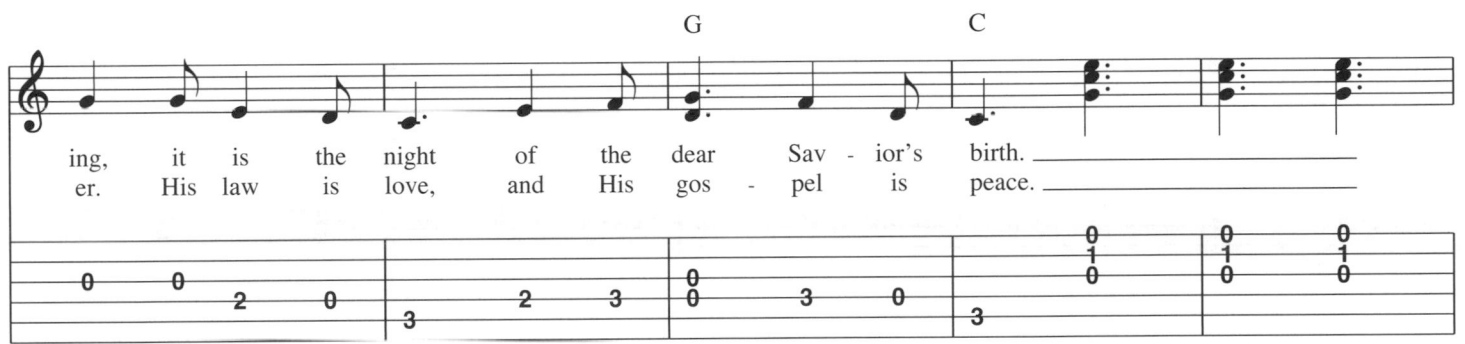

ing, it is the night of the dear Sav - ior's birth. _____
er. His law is love, and His gos - pel is peace. _____

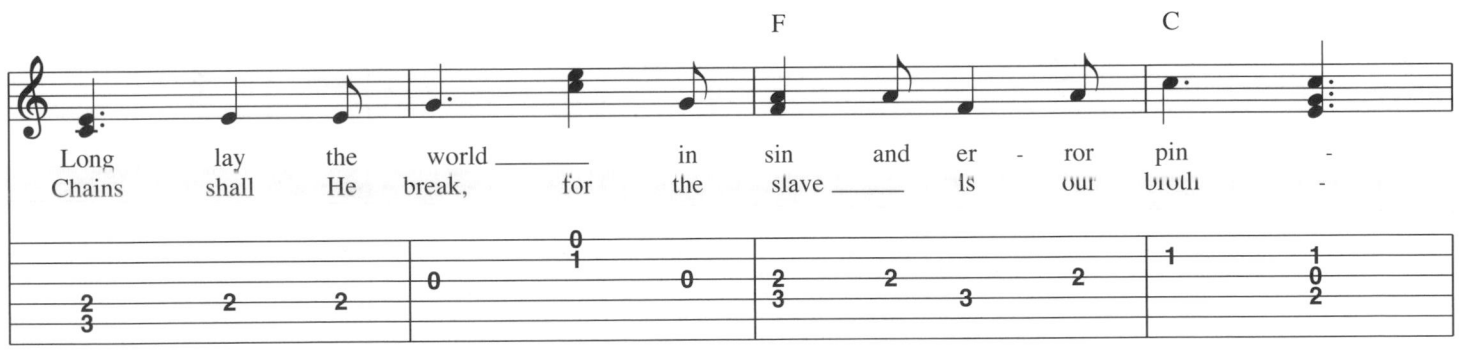

Long lay the world _____ in sin and er - ror pin -
Chains shall He break, for the slave _____ is our broth -

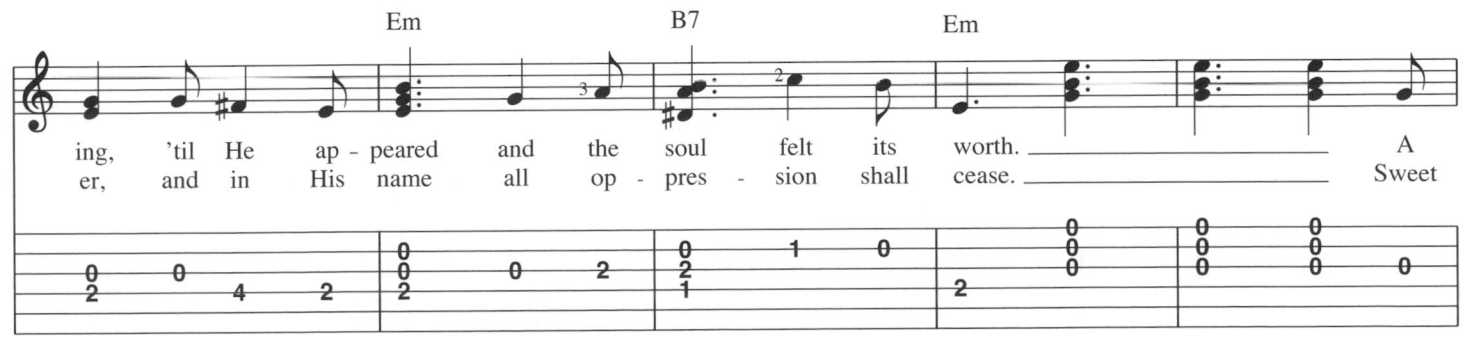

ing, 'til He ap - peared and the soul felt its worth. _____ A
er, and in His name all op - pres - sion shall cease. _____ Sweet

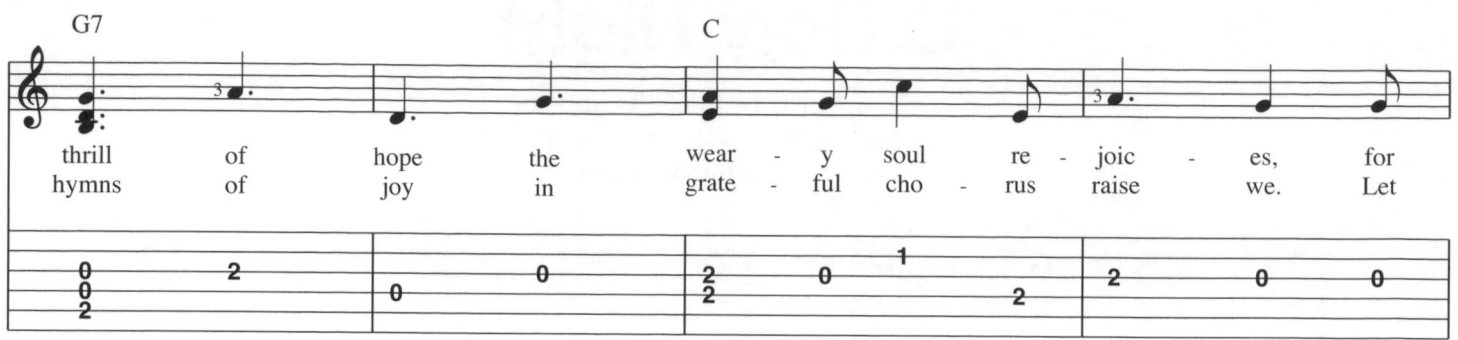

thrill of hope the wear - y soul re - joic - es, for
hymns of joy in grate - ful cho - rus raise we. Let

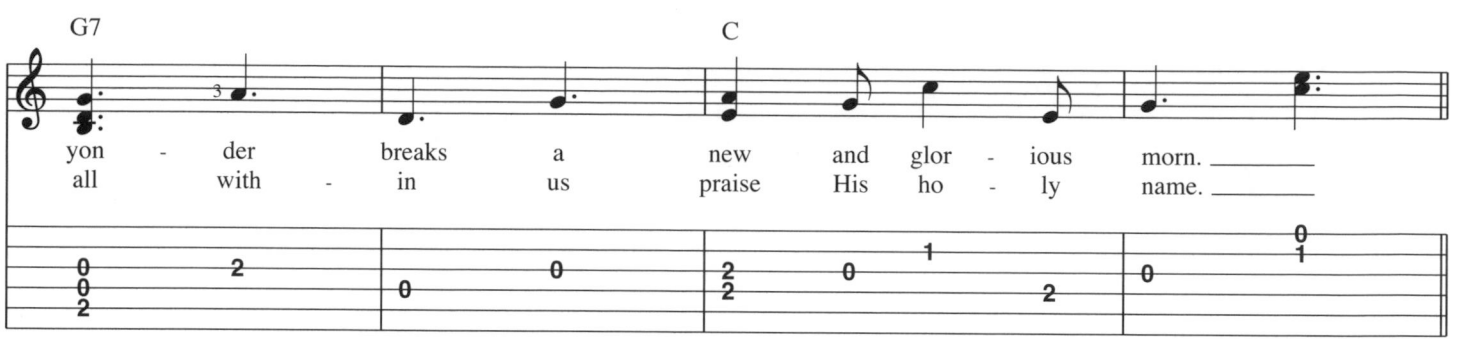

yon - der breaks a new and glor - ious morn. _____
all with - in us new praise His ho - ly name. _____

Chorus

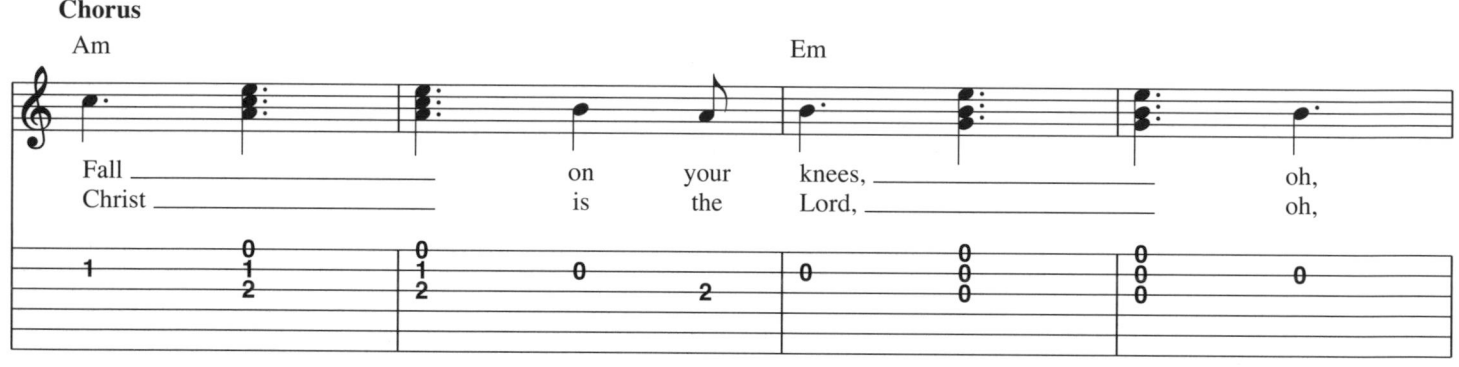

Fall _____ on your knees, _____ oh,
Christ _____ is the Lord, _____ oh,

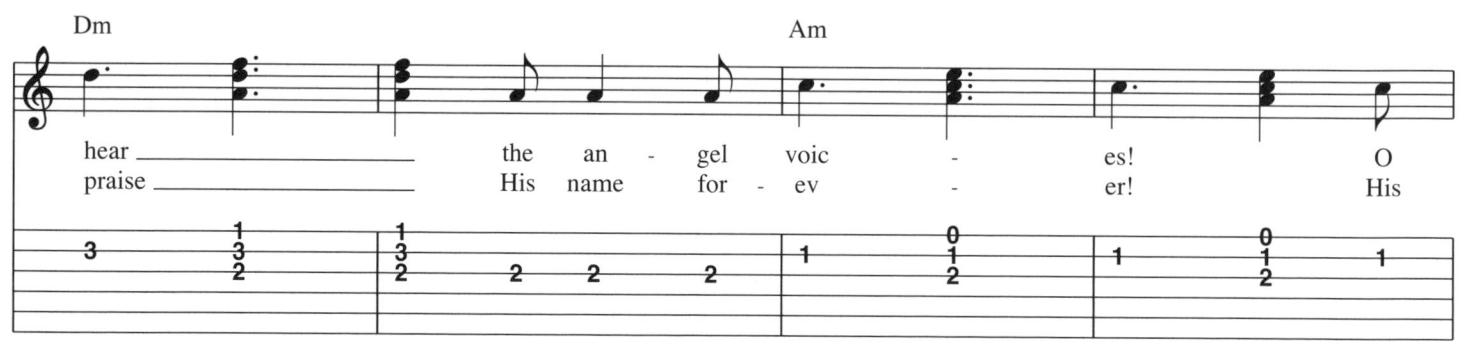

hear _____ the an - gel voic - es! O
praise _____ His name for - ev - er! His

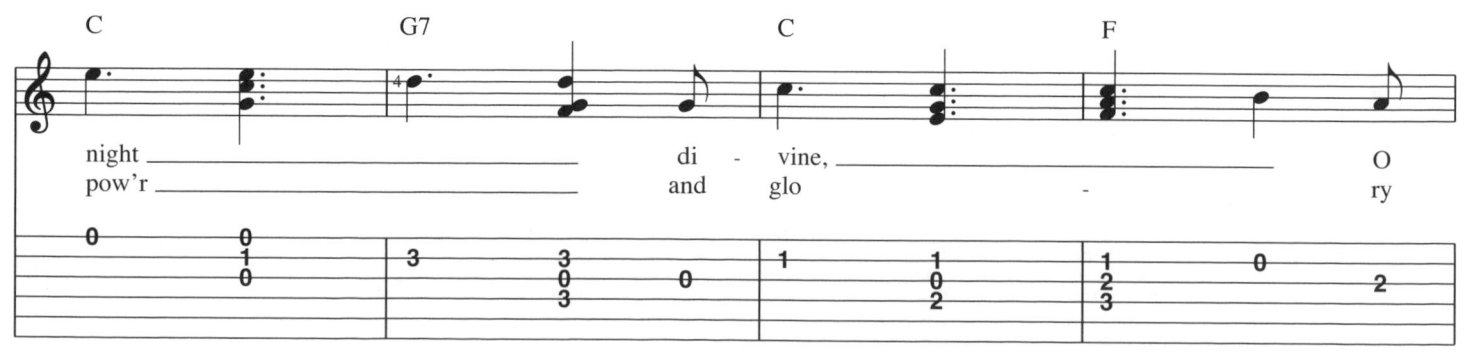

night _____ di - vine, _____ O
pow'r _____ and glo - ry

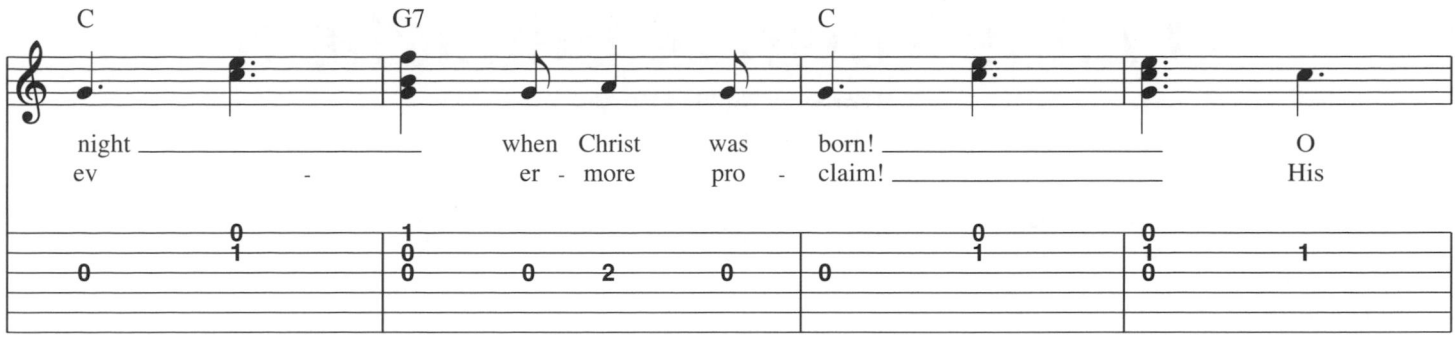

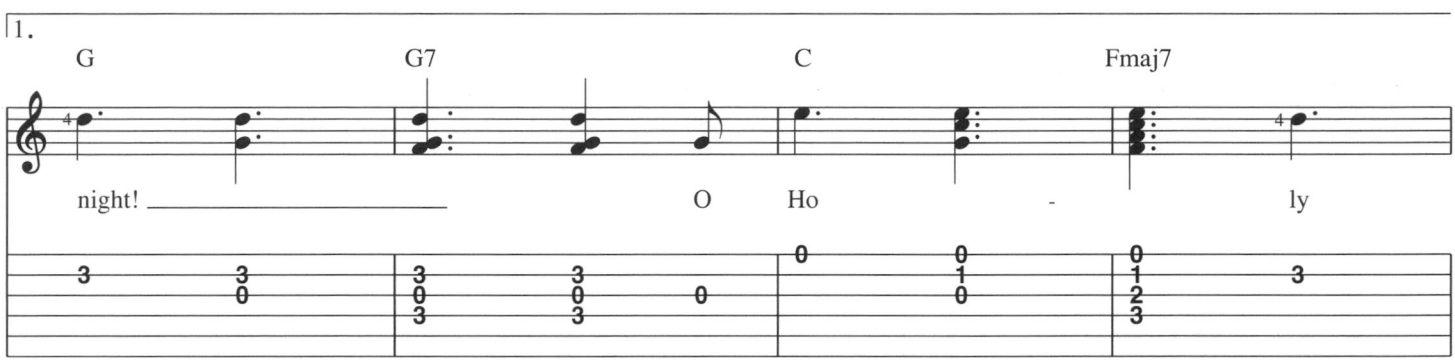

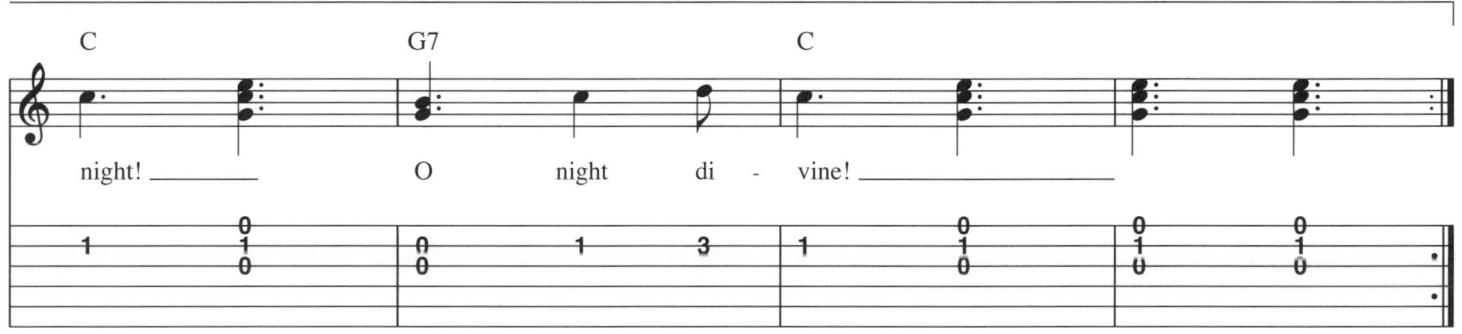

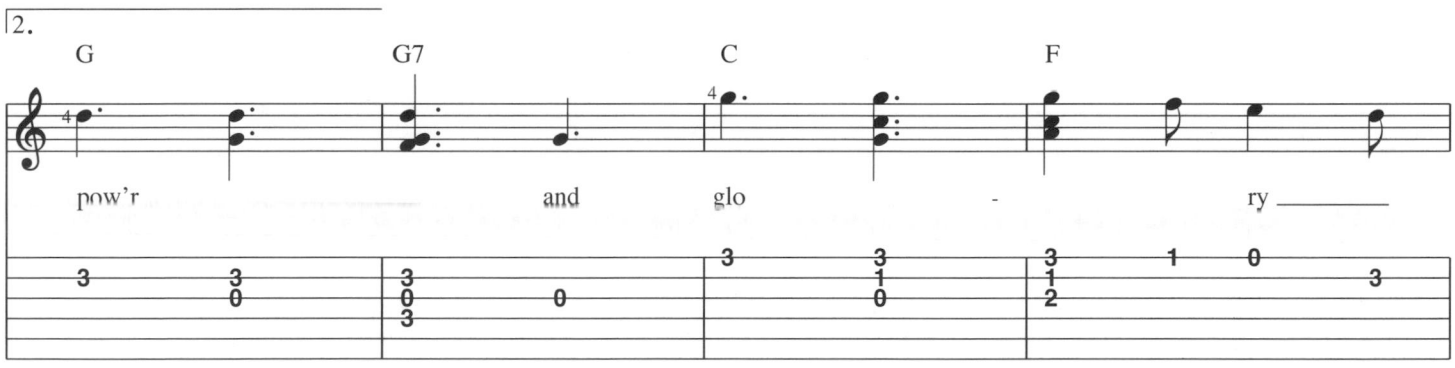

O Little Town of Bethlehem

Words by Phillips Brooks
Music by Lewis H. Redner

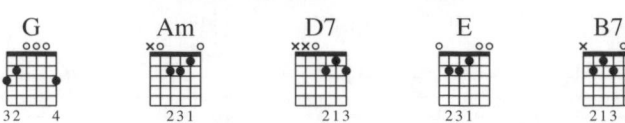

Strum Pattern: 4
Pick Pattern: 5

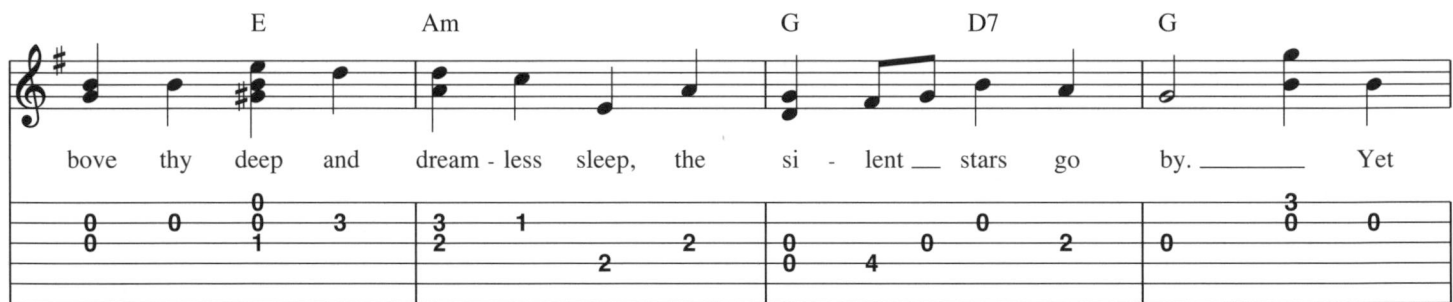

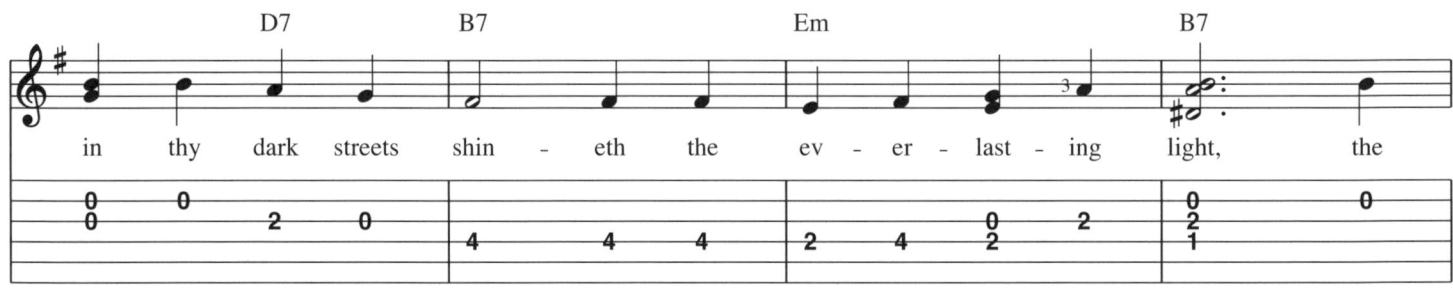

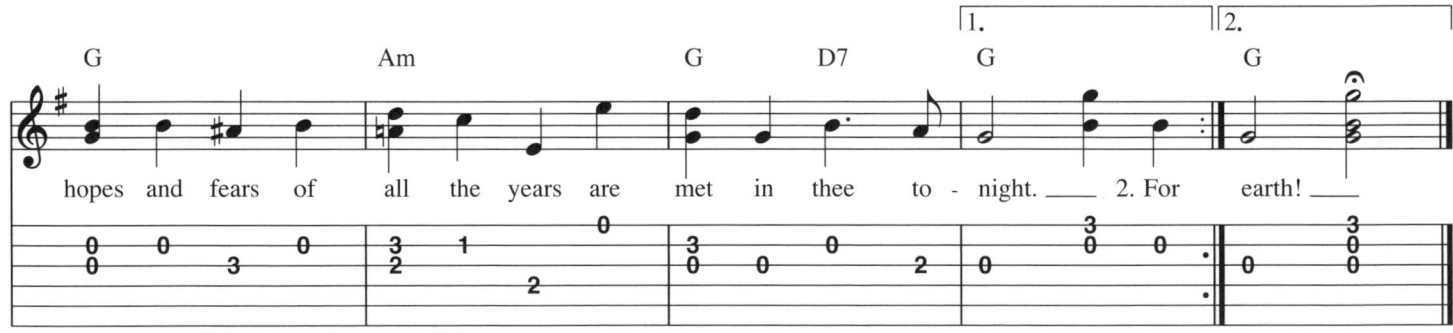

Additional Lyrics

2. For Christ is born of Mary, and gathered all above.
   While mortals sleep the angels keep
   Their watch of wond'ring love.
   O morning stars, together proclaim the holy birth!
   And praises sing to God the King,
   And peace to men on earth!

Pat-A-Pan
(Willie, Take Your Little Drum)

Words and Music by Bernard de la Monnoye

   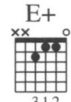

Strum Pattern: 2, 3
Pick Pattern: 2, 3

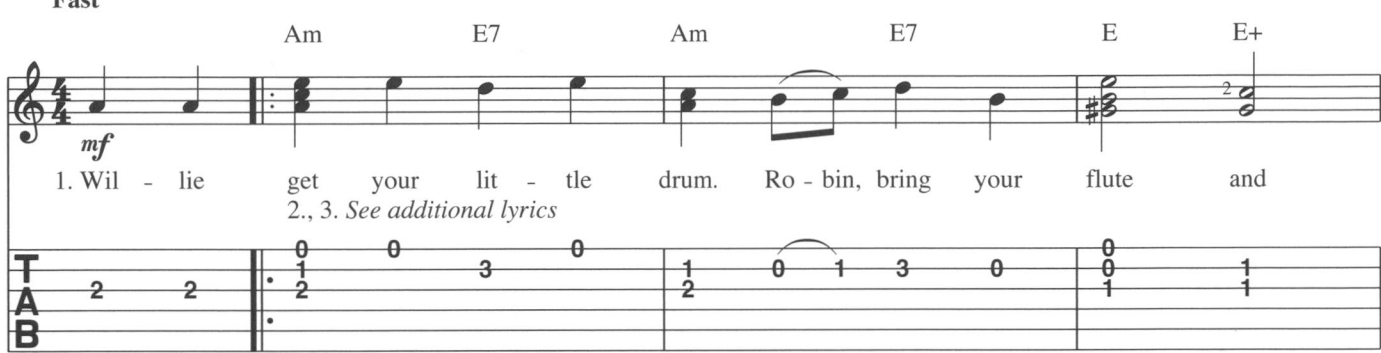

1. Wil - lie get your lit - tle drum. Ro - bin, bring your flute and
2., 3. *See additional lyrics*

come. Aren't they fun to play up - on? Tu - re - lu - re - lu, _____ pat - a - pat - a -

pan. _____ When you play your fife and drum, how can an - y -

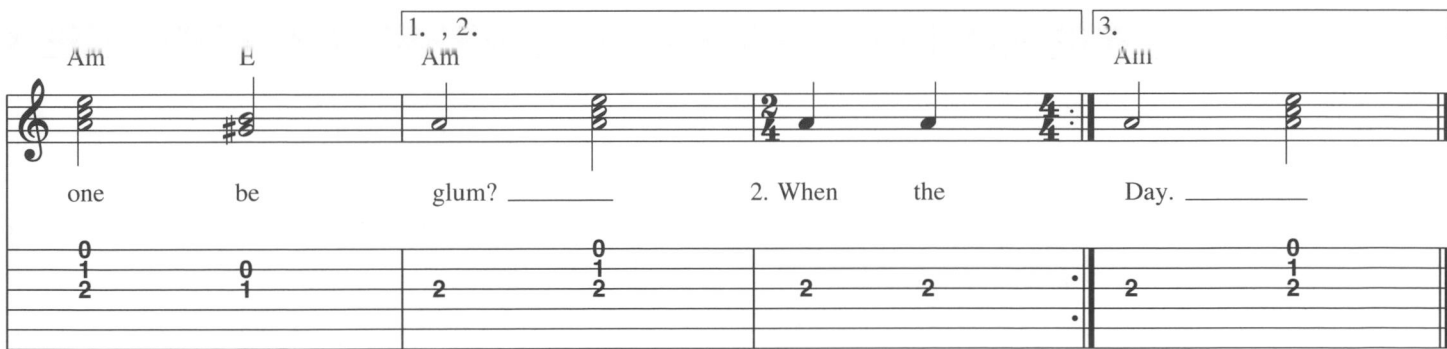

one be glum? _____ 2. When the Day. _____

Additional Lyrics

2. When the men of olden days
   Gave the King of Kings their praise,
   They had pipes to play upon.
   Tu-re-lu-re-lu, pat-a-pat-a-pan.
   And also the drums they'd play.
   Full of joy, on Christmas Day.

3. God and man today become
   Closely joined as flute and drum.
   Let the joyous tune play on!
   Tu-re-lu-re-lu, pat-a-pat-a-pan.
   As the instruments you play,
   We will sing, this Christmas Day.

Rejoice and Be Merry

Traditional English Carol

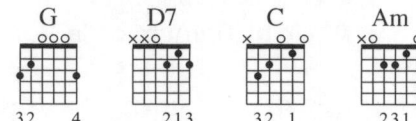

Strum Pattern: 7
Pick Pattern: 7

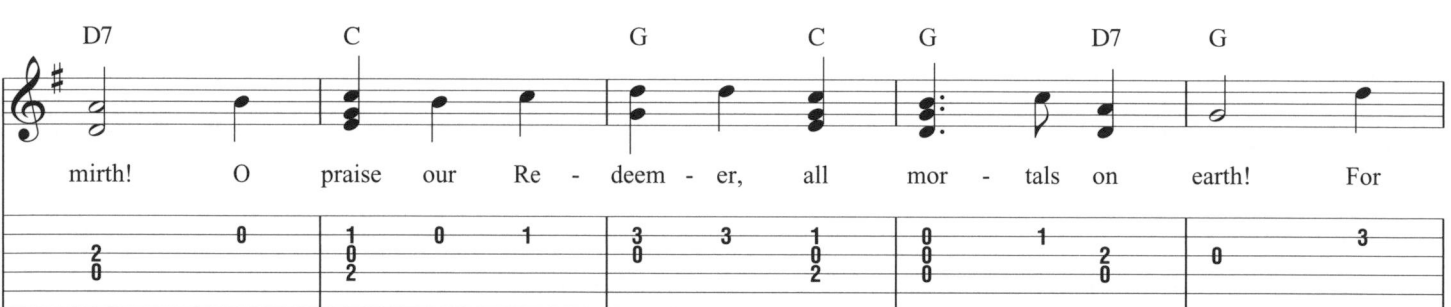

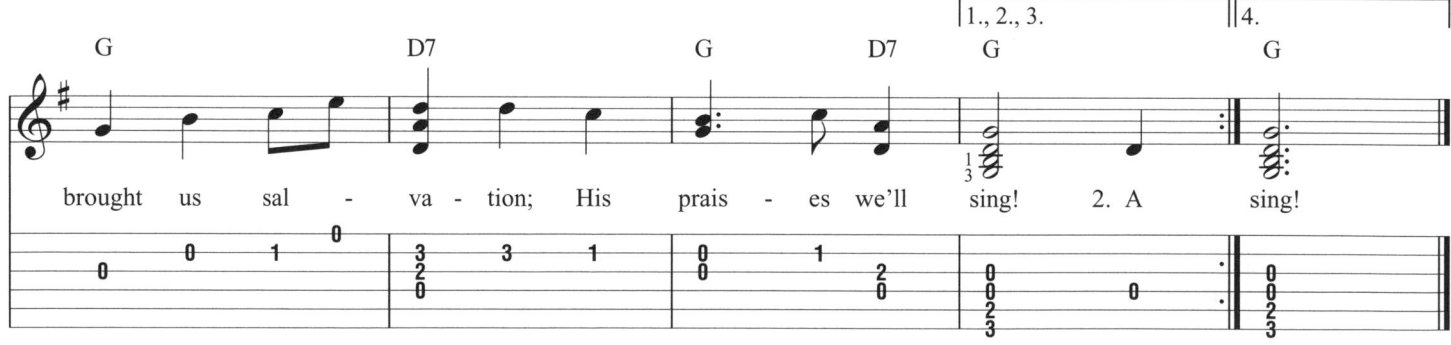

Additional Lyrics

2. A heavenly vision appeared in the sky;
   Vast numbers of angels the shepherds did spy,
   Proclaiming the birthday of Jesus our King,
   Who brought us salvation; His praises we'll sing!

3. Likewise a bright star in the sky did appear,
   Which led the wise men from the east to draw near.
   They found the Messiah, sweet Jesus our King,
   Who brought us salvation; His praises we'll sing!

4. And when they were come, they their treasures unfold,
   And unto Him offered myrrh, incense and gold.
   So blessed forever be Jesus our King,
   Who brought us salvation; His praises we'll sing!

Sing We Now of Christmas

Traditional French Carol

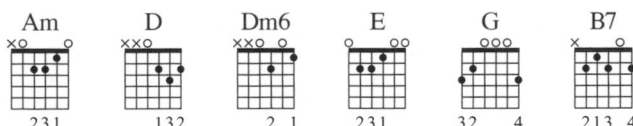

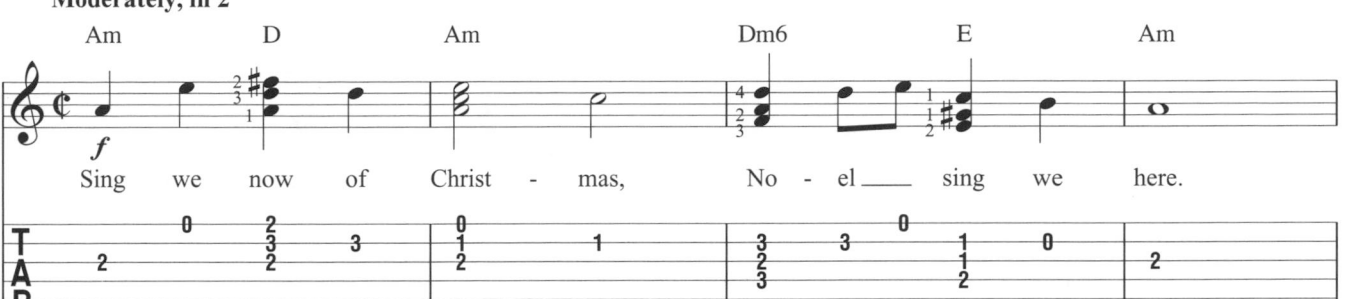

Strum Pattern: 3
Pick Pattern: 3

Verse
Moderately, in 2

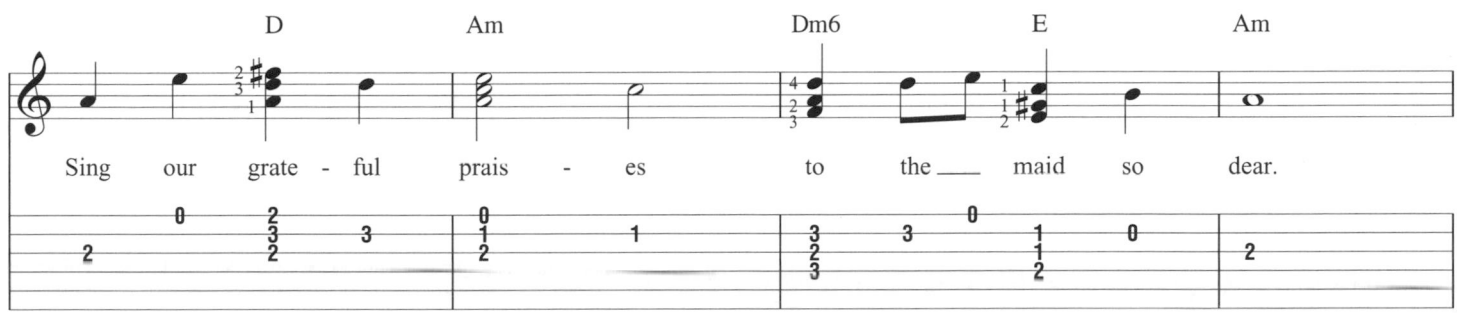

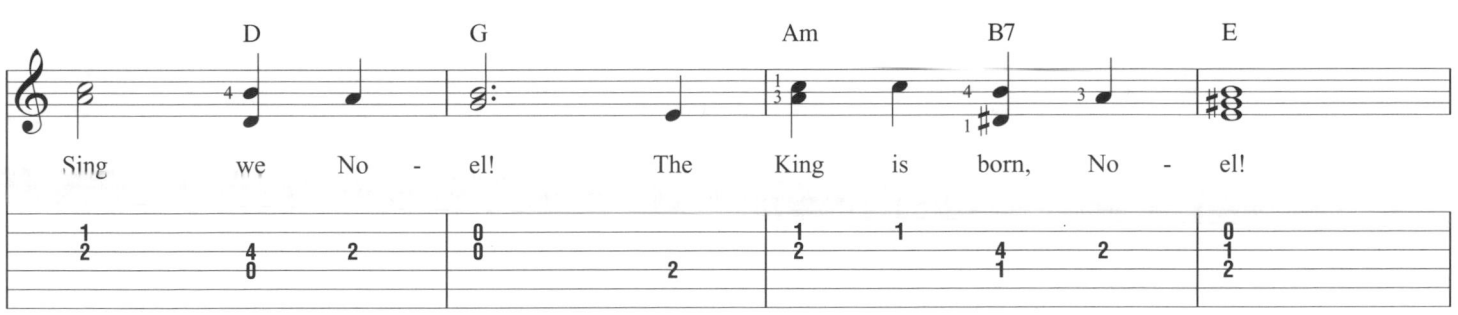

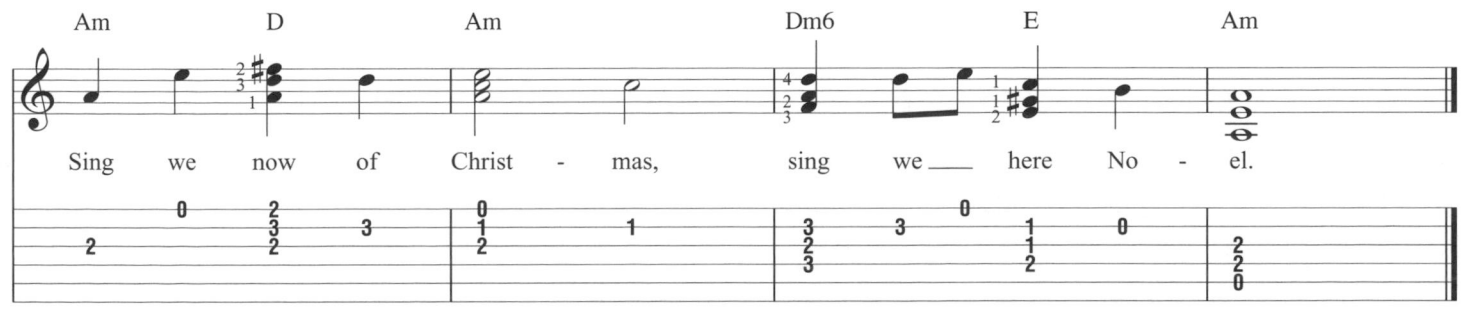

Ring Out, Ye Wild and Merry Bells

Words and Music by C. Maitland

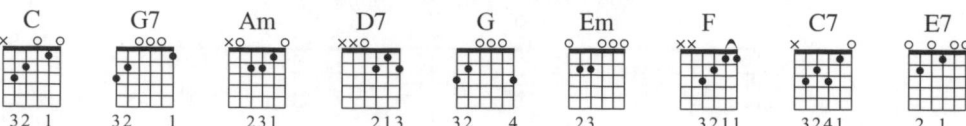

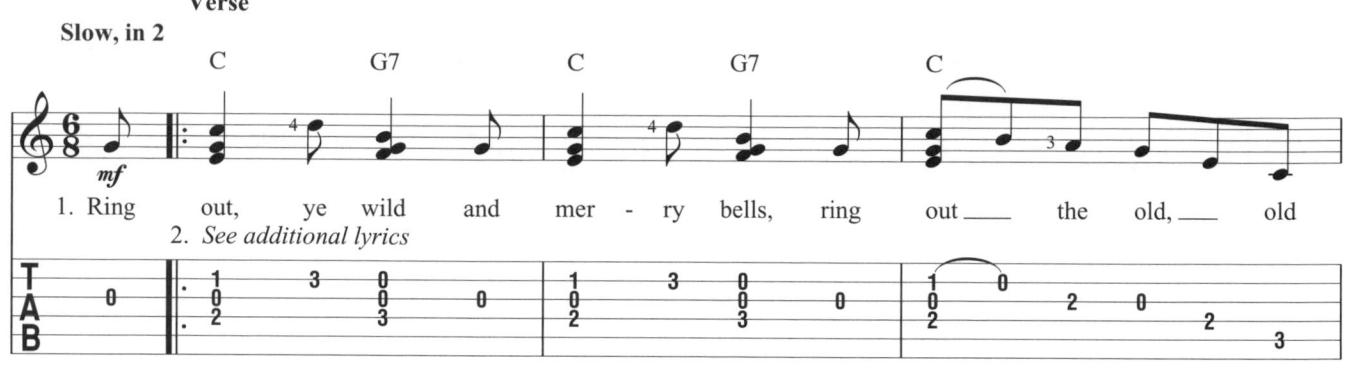

Strum Pattern: 8
Pick Pattern: 8

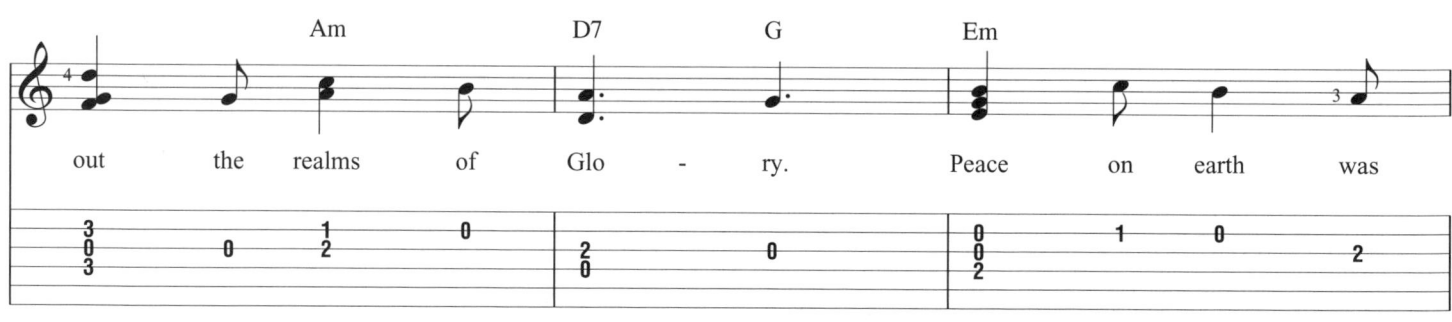

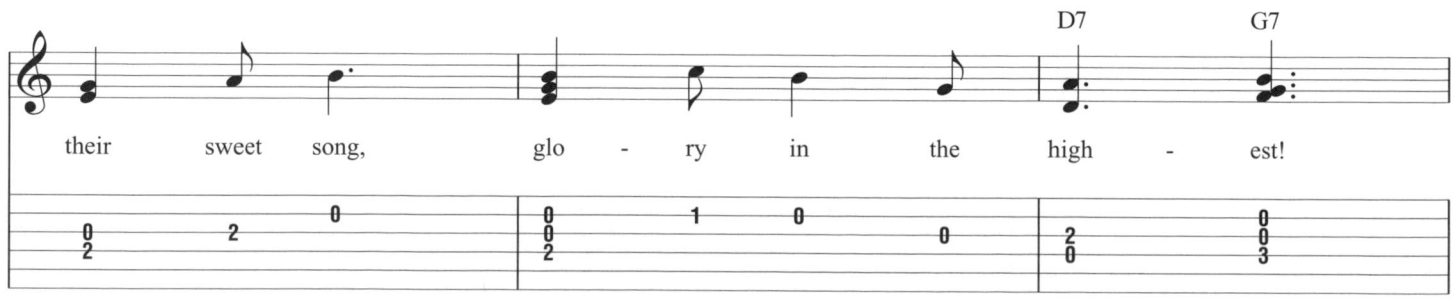

Ech - o - ing all the hills a - way, glo - ry in the

Chorus

high - est! Ring, sweet bells, ring ev - er - more;

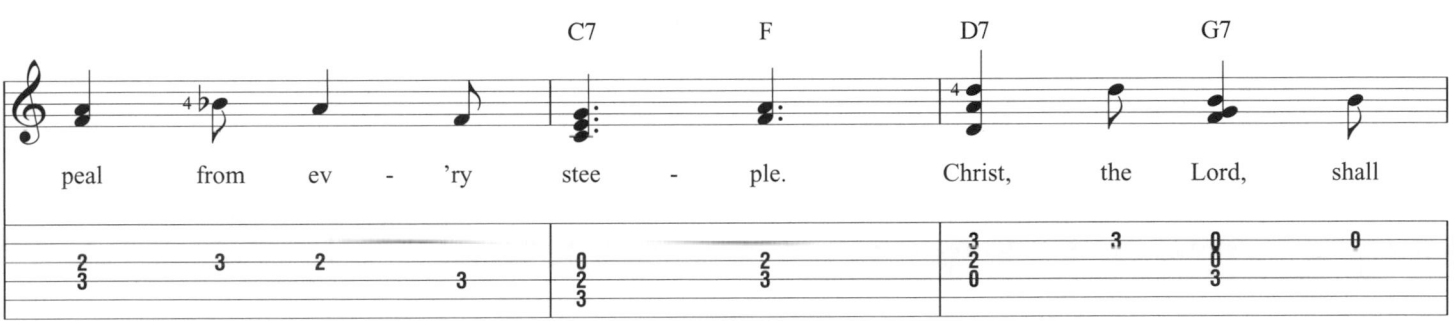

peal from ev - 'ry stee - ple. Christ, the Lord, shall

be our God and we ___ shall be His peo - ple! 2. Ring peo - ple!

Additional Lyrics

2. Ring out, ye silv'ry bells, ring out.
Bring out your exultation
That God with man is reconciled.
Go tell it to the nations!
Therefore let us all today,
Glory in the highest!
Banish sorrow far away,
Glory in the highest!

Rise Up, Shepherd, and Follow

African-American Spiritual

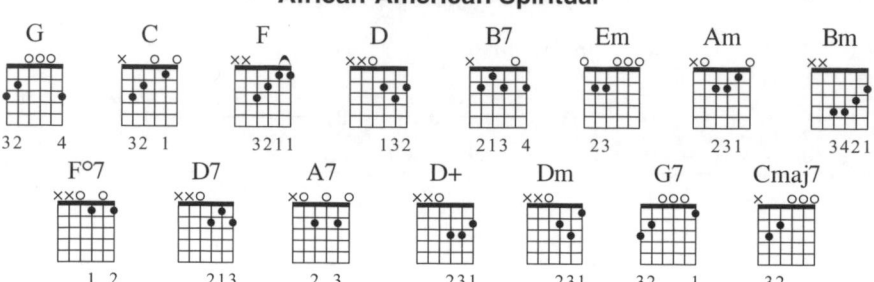

Strum Pattern: 3
Pick Pattern: 3

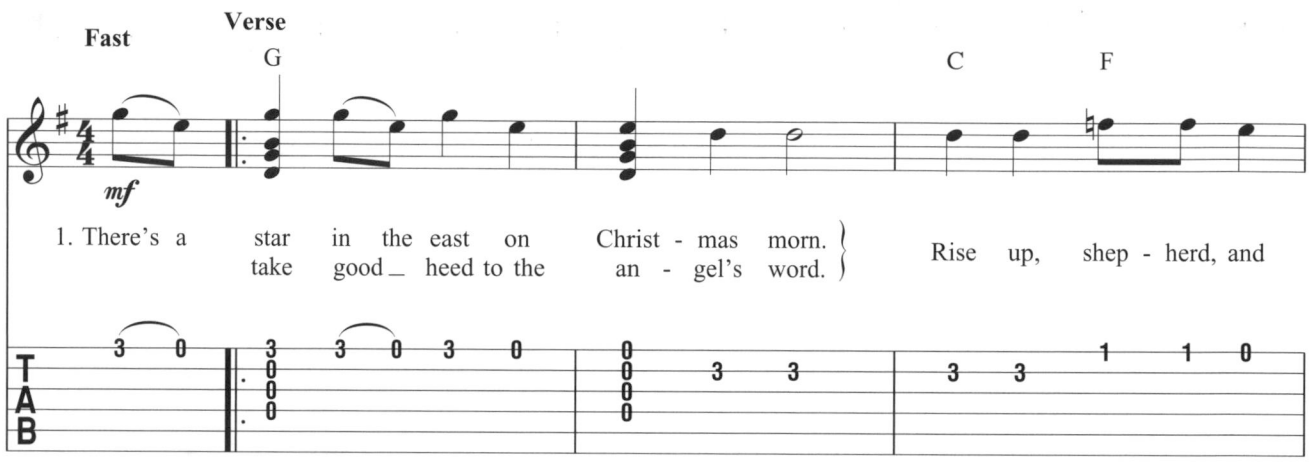

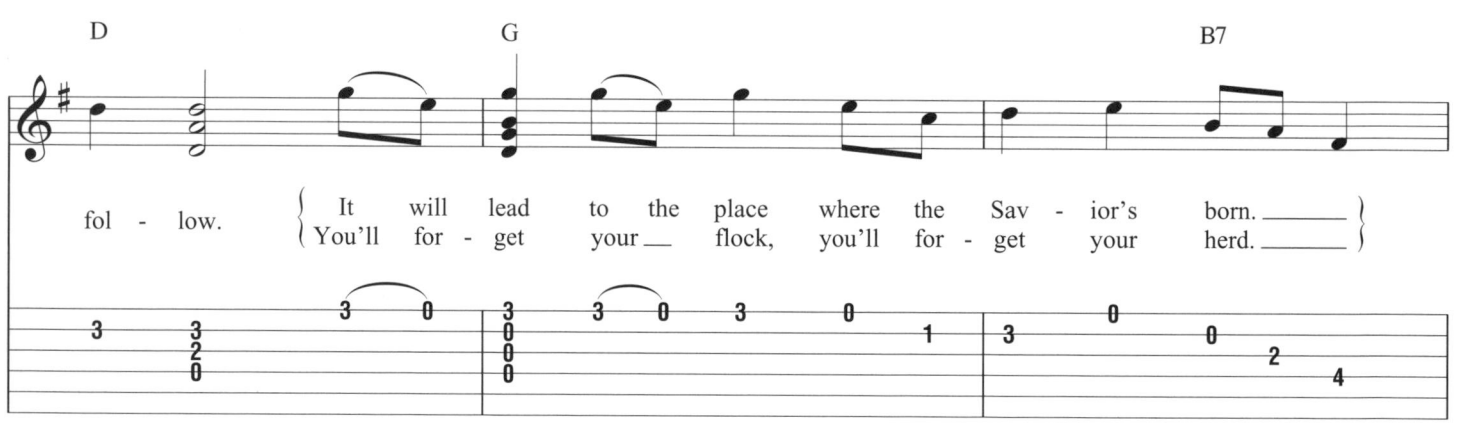

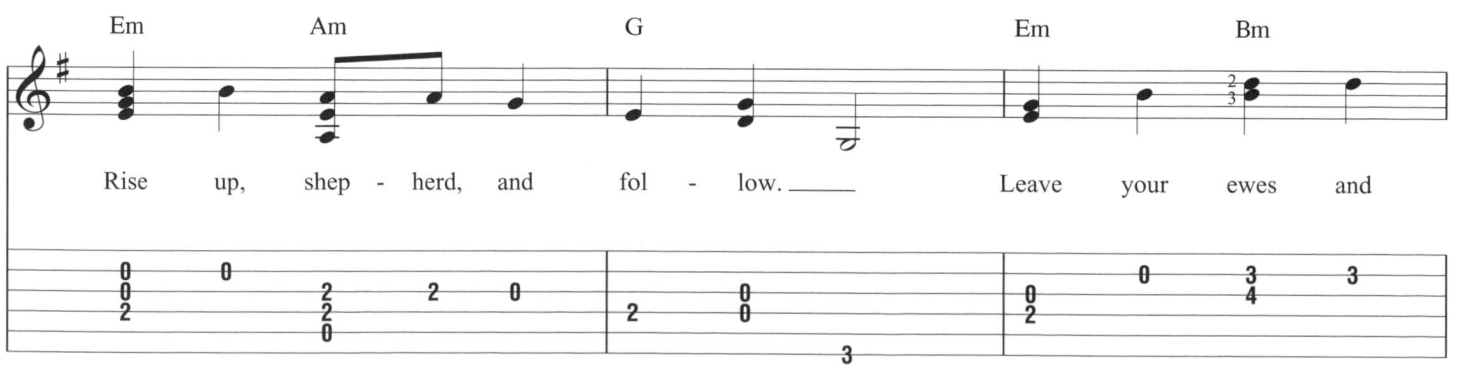

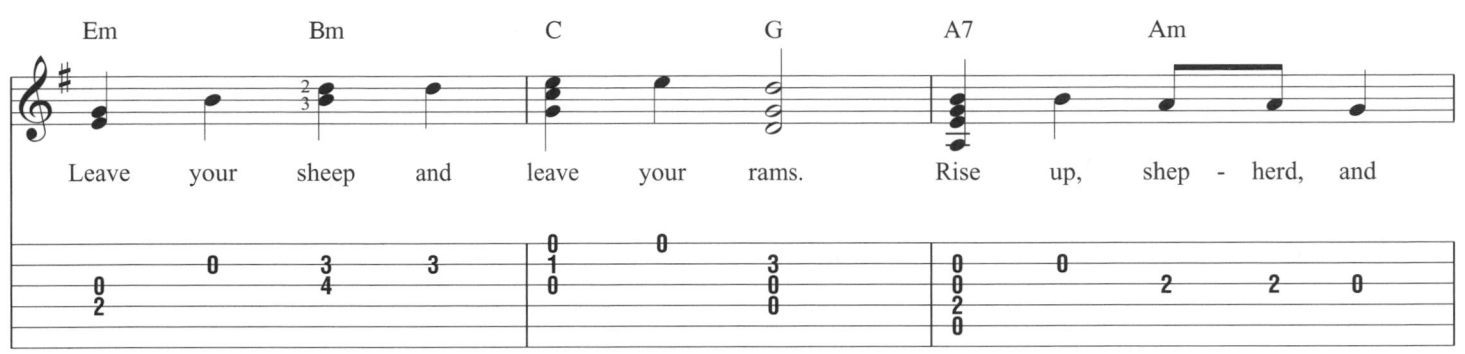

Chorus

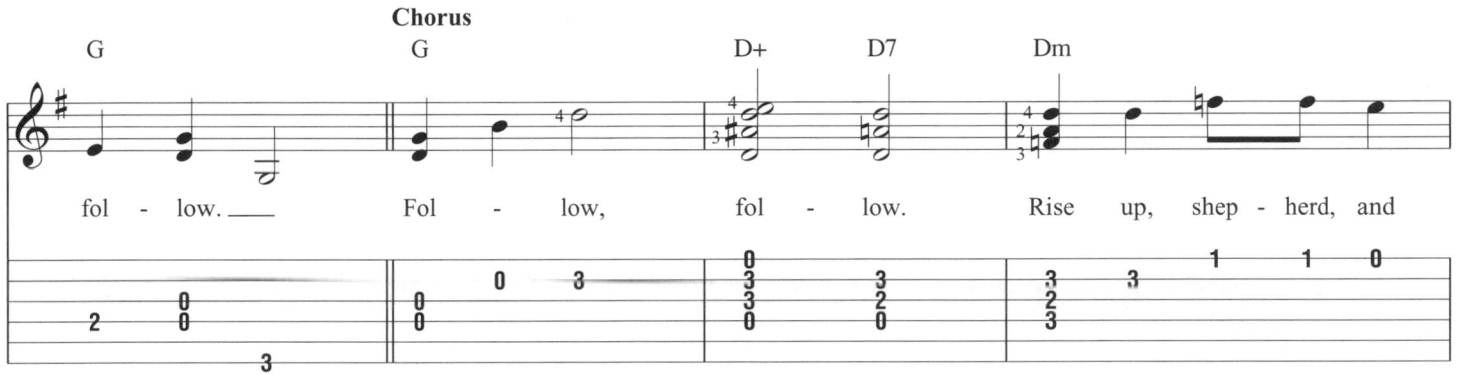

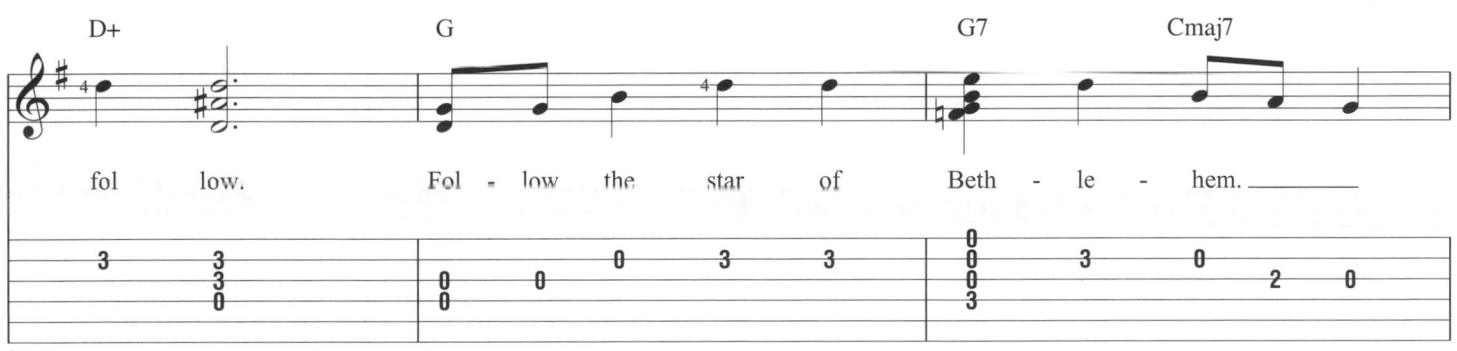

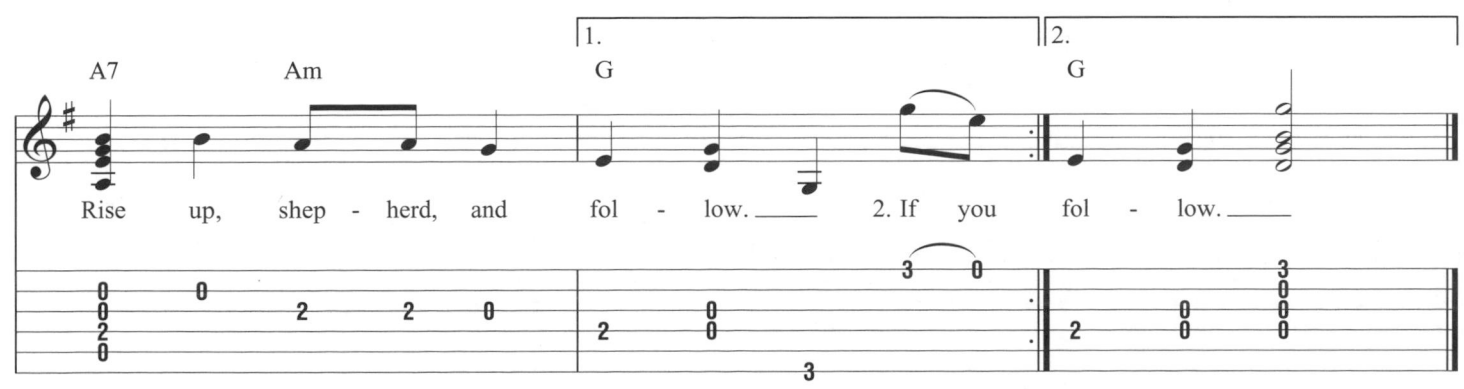

Silent Night

Words by Joseph Mohr
Translated by John F. Young
Music by Franz X. Gruber

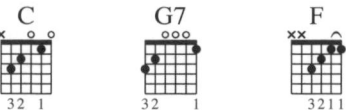

Strum Pattern: 7
Pick Pattern: 9

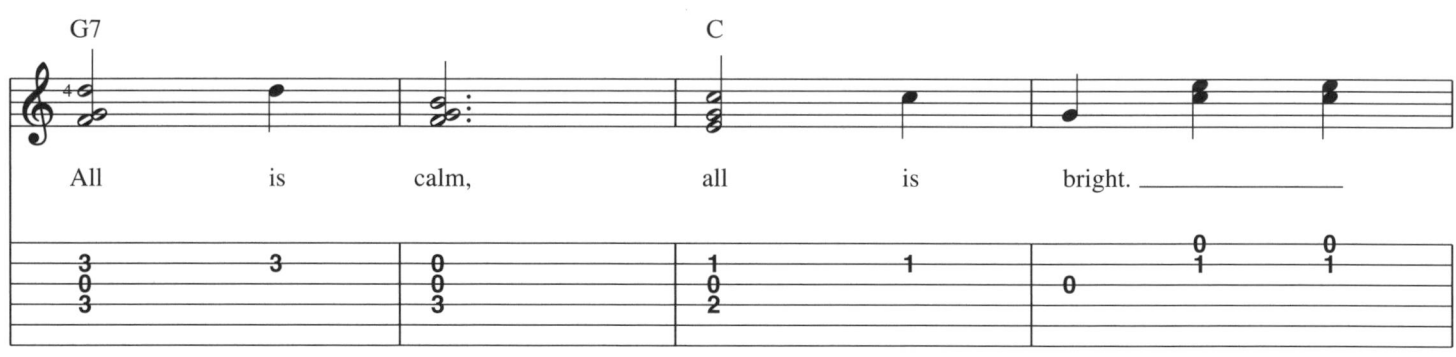

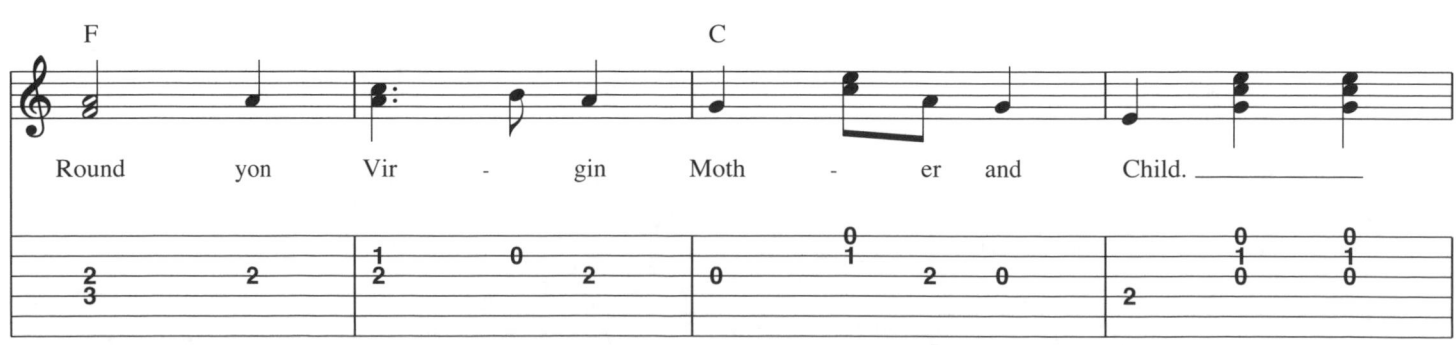

Ho - ly In - fant so ten - der and

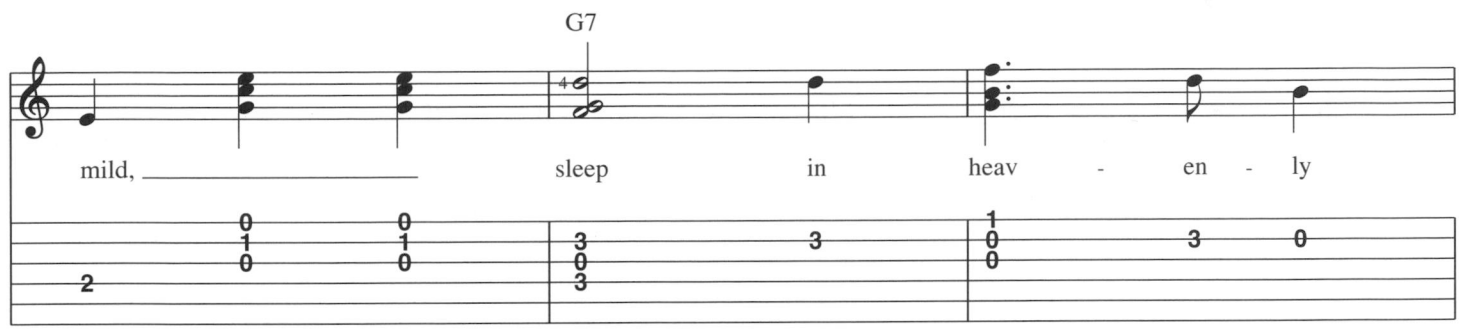

mild, _____ sleep in heav - en - ly

peace. _____ Sleep _____ in heav - en - ly

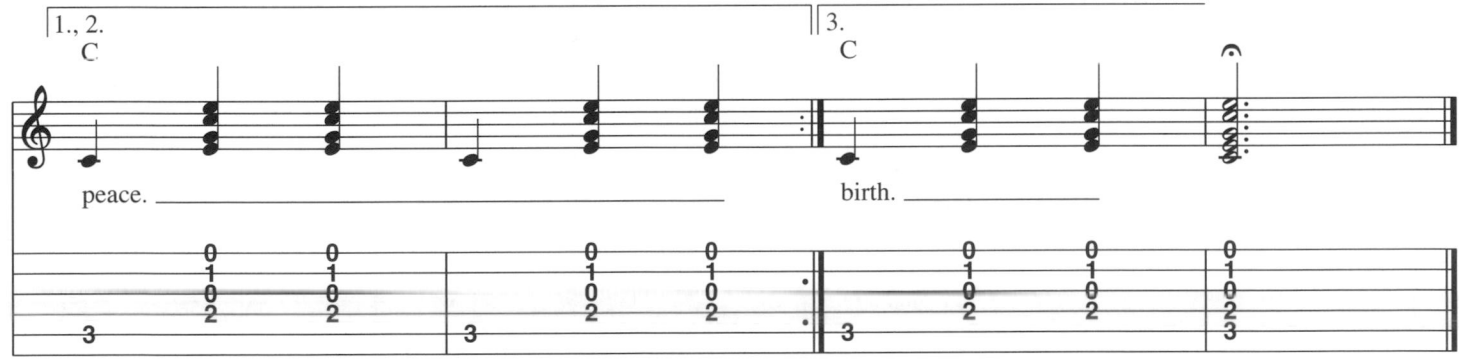

1., 2. peace. _____ 3. birth. _____

Additional Lyrics

2. Silent night, holy night!
   Shepherds quake at the sight.
   Glories stream from heaven afar.
   Heavenly hosts sing Alleluia.
   Christ the Savior is born!
   Christ the Savior is born!

3. Silent night, holy night!
   Son of God, love's pure light.
   Radiant beams from thy holy face
   With the dawn of redeeming grace.
   Jesus Lord at Thy birth.
   Jesus Lord at Thy birth.

The Sleep of the Infant Jesus

Traditional French Carol

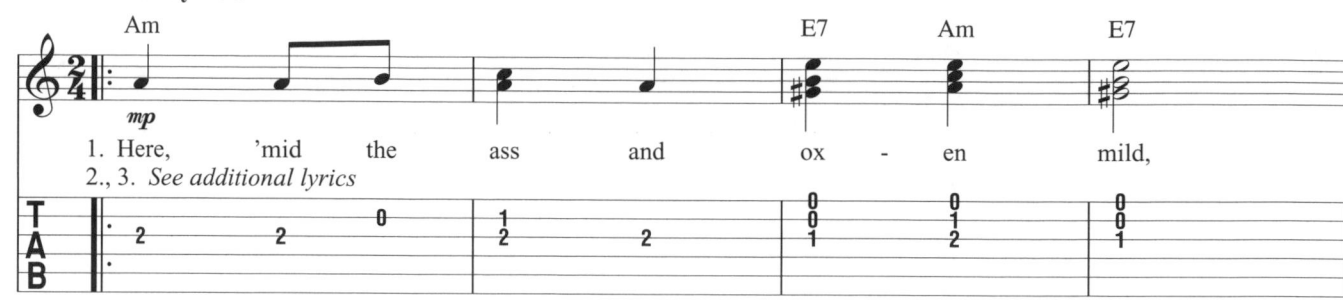

Strum Pattern: 10
Pick Pattern: 10

Verse
Moderately slow

1. Here, 'mid the ass and ox - en mild,
2., 3. *See additional lyrics*

sleep, sleep, sleep, thou ti - ny Child.

Chorus

Thou - sand che - ru - bim, thou - sand ser - a - phim

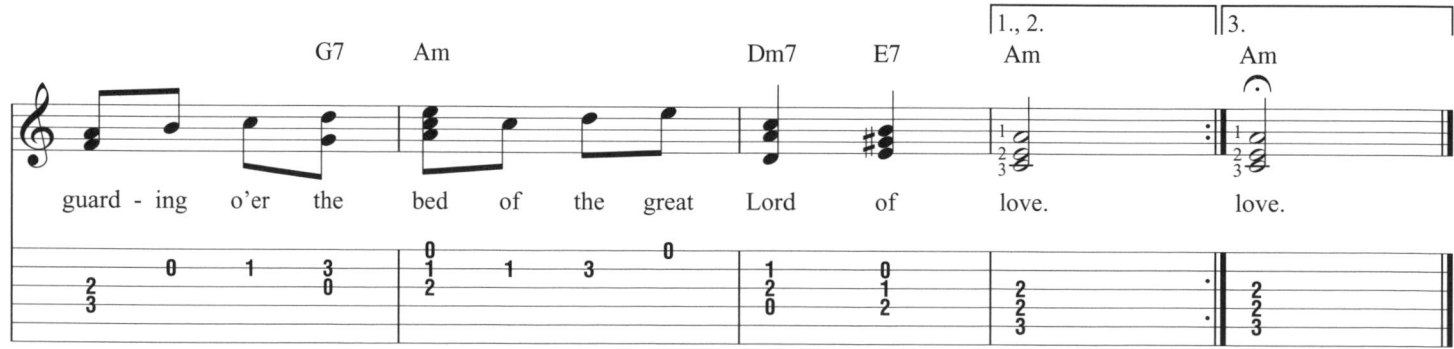

guard - ing o'er the bed of the great Lord of love. love.

Additional Lyrics

2. Here, 'mid the rose and lily bright,
   Sleep, sleep, sleep thou tiny Child.

3. Here, 'mid the shepherds' glad delight,
   Sleep, sleep, sleep thou tiny Child.

Star of the East

Words by George Cooper
Music by Amanda Kennedy

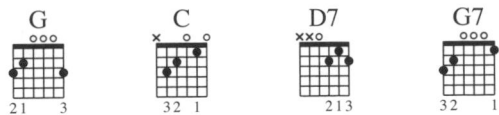

Strum Pattern: 9
Pick Pattern: 9

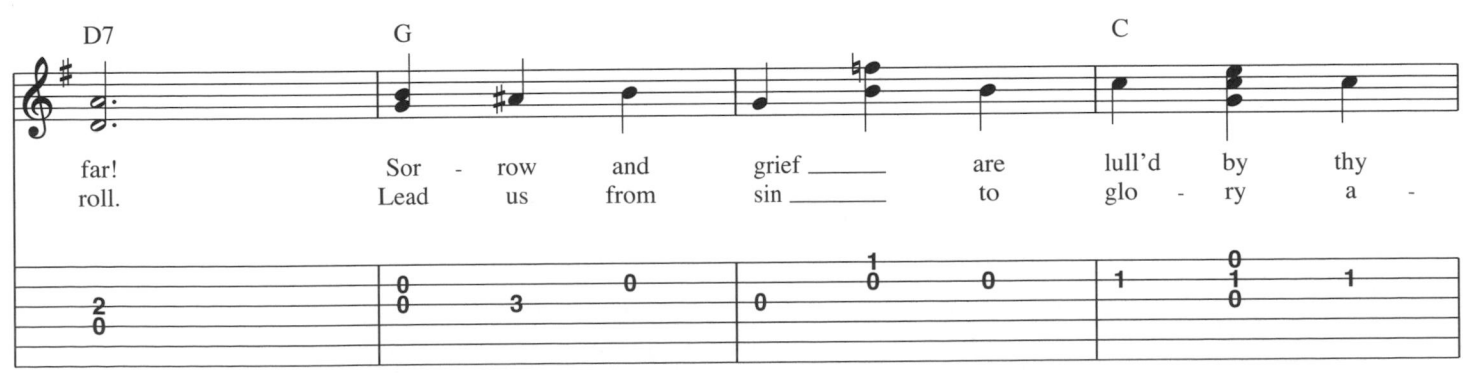

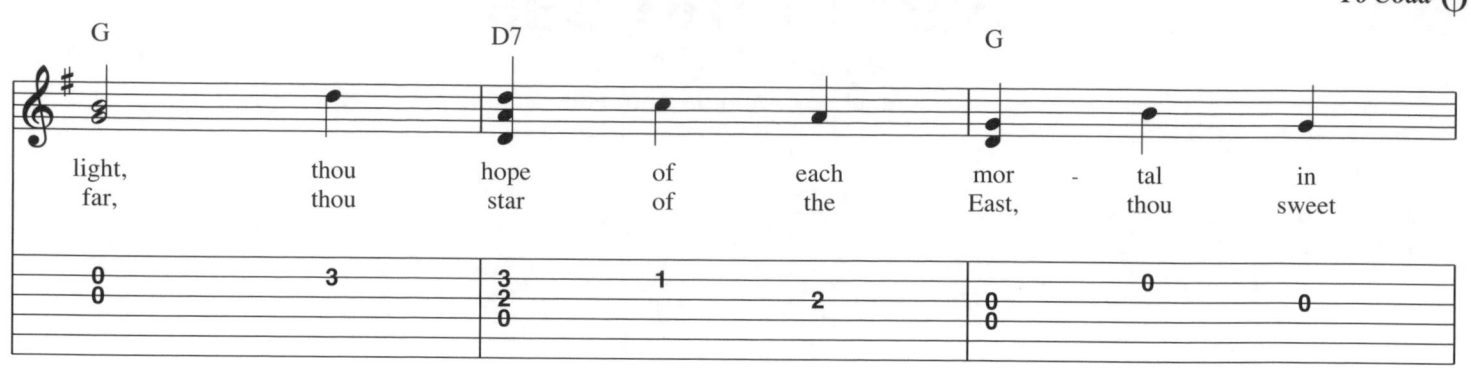

light, thou hope of each mor - tal in
far, thou star of the East, thou sweet

death's lone - ly night. _____ Fear - less and

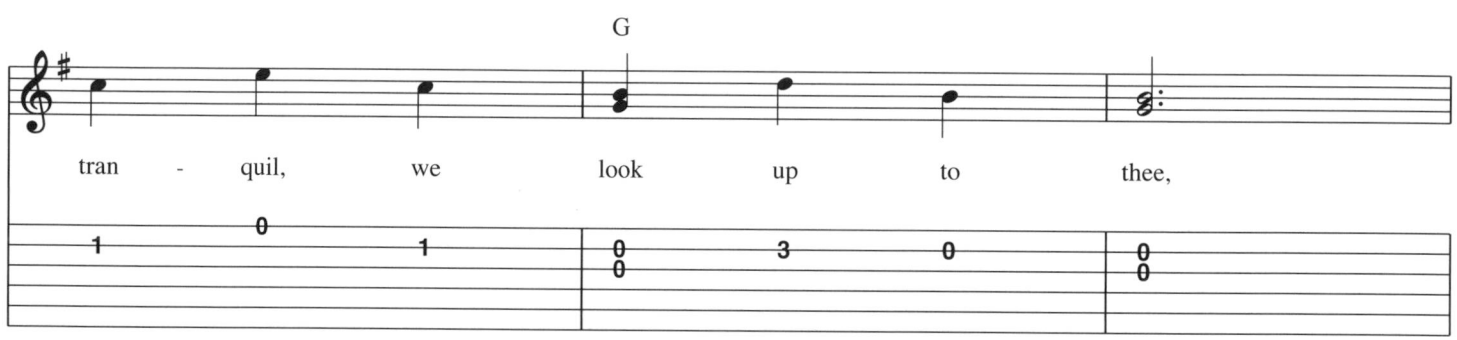

tran - quil, we look up to thee,

know - ing thou beam'st thro' e - ter - ni - ty!

Help us to fol - low where thou still dost guide.

⊕ Coda

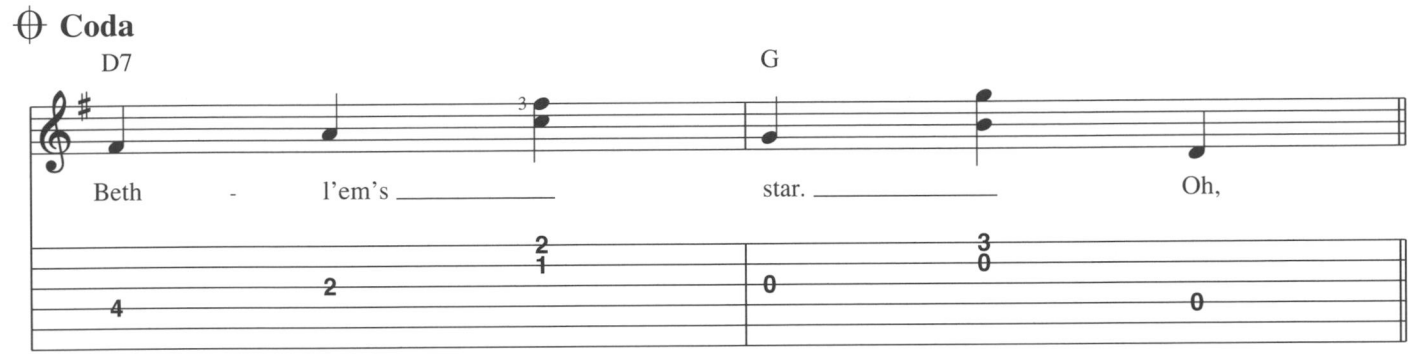

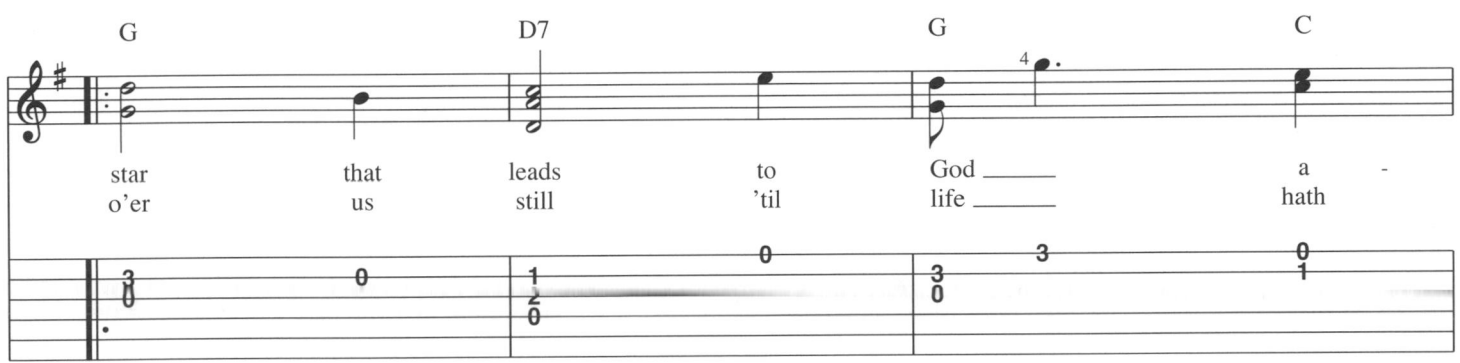

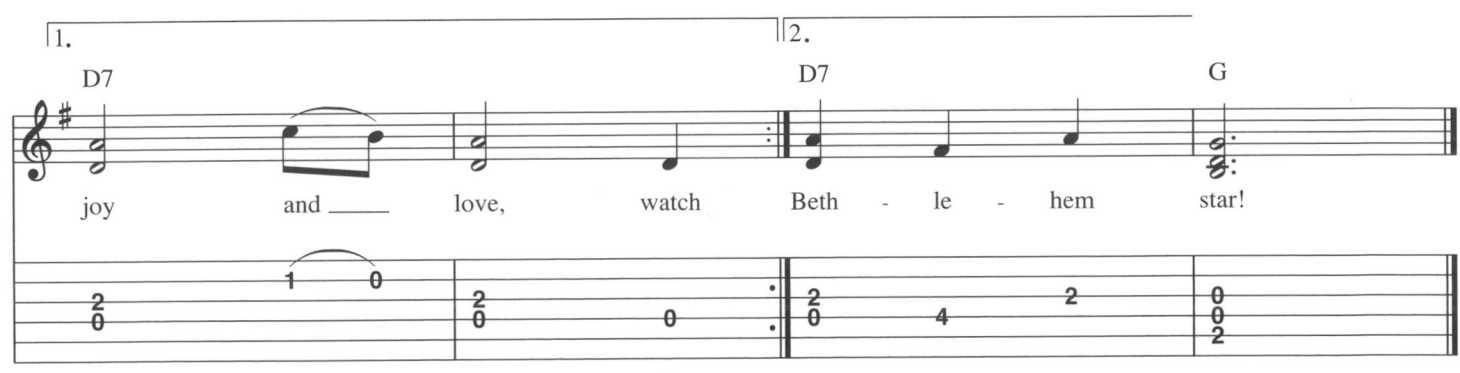

The Snow Lay on the Ground

Traditional Irish Carol

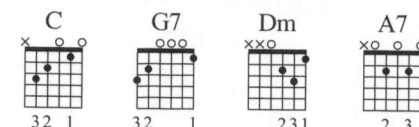

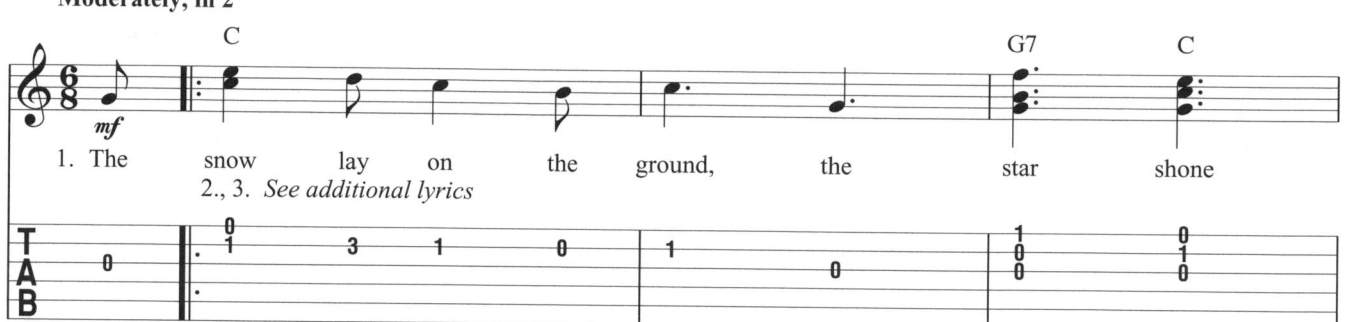

Strum Pattern: 8
Pick Pattern: 8

Verse
Moderately, in 2

1. The snow lay on the ground, the star shone
2., 3. *See additional lyrics*

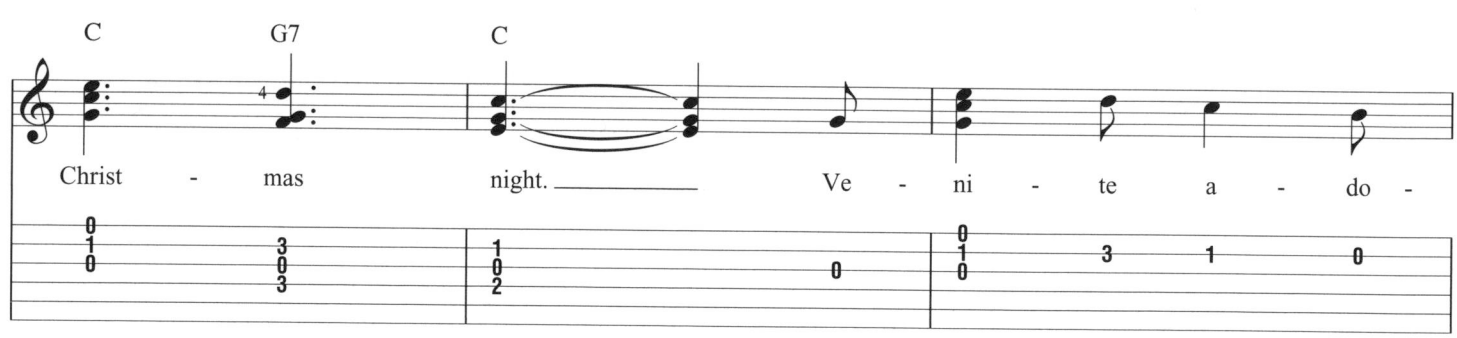

bright, _____ when Christ our Lord was born on

Christ - mas night. _____ Ve - ni - te a - do -

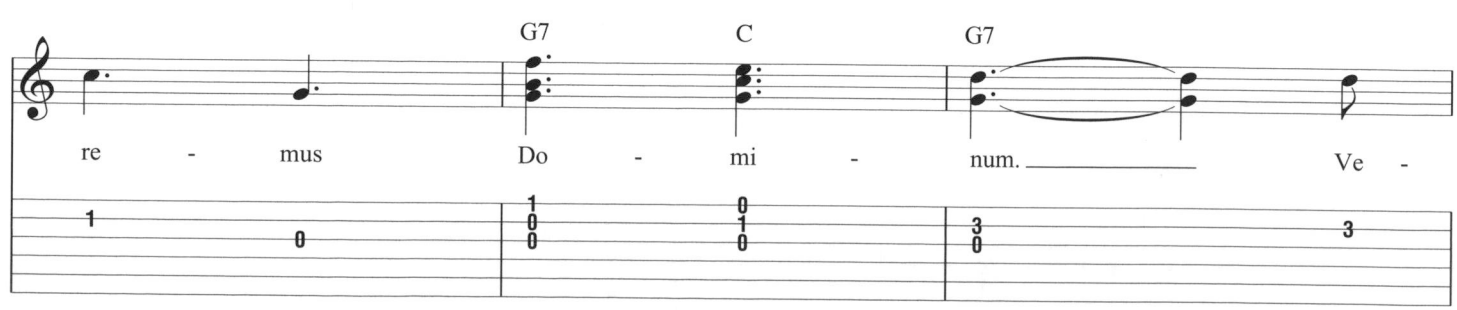

re - mus Do - mi - num. _____ Ve -

ni - te a - do - re - mus Do - mi -

Chorus

num. _____ Ve - ni - te a - do - re - mus

Do - mi - num. _____ Ve - ni - te a - do -

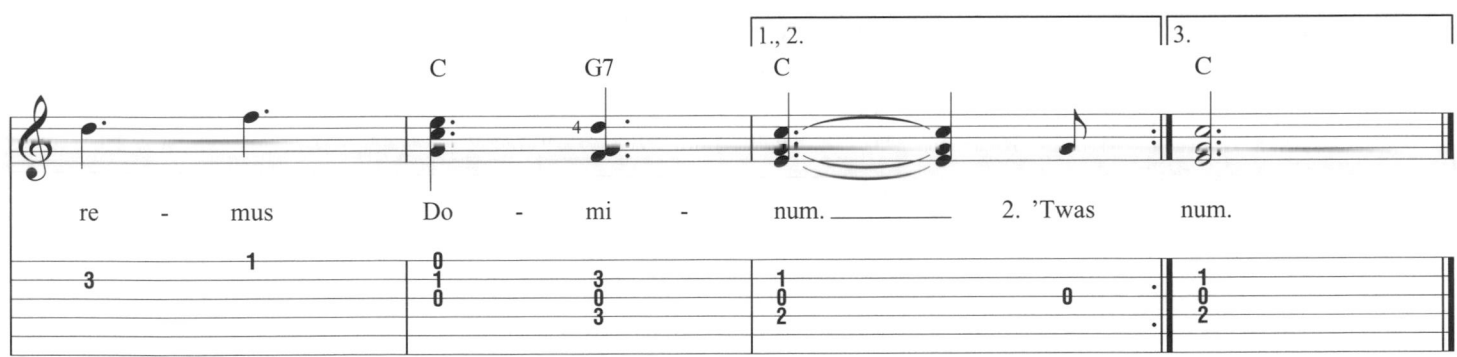

re - mus Do - mi - num. _____ 2. 'Twas num.

Additional Lyrics

2. 'Twas Mary, virgin pure of Holy Anne
   That brought into this world the God-made man.
   She laid Him in a stall at Bethlehem.
   The ass and oxen share the roof with them.

3. Saint Joseph too, was by to tend the Child,
   To guard Him and protect His mother mild.
   The angels hovered 'round and sang this song:
   Venite adoremus Dominum.

Still, Still, Still

Salzburg Melody, c.1819
Traditional Austrian Text

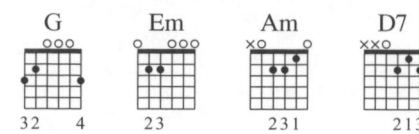

Strum Pattern: 4
Pick Pattern: 3

Verse
Moderately slow

1. Still, ___ still, ___ still, to ___ sleep is ___ now His ___
2. Sleep, ___ sleep, ___ sleep, while __ we Thy ___ vig - il ___

will. On Mar - y's ___ breast He rests in ___ slum - ber,
keep. And an - gels ___ come He from heav - en ___ sing - ing

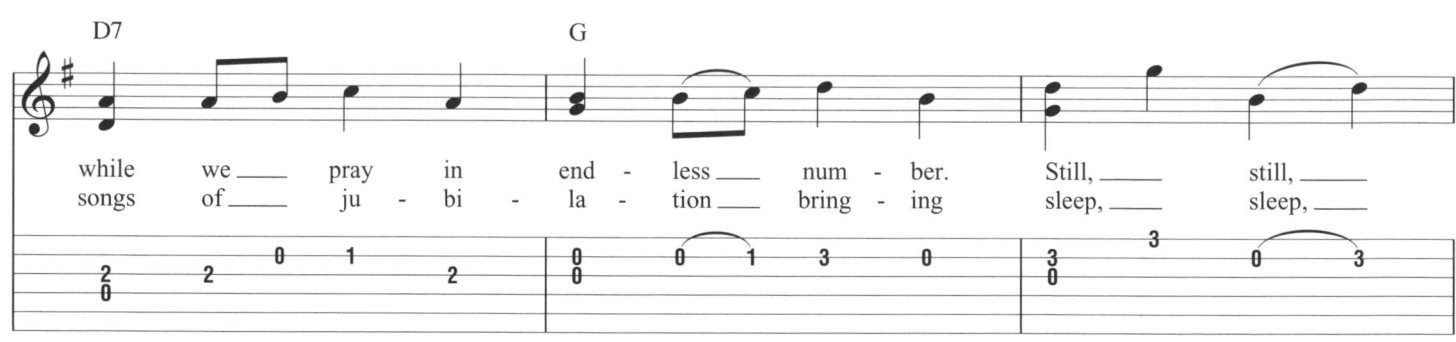

while we ___ pray in end - less ___ num - ber. Still, ___ still, ___
songs of ___ ju - bi - la - tion ___ bring - ing sleep, ___ sleep, ___

still, to ___ sleep is ___ now His ___ will.
sleep, while __ we Thy ___ vig - il ___ keep.

There's a Song in the Air

Words and Music by Josiah G. Holland and Karl P. Harrington

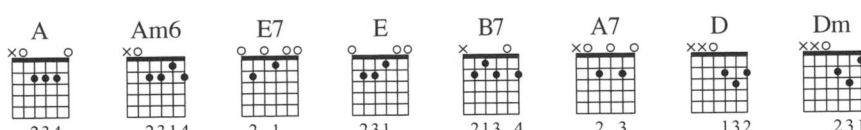

Strum Pattern: 8
Pick Pattern: 8

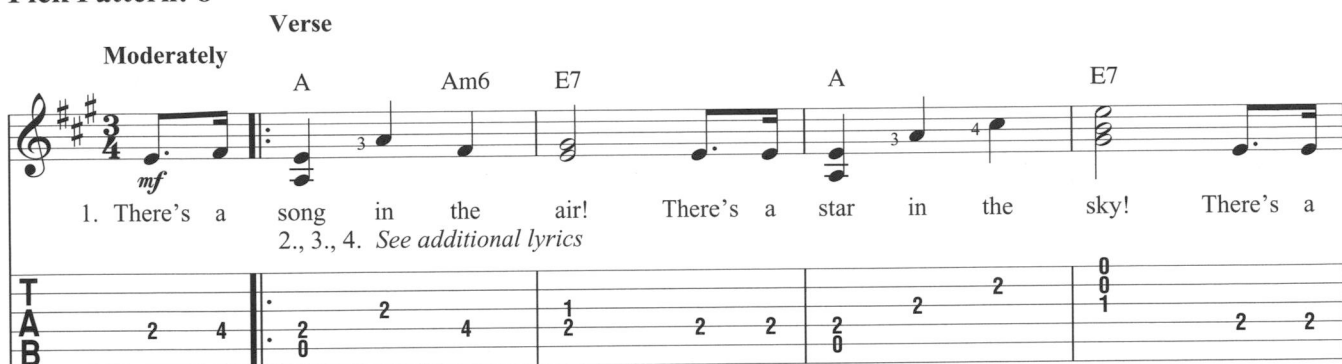

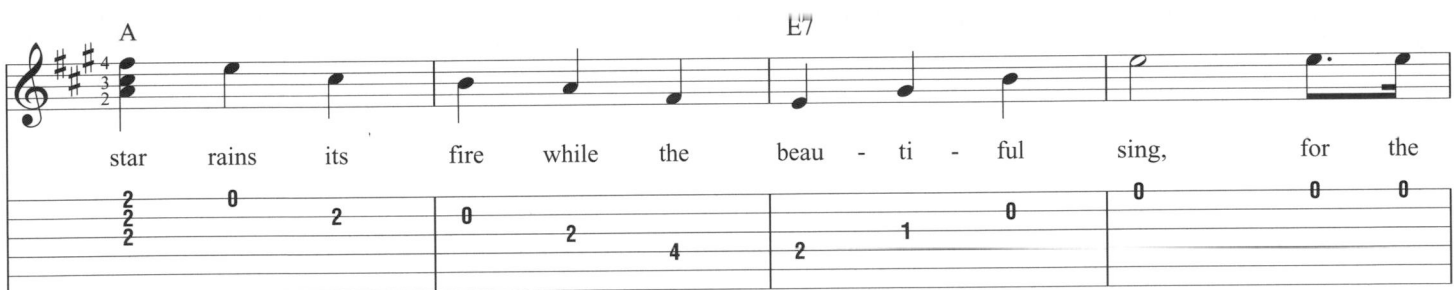

Additional Lyrics

2. There's a tumult of joy o'er the wonderful birth,
   For the Virgin's sweet boy is the Lord of the earth.
   Ay! The star rains its fire while the beautiful sing,
   For the manger of Bethlehem cradles a King!

3. In the light of that star lie the ages impearled,
   And that song from afar has swept over the world.
   Ev'ry hearth is aflame, and the beautiful sing
   In the homes of the nations that Jesus is King!

4. We rejoice in the light, and we echo the song
   That comes down thro' the night from the heavenly throng.
   Ay! We shout to the lovely evangel they bring,
   And we greet in His cradle our Savior and King!

Toyland

from BABES IN TOYLAND

Words by Glen MacDonough
Music by Victor Herbert

 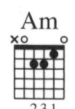  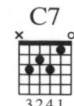 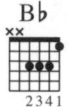 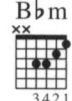

Strum Pattern: 8
Pick Pattern: 8

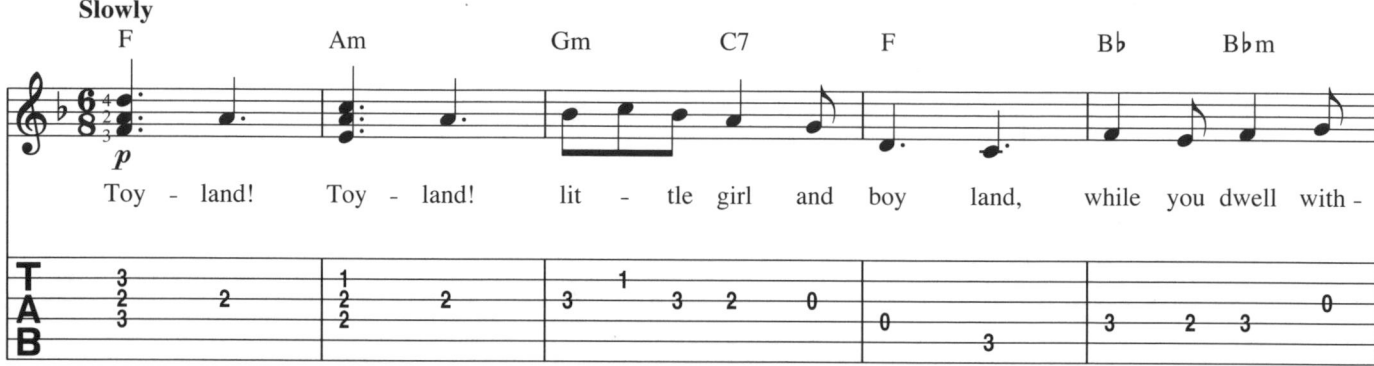

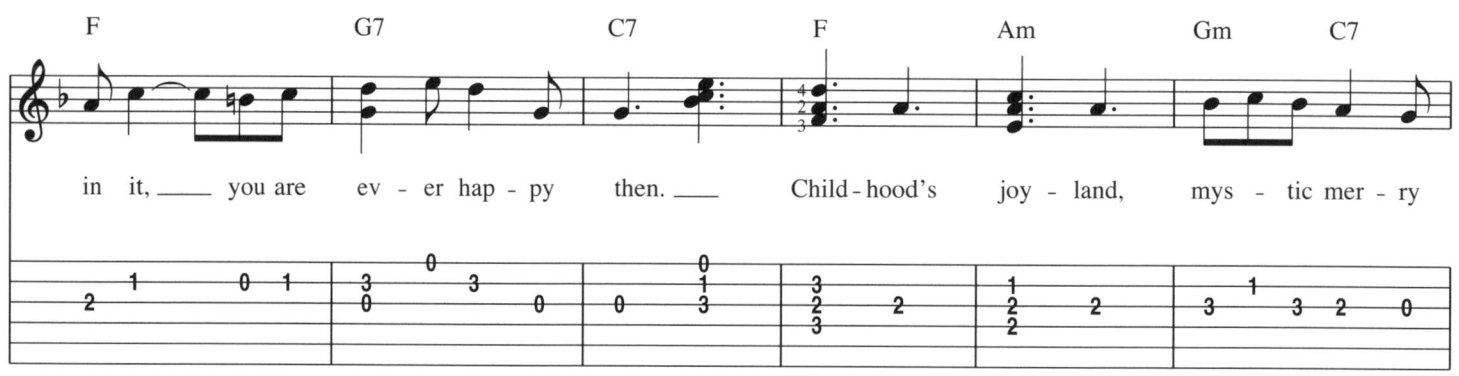

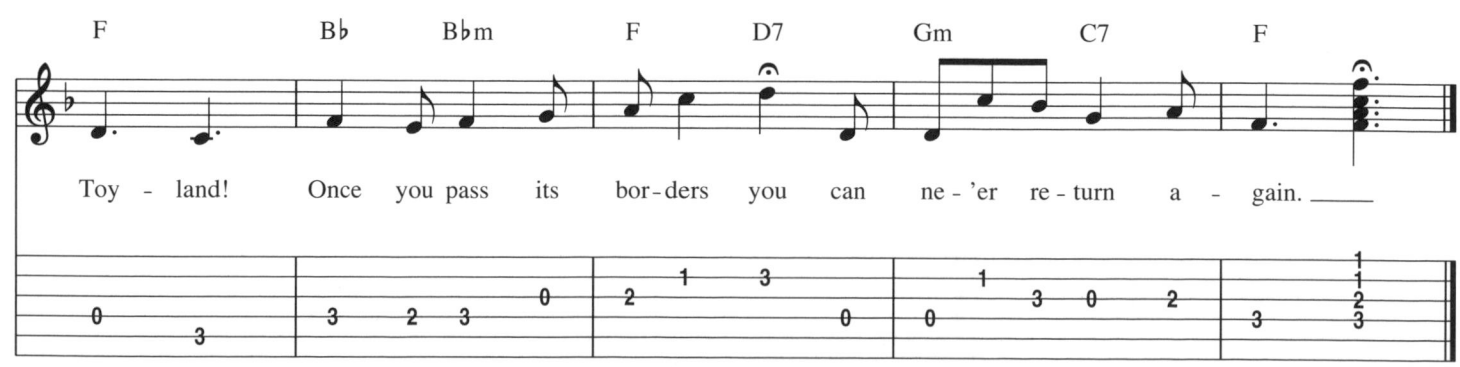

The Twelve Days of Christmas

Traditional English Carol

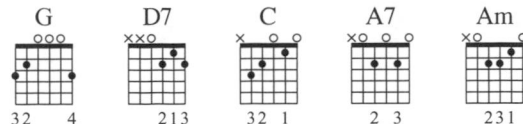

Strum Pattern: 3
Pick Pattern: 3

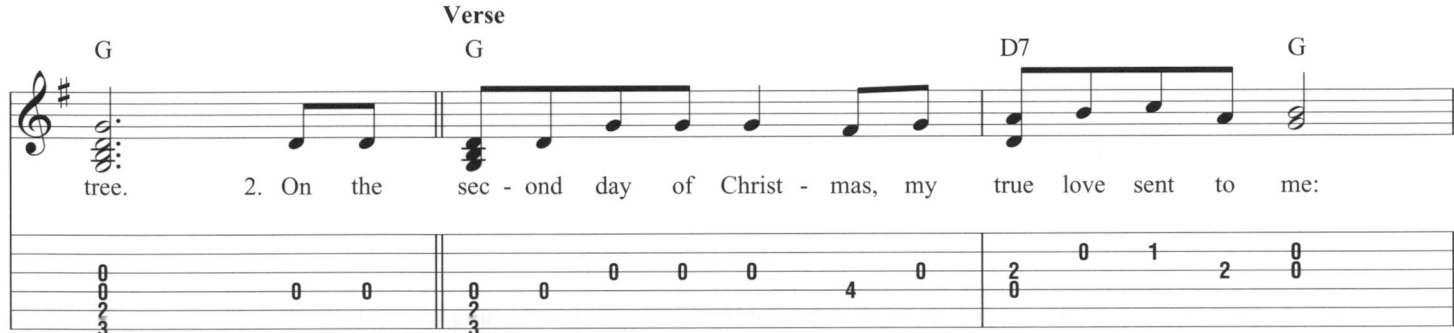

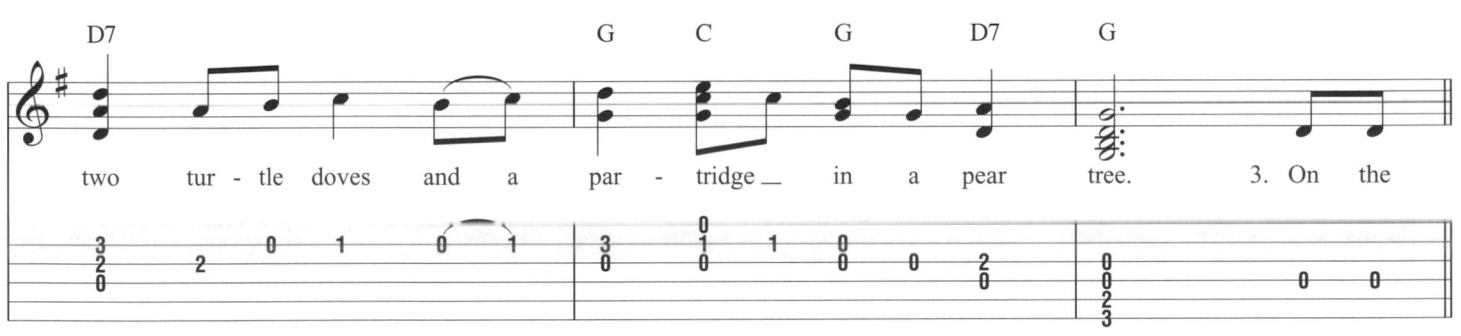

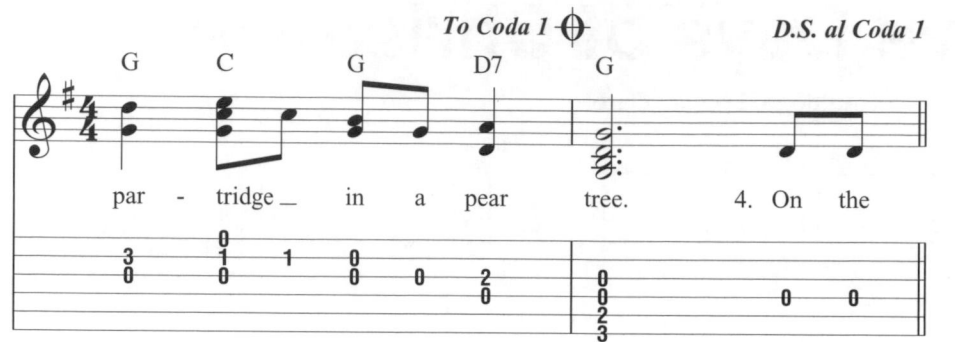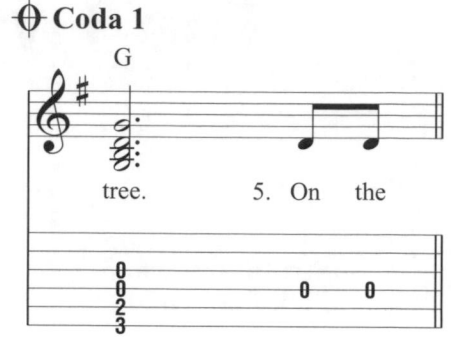

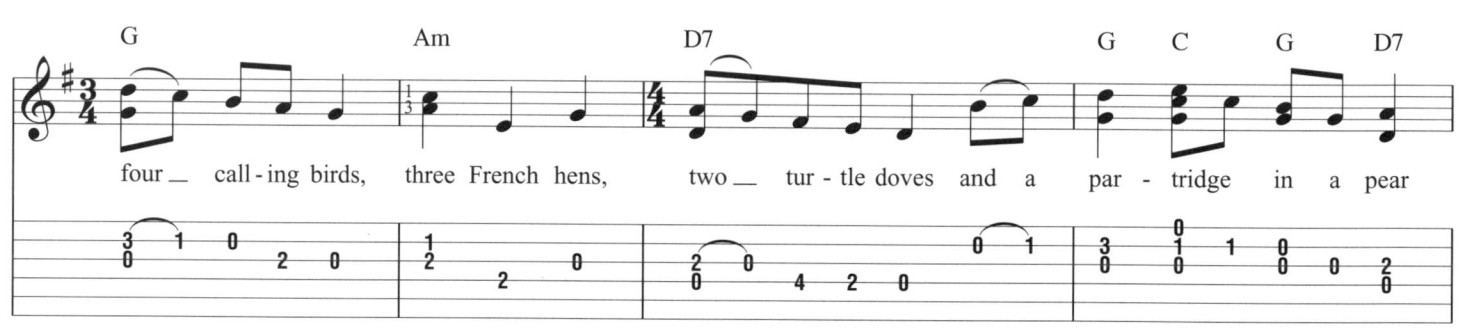

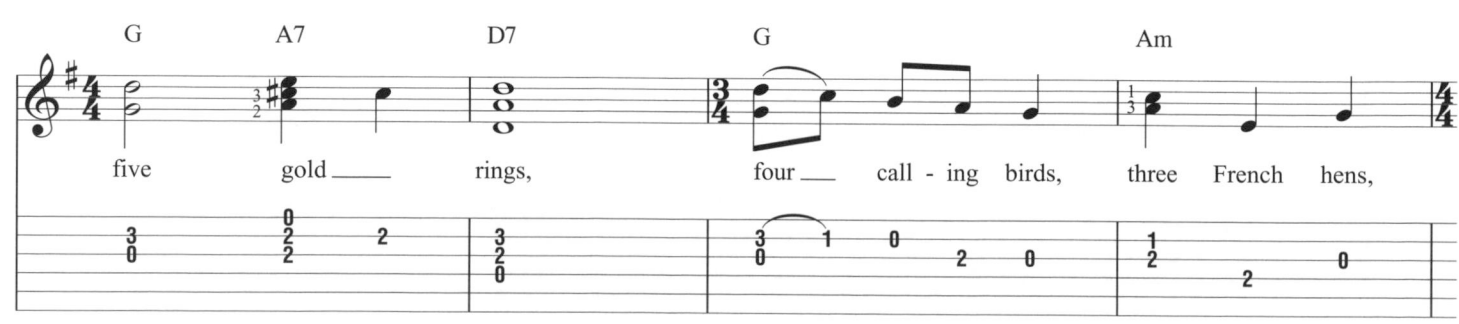

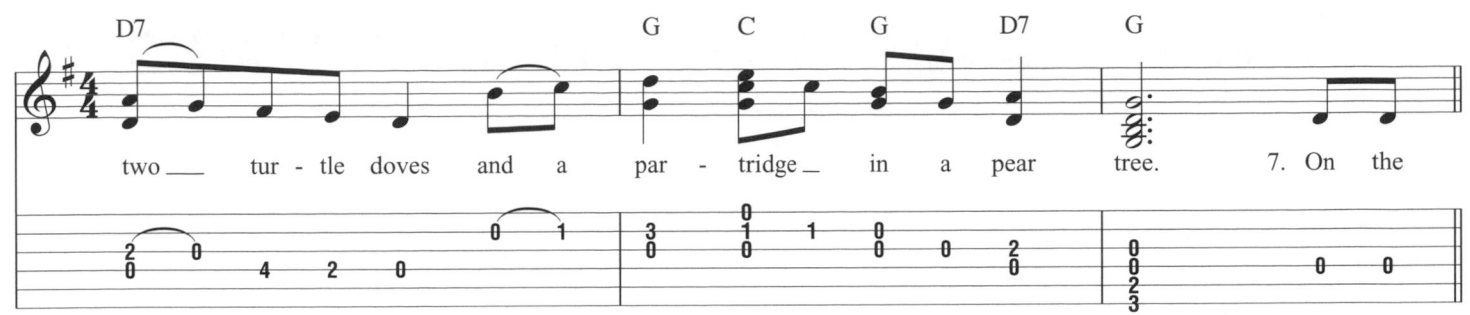

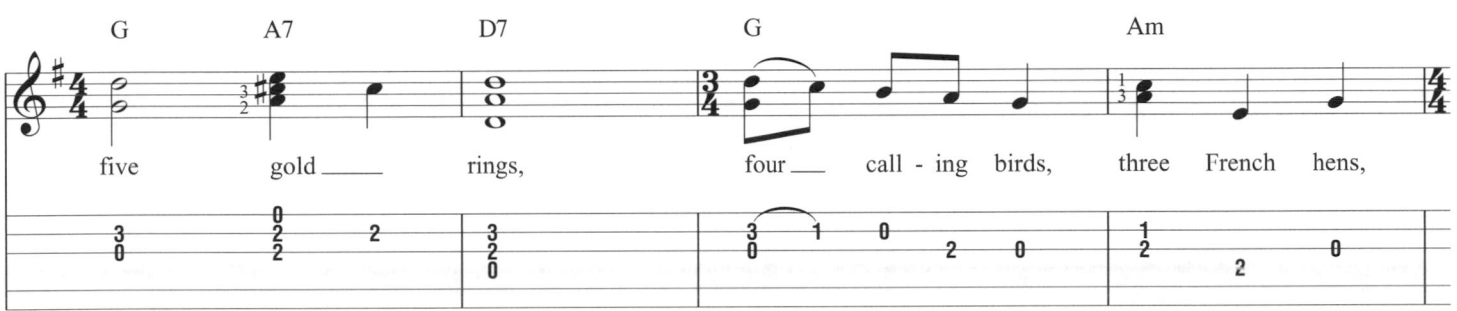

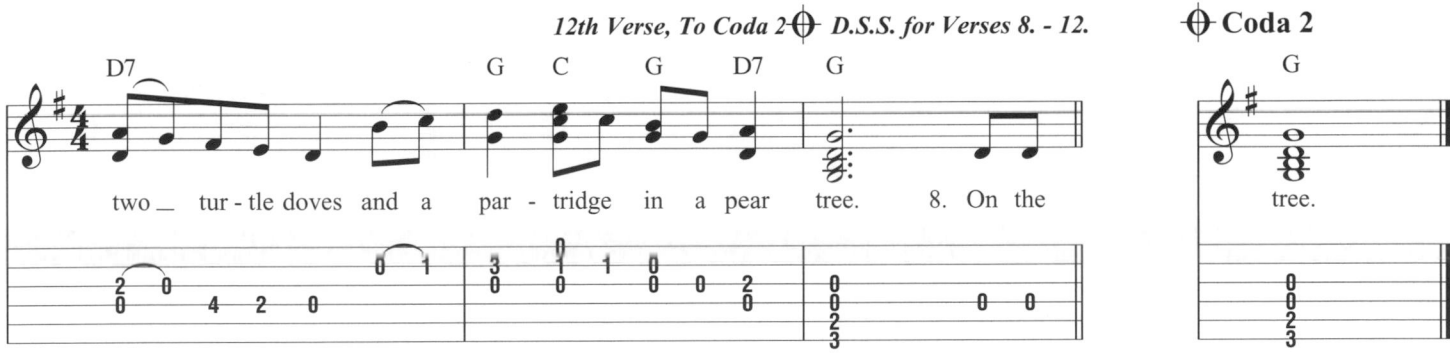

Additional Lyrics

4. On the fourth day of Christmas, my true love gave to me:
Four calling birds, three French hens, two turtle doves and a partridge in a pear tree.

8. On the eighth day of Christmas, my true love gave to me: eight maids a milking,...

9. On the ninth day of Christmas, my true love gave to me: nine ladies dancing,...

10. On the tenth day of Christmas, my true love gave to me: ten lords a leaping,...

11. On the 'leventh day of Christmas, my true love gave to me: 'leven pipers piping,...

12. On the twelfth day of Christmas, my true love gave to me: twelve drummers drumming,...

'Twas the Night Before Christmas

Words by Clement Clark Moore
Music by F. Henri Klickman

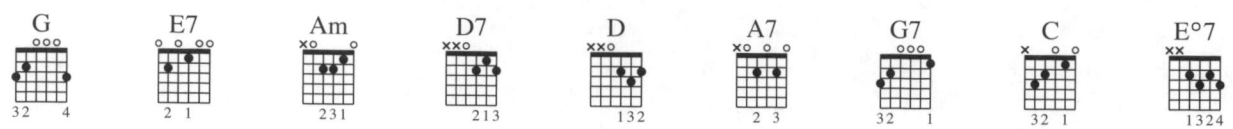

Strum Pattern: 4
Pick Pattern: 5

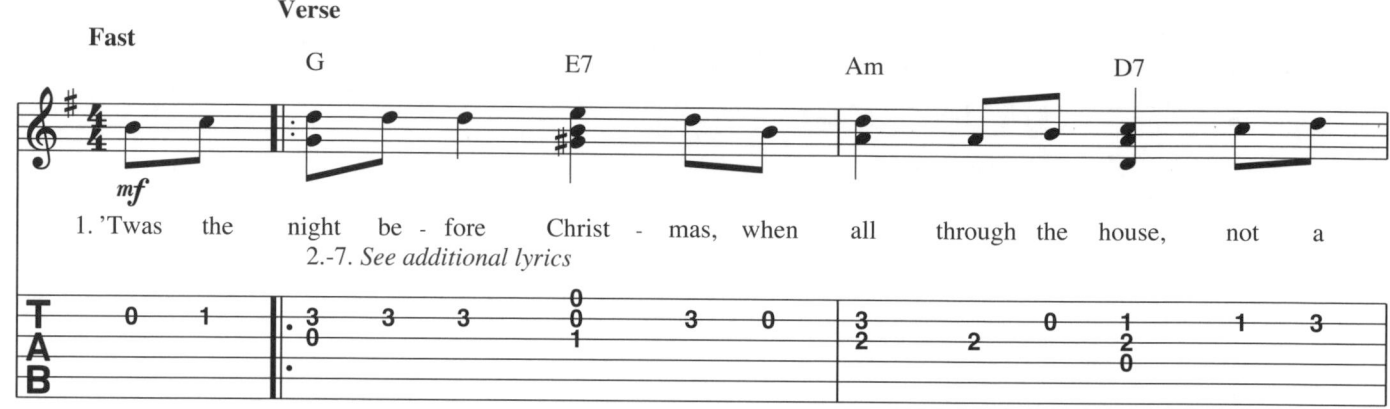

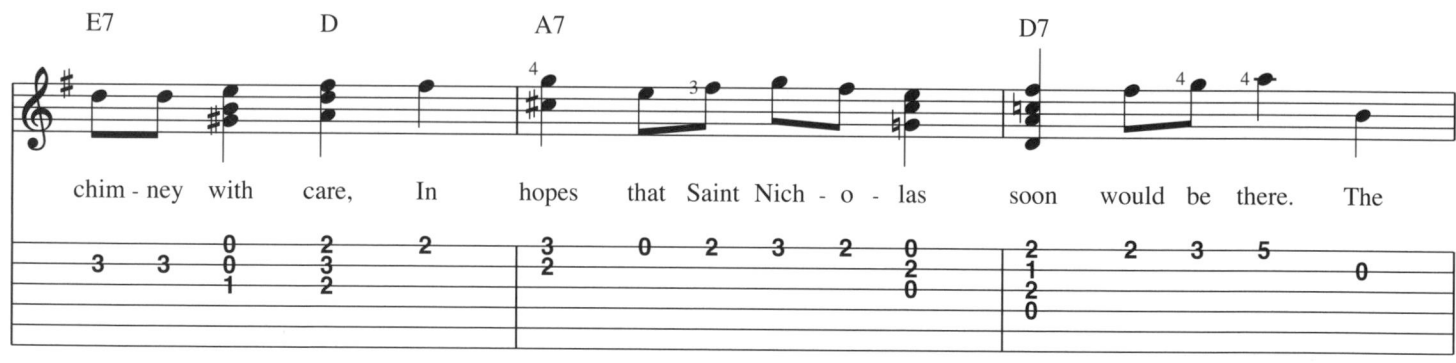

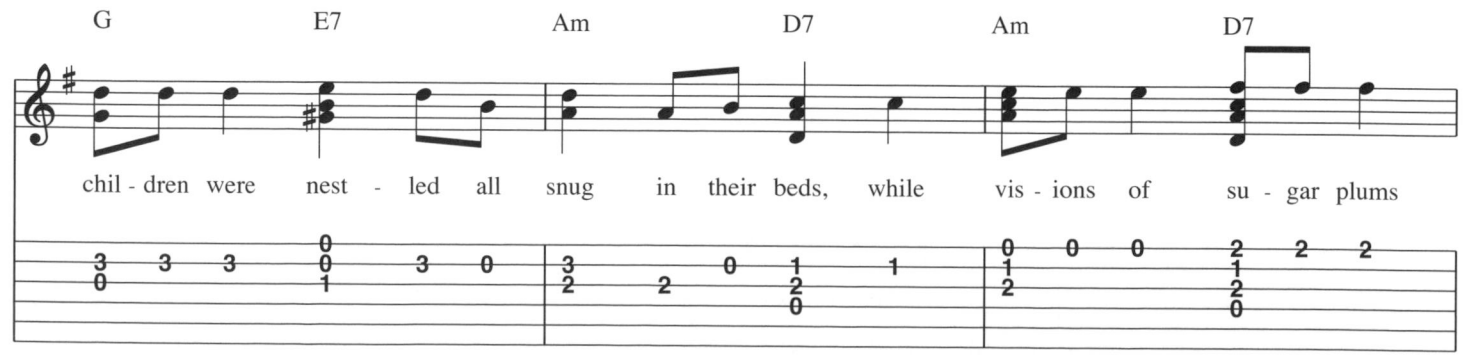

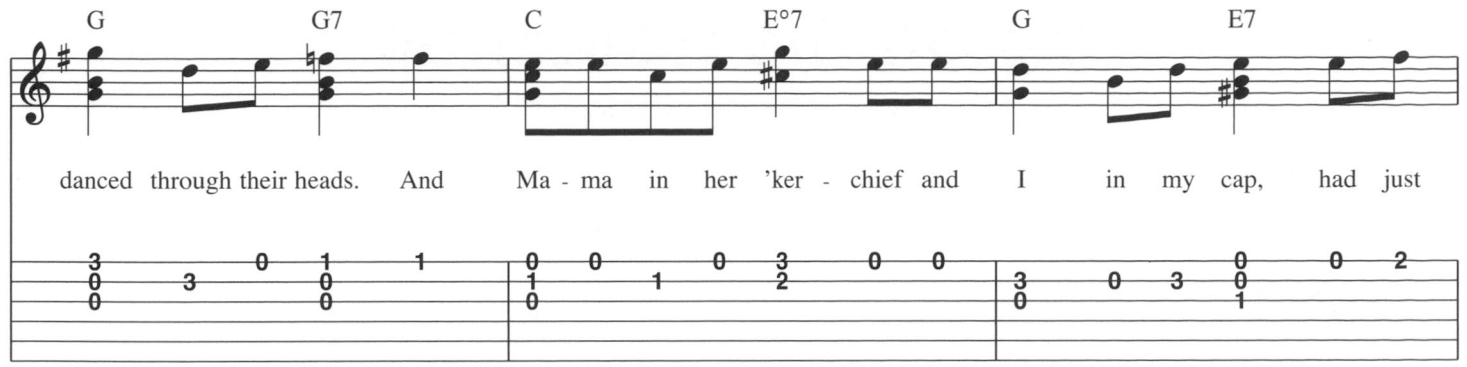

danced through their heads. And Ma - ma in her 'ker - chief and I in my cap, had just

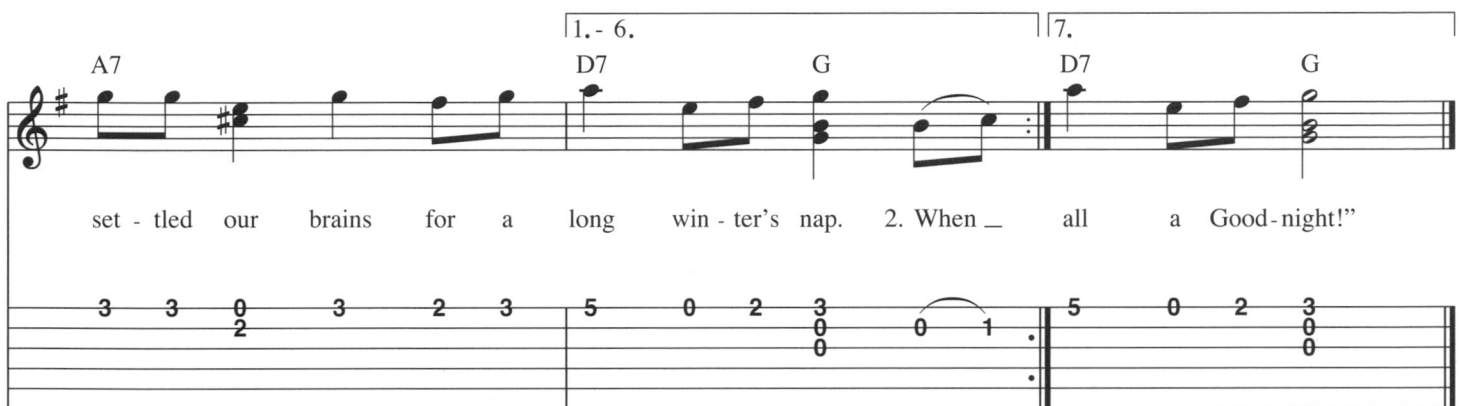

set - tled our brains for a long win - ter's nap. 2. When ___ all a Good-night!"

Additional Lyrics

2. When out on the lawn there arose such a clatter;
   I sprang from my bed to see what was the matter.
   Away to the window I flew like a flash,
   Tore open the shutters and threw up the sash.
   The moon, on the breast of the new-fallen snow,
   Gave a lustre of midday to objects below.
   When what to my wondering eyes should appear
   But a miniature sleigh and eight tiny reindeer.

3. With a little old driver, so lively and quick,
   I knew in a moment it must be Saint Nick.
   More rapid than eagles, his coursers they came
   And he whistled and shouted and called them by name:
   "Now, Dasher, Now, Dancer! Now, Prancer! Now, Vixen!
   On Comet! On, Cupid! On Donner and Blitzen!
   To the top of the porch, to the top of the wall!
   Now dash away, dash away, dash away all!"

4. As dry leaves that before the wild hurricane fly,
   When they meet with an obstacle, mount to the sky.
   So up to the house-top the coursers they flew,
   With the sleigh full of toys and Saint Nicholas, too.
   And then in a twinkling I heard on the roof
   The prancing and pawing of each little hoof.
   As I drew in my head, and was turning around,
   Down the chimney Saint Nicholas came with a bound.

5. He was dressed all in fur from his head to his foot
   And his clothes were all tarnished with ashes and soot.
   A bundle of toys he had flung on his back
   And he looked like a peddler just opening his pack.
   His eyes how they twinkled! His dimples how merry!
   His cheeks were like roses, his nose like a cherry,
   His droll little mouth was drawn up like a bow
   And the beard of his chin was as white as the snow.

6. The stump of a pipe he held tight in his teeth
   And the smoke, it encircled his head like a wreath.
   He had a broad face and a round little belly
   That shook, when he laughed, like a bowl full of jelly.
   He was chubby and plump, a right jolly old elf,
   And I laughed when I saw him, in spite of myself.
   A wink of his eye and a twist of his head,
   Soon gave me to know I had nothing to dread.

7. He spoke not a word but went straight to his work
   And filled all the stockings, then turned with a jerk,
   And laying his finger aside of his nose,
   And giving a nod, up the chimney he rose.
   He sprang to his sleigh, to his team gave a whistle
   And away they all flew like the down of a thistle.
   But I heard him exclaim, 'ere he drove out of sight:
   "Happy Christmas to all, and to all a Good-night!"

Up on the Housetop

Words and Music by B.R. Handy

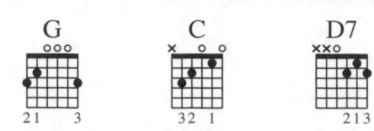

Strum Pattern: 3, 4
Pick Pattern: 3, 5

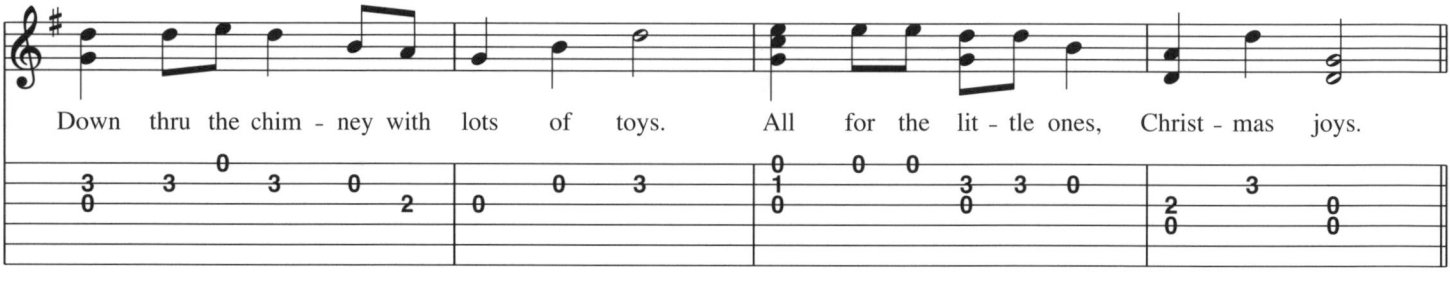

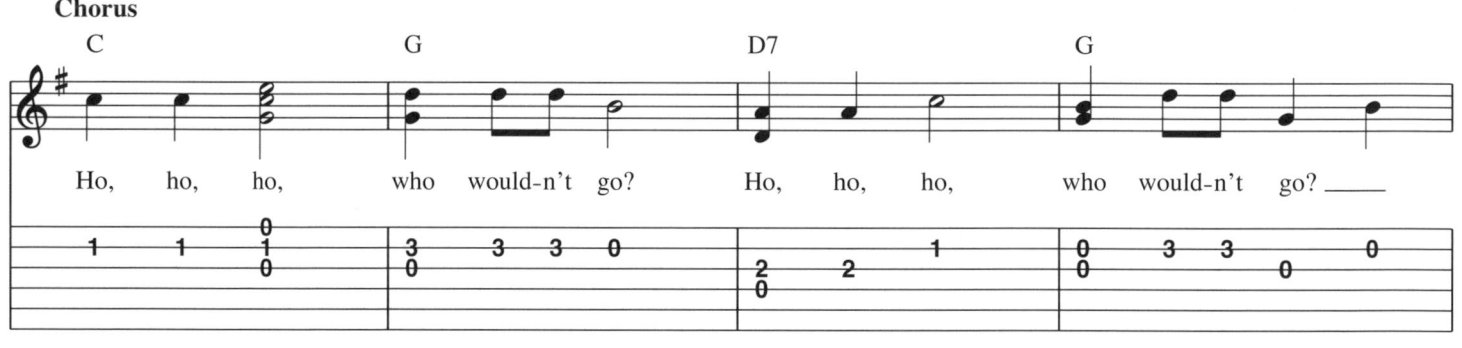

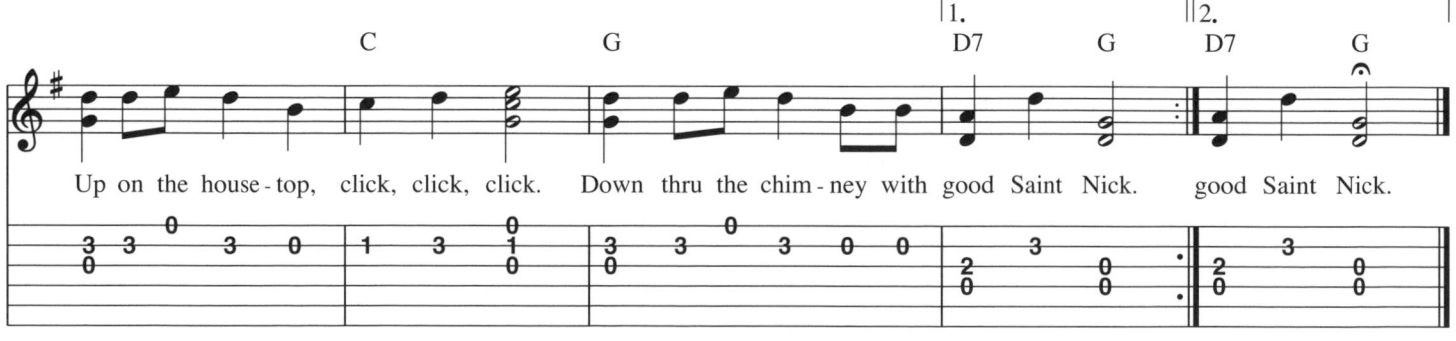

Additional Lyrics

2. First comes the stocking of Little Nell,
Oh, dear Santa, fill it well.
Give her a dollie that laughs and cries,
One that will open and shut her eyes.

We Wish You a Merry Christmas

Traditional English Folksong

Strum Pattern: 8, 9
Pick Pattern: 8, 9

Additional Lyrics

2. We all know that Santa's coming.
   We all know that Santa's coming.
   We all know that Santa's coming
   And soon will be here.

We Three Kings of Orient Are

Words and Music by John H. Hopkins, Jr.

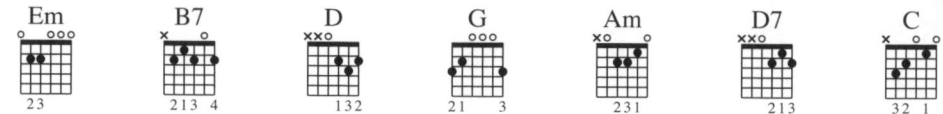

Strum Pattern: 8
Pick Pattern: 8

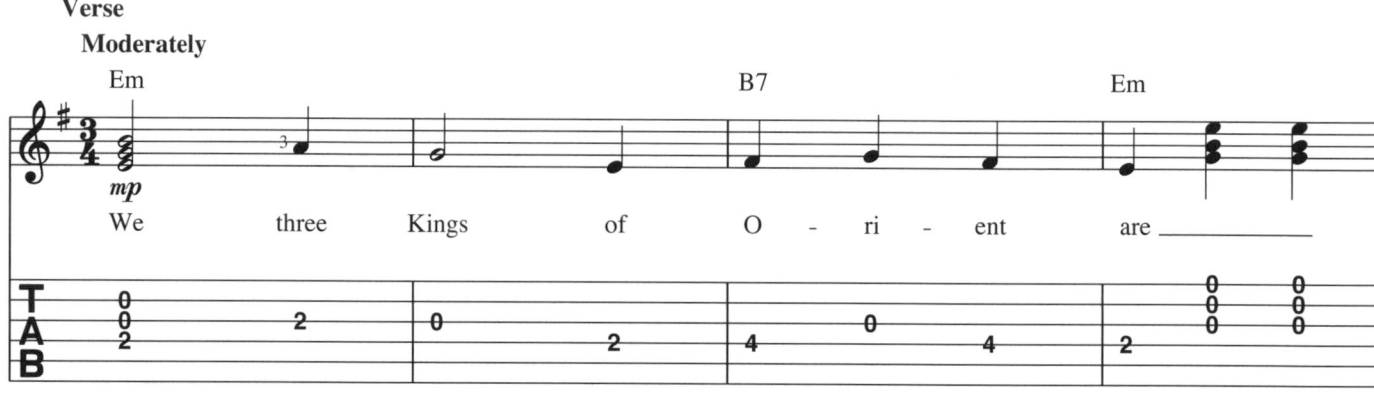

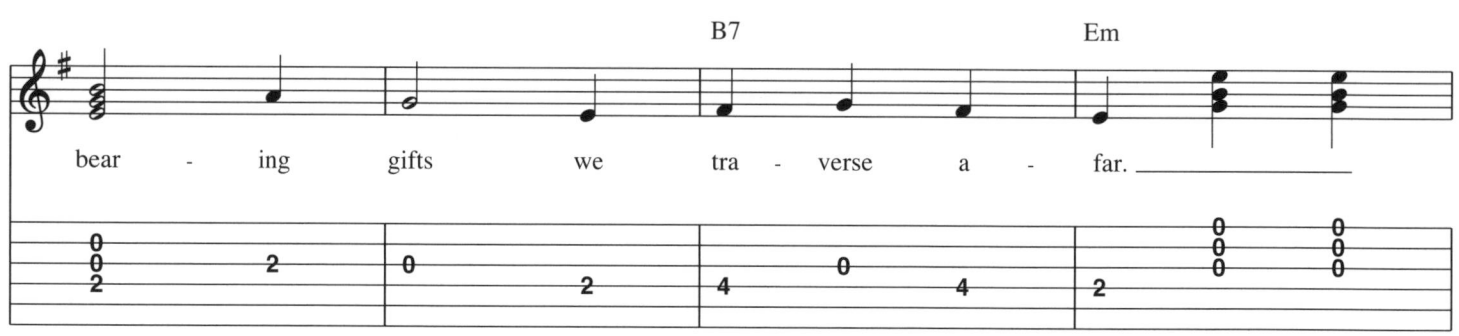

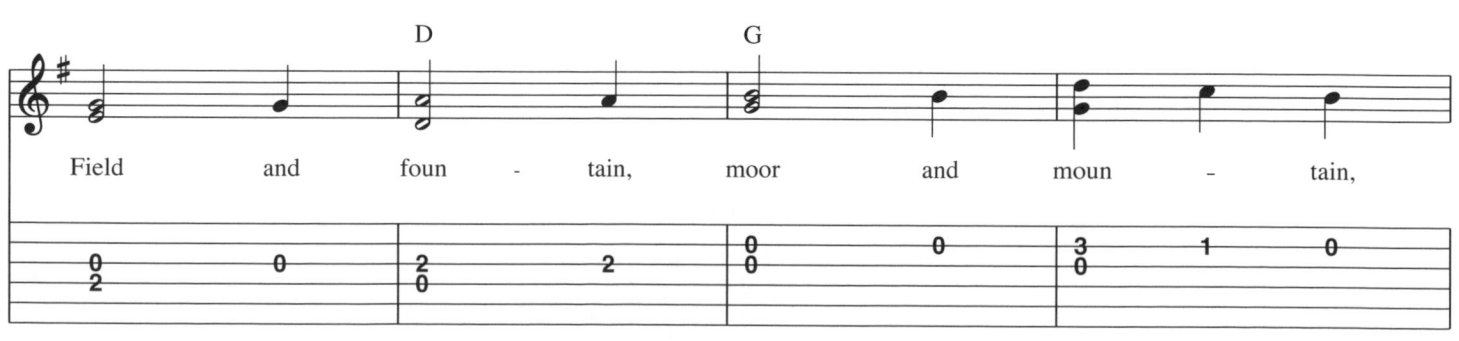

fol - low - ing yon - der star. _____ O, _____

Chorus

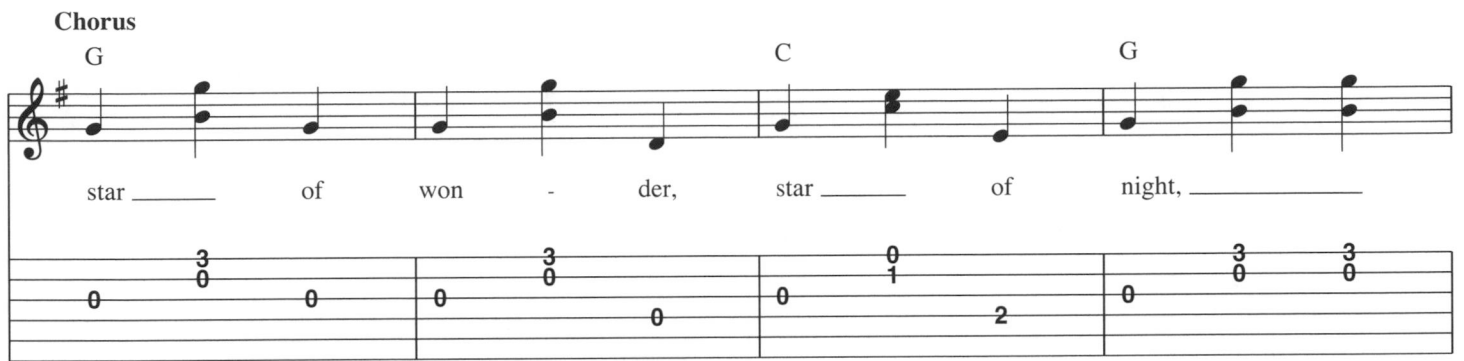

star _____ of won - der, star _____ of night, _____

star _____ with roy - al beau - ty bright. _____

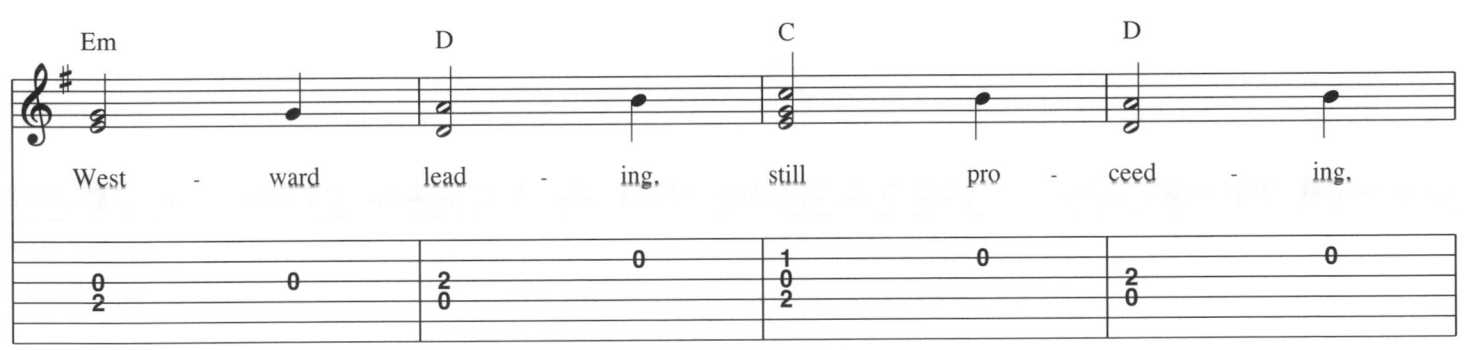

West - ward lead - ing, still pro - ceed - ing,

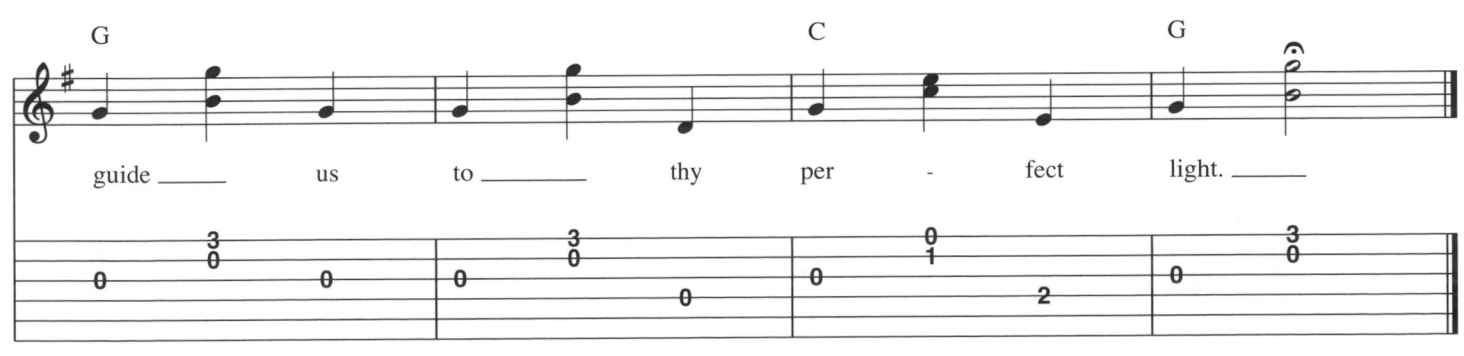

guide _____ us to _____ thy per - fect light. _____

Welsh Carol

Words by Pastor K.E. Roberts
Traditional Welsh Carol

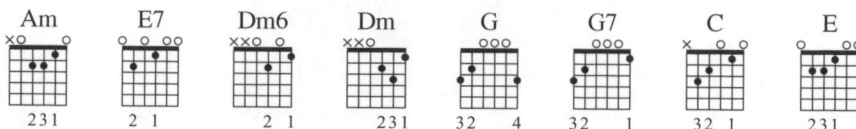

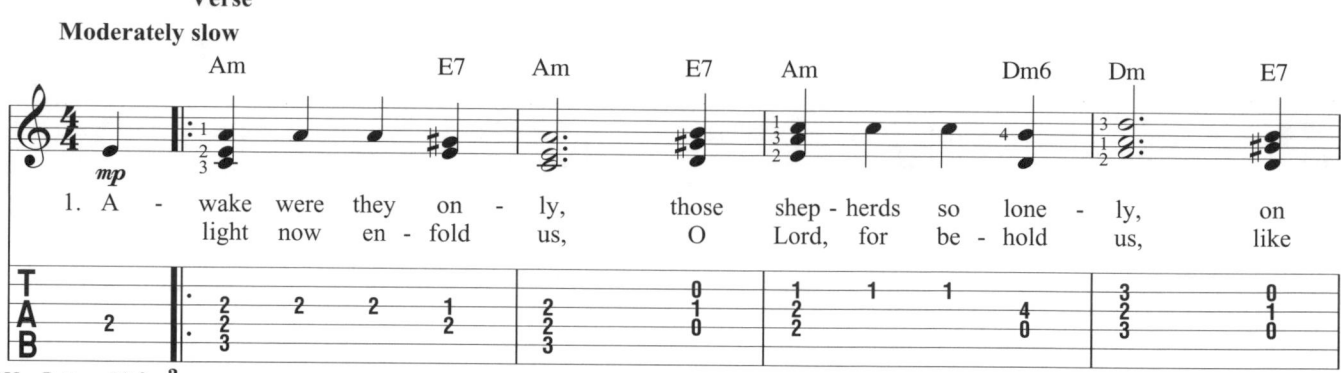

*Strum Pattern: 4
*Pick Pattern: 4

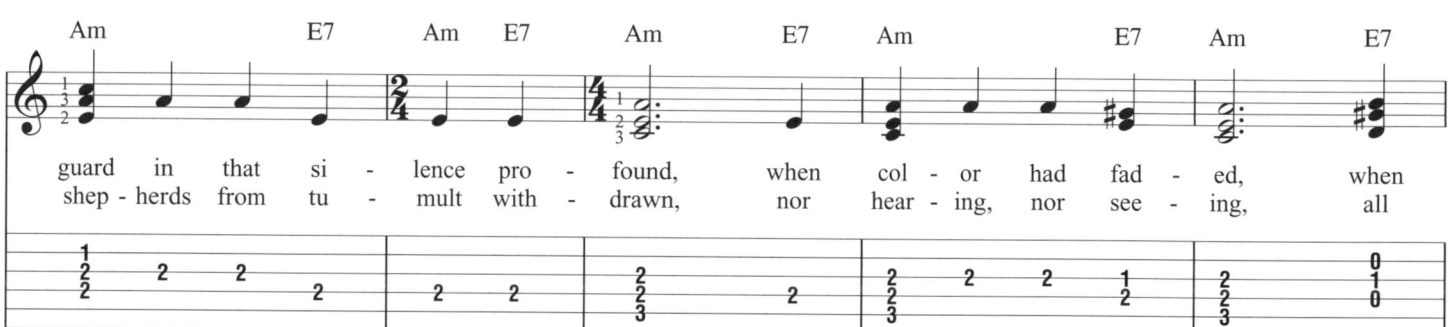

*Use Pattern 10 for 2/4 meas.

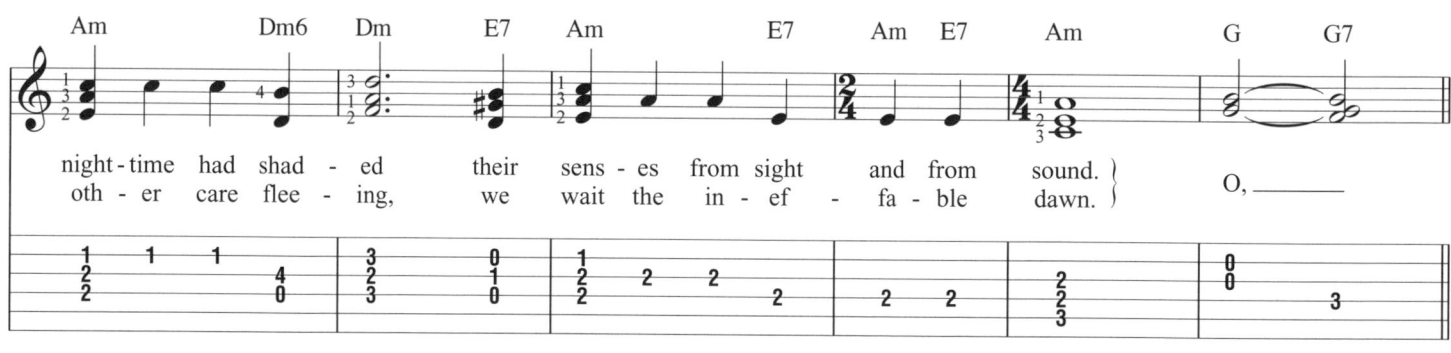

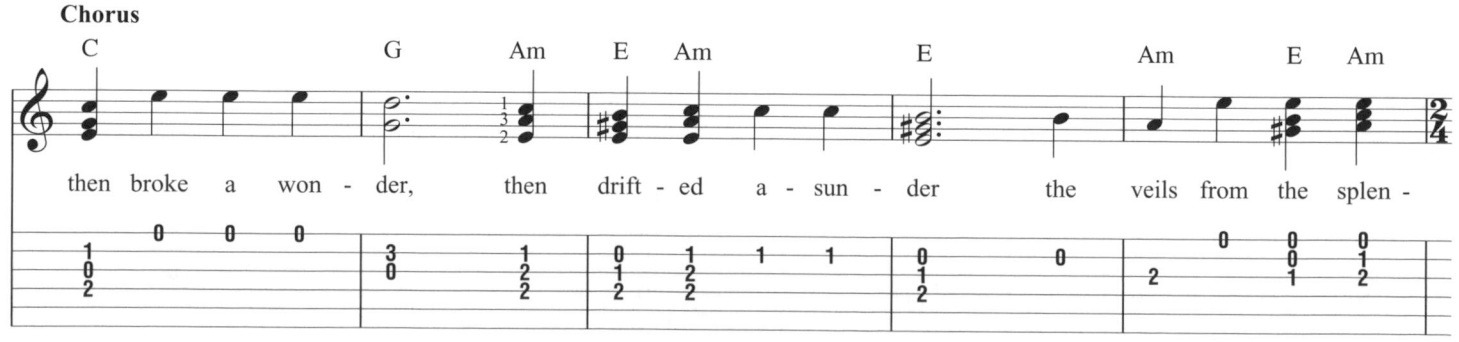

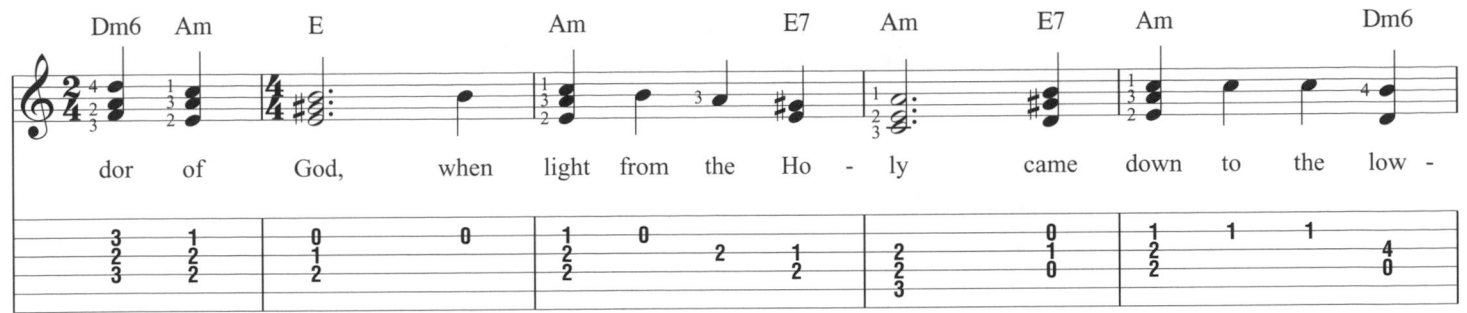

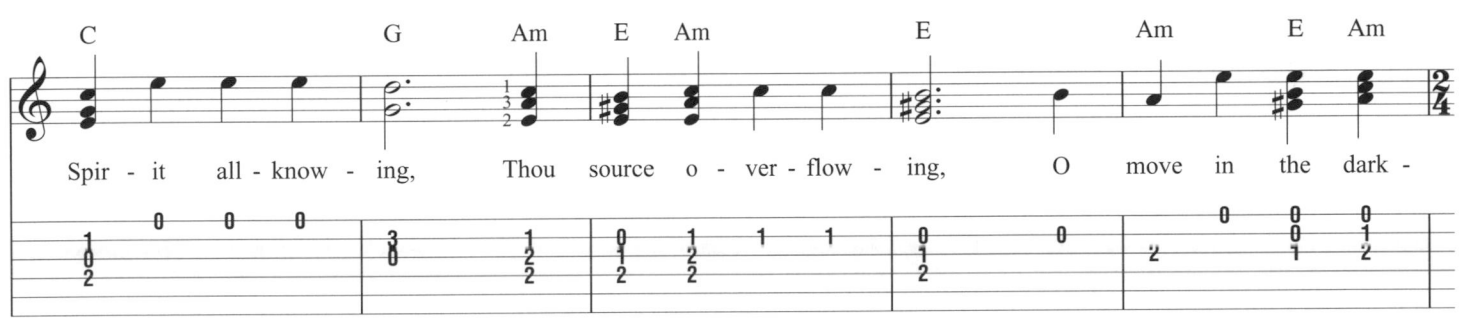

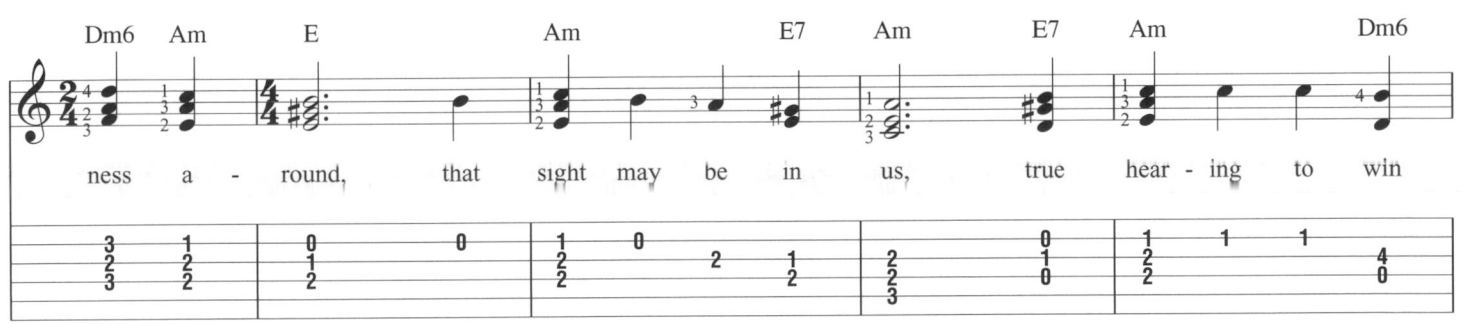

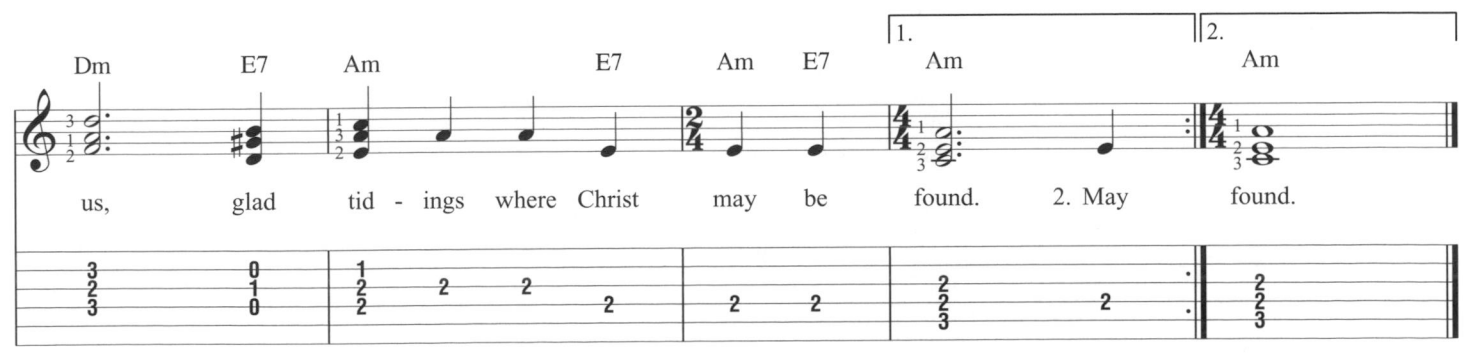

Wexford Carol

Traditional Irish Carol

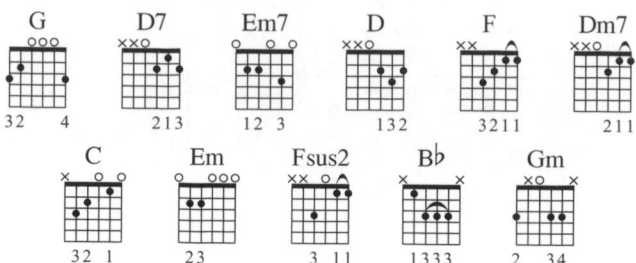

Strum Pattern: 7
Pick Pattern: 7

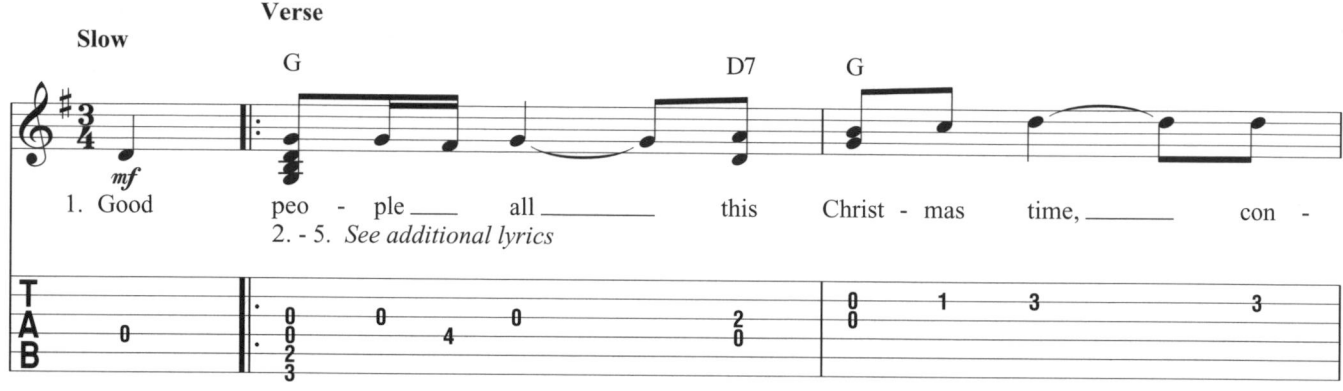

2. - 5. *See additional lyrics*

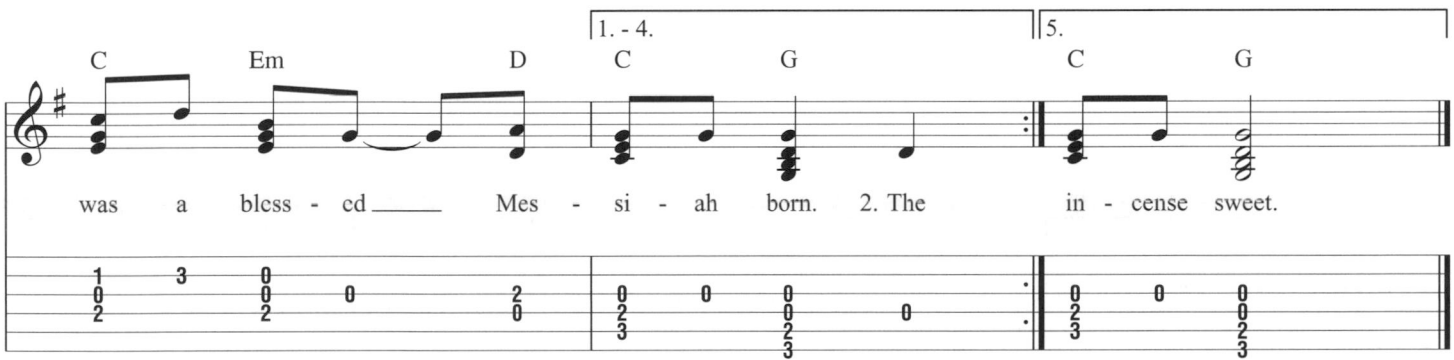

Additional Lyrics

2. The night before that happy tide,
   The noble virgin and her guide
   Were long time seeking up and down
   To find a lodging in the town.
   But mark how all things came to pass,
   From ev'ry door repell'd alas!
   As long foretold, their refuge all
   Was but a humble ox's stall.

3. Near Bethlehem did shepherds keep
   Their flocks of lambs and feeding sheep
   To whom God's angels did appear,
   Which put the shepherds in great fear.
   "Prepare and go," the angels said,
   "To Bethlehem, be not afraid,
   For there you'll find, this happy morn,
   A princely Babe, sweet Jesus born."

4. With thankful heart and joyful mind,
   The shepherds went the Babe to find,
   And as God's angel had foretold,
   They did our Savior Christ behold.
   Within a manger He was laid,
   And by His side, the virgin maid
   Attending on the Lord of life,
   Who came on earth to end all strife.

5. There were three wise men from afar
   Directed by a glorious star,
   And on they wandered night and day,
   Until they came where Jesus lay.
   And when they came unto that place,
   Where our beloved Messiah was,
   They humbly cast them at His feet,
   With gifts of gold and incense sweet.

What Child Is This?

Words by William C. Dix
16th Century English Melody

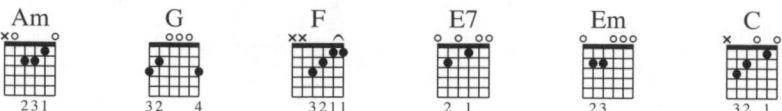

Strum Pattern: 7, 8
Pick Pattern: 8, 9

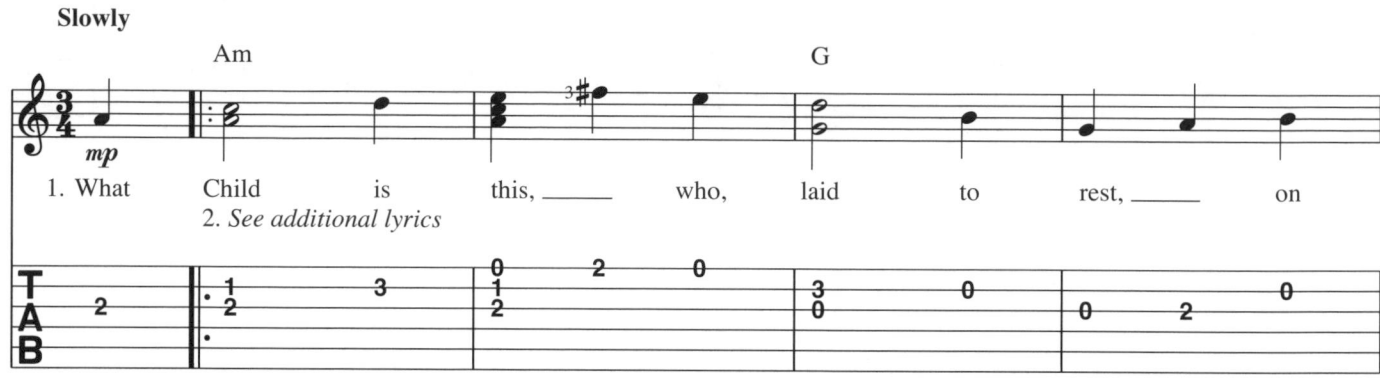

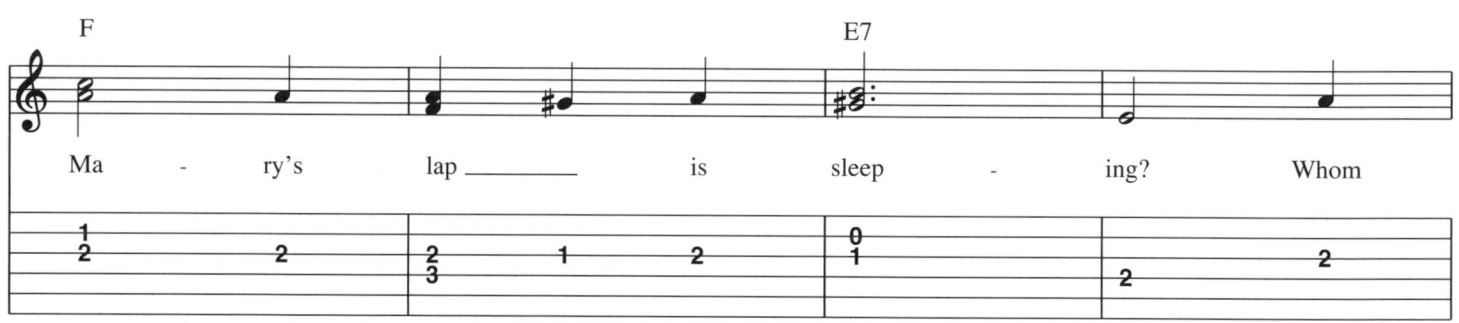

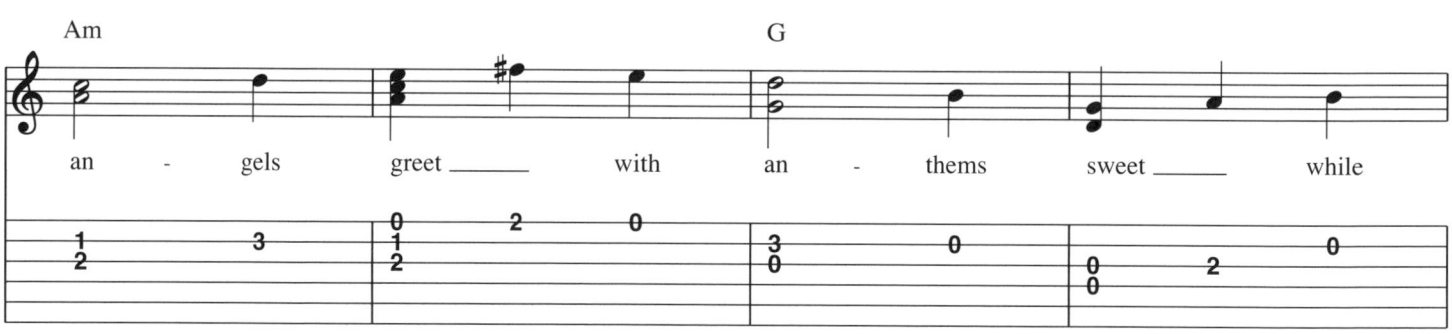

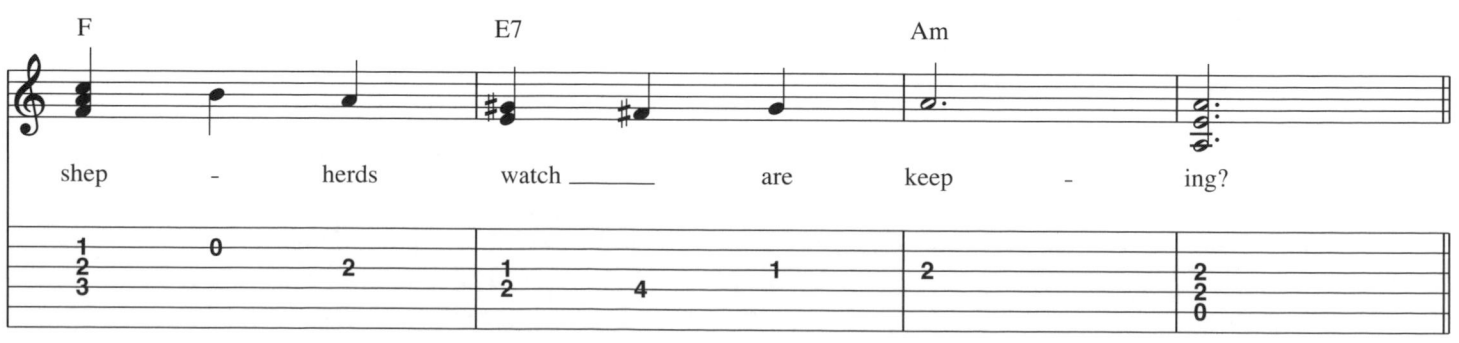

Chorus

This, this _____ is Christ the King, _____ whom
See additional lyrics

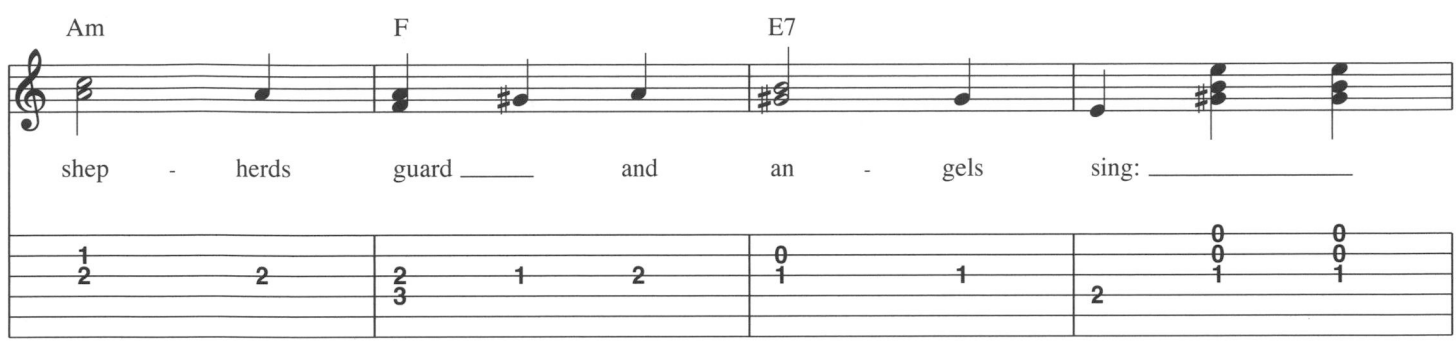

shep - herds guard _____ and an - gels sing: _____

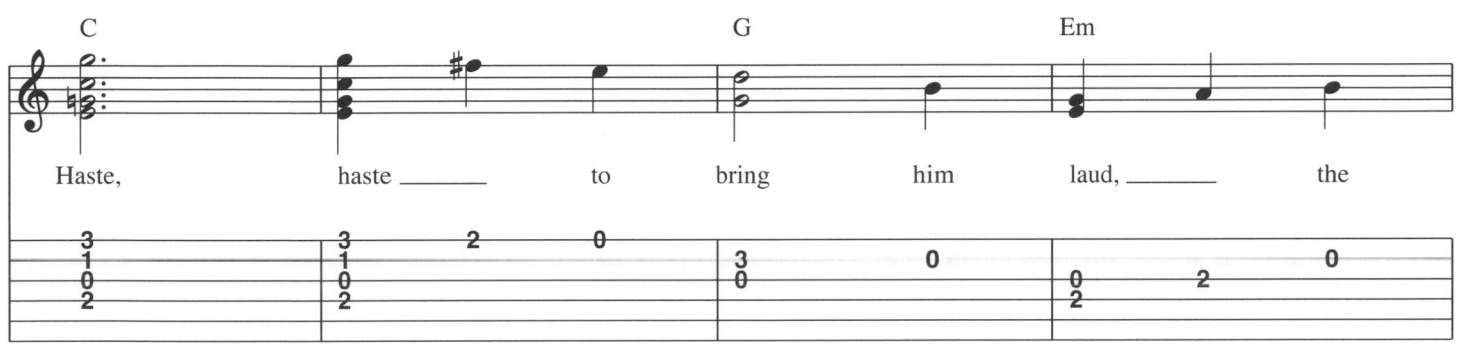

Haste, haste _____ to bring him laud, _____ the

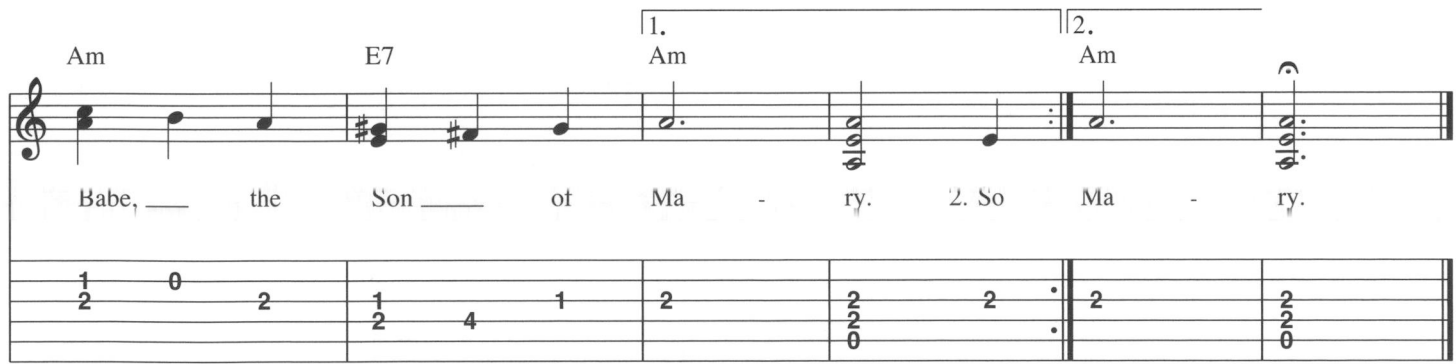

Babe, ___ the Son ___ of Ma - ry. 2. So Ma - ry.

Additional Lyrics

2. So bring Him incense, gold and myrrh,
   Come peasant king to own Him;
   The King of kings salvation brings.
   Let loving hearts enthrone Him.

Chorus   Raise, raise the song on high,
   The Virgin sings her lullaby;
   Joy, joy for Christ is born,
   The Babe, the Son of Mary.

While Shepherds Watched Their Flocks

Words by Nahum Tate
Music by George Frideric Handel

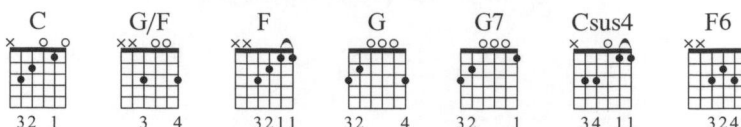

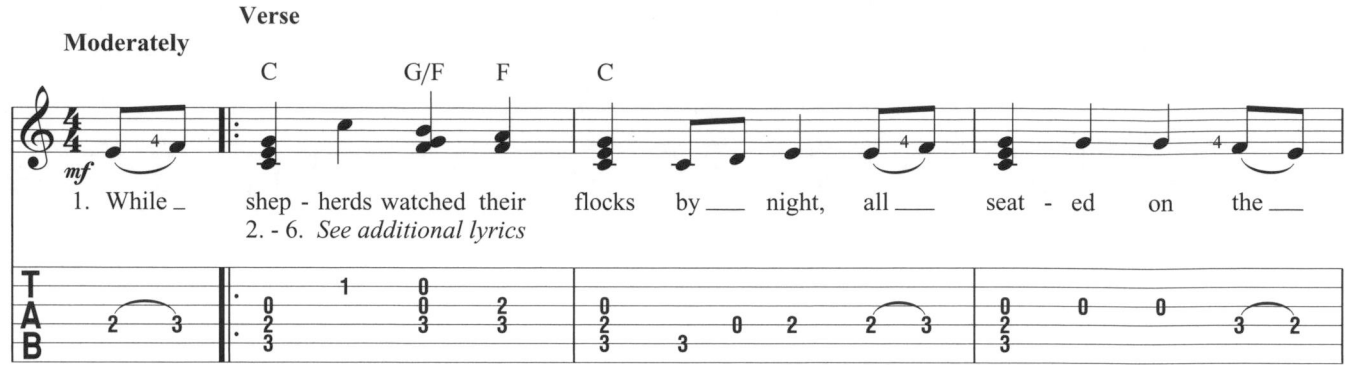

Strum Pattern: 3
Pick Pattern: 3

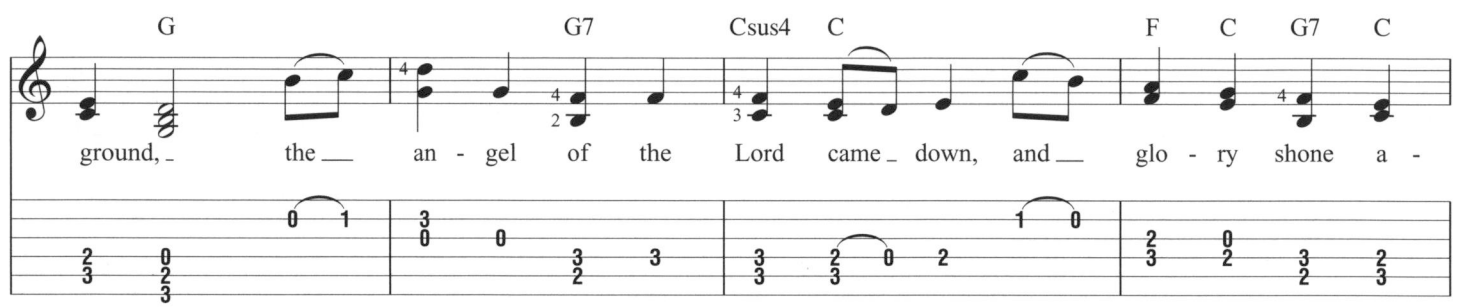

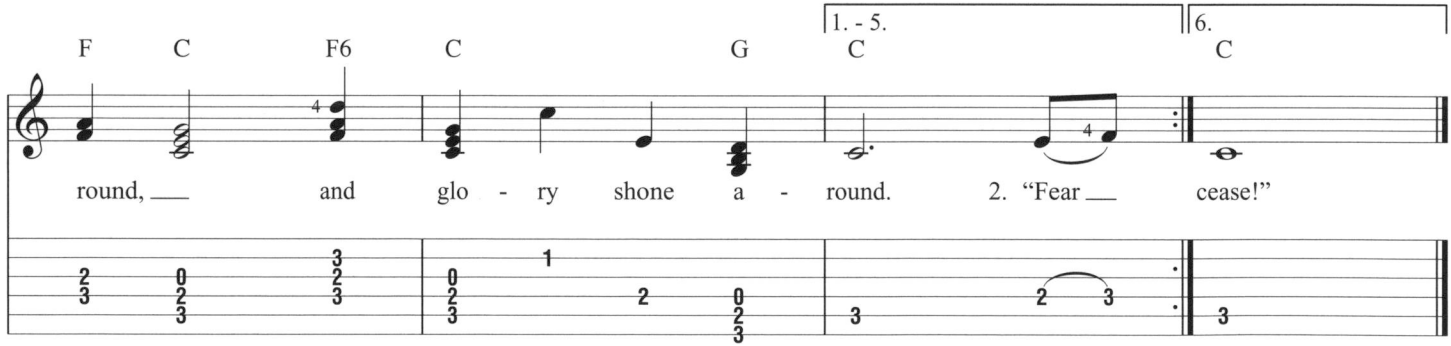

Additional Lyrics

2. "Fear not!" said he, for mighty dread
   Had seized their troubled mind.
   "Glad tidings of great joy I bring
   To you and all mankind,
   To you and all mankind.

3. "To you, in David's town this day,
   Is born of David's line,
   The Savior, who is Christ the Lord;
   And this shall be the sign,
   And this shall be the sign:

4. "The heavenly Babe you there shall find
   To human view displayed,
   All meanly wrapped in swathing bands,
   And in a manger laid,
   And in a manger laid."

5. "All glory be to God on high,
   And to the earth be peace;
   Good will henceforth from heaven to men,
   Begin and never cease,
   Begin and never cease!"

6. "All glory be to God on high,
   And to the earth be peace;
   Good will henceforth from heaven to men,
   Begin and never cease,
   Begin and never cease!"